Unless otherwise indicated, all scripture quotations are arranged throughout the book in italics and taken from the *New King James Version* of the Bible.

You may contact D.E. Paulk at:
Spirit and Truth Sanctuary
2915 Midway Road
Decatur, GA 30030
(404) 243-5020
info@mytruthsanctuary.com
www.mytruthsanctuary.com

Follow D.E. on social media:
Facebook: Donald Earl Paulk and @SpiritandTruthSanctuary
Instagram: @d.e.paulk and @spiritandtruthsanctuary
Twitter: @depaulk
YouTube: youtube.com/spiritandtruthsanctuary

FULLY AWAKE
365 Days That Will Challenge Your Mind, Channel Your Power and Change Your Life.
Copyright © 2022 by D.E. Paulk

Other books by D.E. Paulk:
The Holy Bible of Inclusion
I Don't Know... The Way of Knowing

Printed in the United States of America.
All rights reserved under International Copyright Law.
Contents and/or cover may not be reproduced in whole or in part in any form without the express written consent of the author.

D.E. PAULK'S BIO

D. E. Paulk is the Senior Pastor of Spirit and Truth Sanctuary in Atlanta, GA. where he successfully transitioned an Evangelical Charismatic church into a thriving multicultural, interfaith, LGBTQ+ affirming congregation. D. E. holds a Master of Theological Studies (M.T.S.) in Global Religions from Emory University's Candler School Of Theology and is widely known as a radically inclusive minister who believes that the Christ Spirit is present in all of creation and cannot be defined by, nor confined to, Christianity.

> *"D.E.'s preaching is as easy-going as the church's approach to differences. No wagging fingers or thunderous revelations. He treats parishioners as fellow companions on a spiritual journey. He sprinkles his conversational sermons with references to everyone from the Buddha to Teddy Pendergrass."* -John Blake, CNN Enterprise writer/producer

> *"Descended from generations of Southern preachers, Donnie Earl is now a preacher himself, though a different breed"* (Katherine Marsh, Rolling Stone Magazine, from the article Son of a Preacher Man).

> *"Donnie Earl is progressive, young, hip"* (Mara Shalhoup, Creative Loafing, from the article The Young Shepherd).

His family founded Chapel Hill Harvester Church (formerly The Cathedral of the Holy Spirit) in 1960. The Paulks have always been known for their ministry of restoration. For over 62 years, the Spirit and Truth Sanctuary has opened its doors to people from every walk of life. This has served as the foundation of who D.E. is today.

D. E. has been the recipient of numerous community, civic and service awards. In 2008, D.E. was inducted into the Morehouse College Dr. Martin Luther King, Jr. International Board of Preachers. In 2009, he was honored by Cornerstone University in Lake Charles, Louisiana with an honorary doctorate degree for his in-depth theological research and writings. In 2010, D. E. began serving as a National Board Member for the Southern Christian Leadership Conference (S.C.L.C.), the historic civil rights organization founded by Dr. Martin Luther King, Jr. He has authored several books including *I DON'T KNOW... THE WAY OF KNOWING, THE HOLY BIBLE OF INCLUSION* and his most recent release, F*ULLY AWAKE* (a 100 day devotional aimed at challenging the mind, channeling power, and changing paradigm). All of D.E.'s books are available for purchase in paperback on Amazon and PayPal and as E-books on Amazon, Kindle, Nook, Google Play and Apple Books.

D.E. Paulk makes his home in suburban Atlanta along with his wife, Brandi, and children, Esther and Micah.

LADONNA PAULK DIAZ'S BIO

LaDonna Paulk Diaz is a 5th generation pastor who has served in full time ministry for over 40 years at Spirit and Truth Sanctuary in Decatur, Georgia. Throughout her adult life LaDonna has worked to provide a wide variety of ministry to the local congregation as well as to the broader community of faith. As a teacher and a writer she has excelled at presenting a healthy balance of spiritual guidance and practical life lessons to our Youth Ministry, Children's Ministry, Academy and entire Congregation. Her contribution to the ministry of Worship and the Arts has been a key ingredient to our ministry for decades.   And in the area of pulpit ministry, she chooses to allow Spirit to flow to her and through her by honoring the biblical concepts on which she has been raised while also exploring the truths and Christ-like concepts found in other faith paths. She truly has a gift of gathering insight from many sources and presenting a well sculpted message that encourages and equips personal and corporate growth. LaDonna celebrates life as a dedicated daughter, sister, wife, mother and friend.

UPDATE FROM THE AUTHOR

When Covid-19 arrived on all of our doorsteps our local church, Spirit and Truth Sanctuary, had to make some very quick, abrupt changes. Our services were completely virtual for a year. During this time of physical separation, we began to miss one another. We desired to hear each other's voices and to have a daily time of fellowship. So, I was inspired to write a one-hundred-day devotional that would help to facilitate a daily morning connection. This devotional, *Fully Awake: 100 Days That Will Challenge Your Mind, Channel Your Power And Change Your Life*, grew out of a need. The old saying is "necessity is the mother of invention." After one-hundred straight days of devotion there was a growing desire, and even demand, to continue this daily connection for an entire year. Each of the one-hundred days brought us joy and laughter and helped us begin our days in a high vibration of gratitude and mindfulness. Which ultimately meant, I had to write two-hundred sixty-five more days of devotion.

It just so happened that during this time I was also in school at Emory University, Candler School of Theology, working on a Master of Theological Studies. So, I recruited my sister, Pastor LaDonna Diaz, to help me write many of the new devotionals. In the end, I wrote two-hundred days and she wrote one-hundred sixty-five. Here is the beauty of vibration: my sister and I think so much alike that I challenge you to see if you can decipher which one of us wrote which devotionals.

I am so glad to share this journey with you…the journey to your Self! Each day is designed to comfort and encourage you. Each day is also designed to incorporate challenge, channel and change into the creation of your life experience. As we begin, remember that we all change, but at our own pace and in our own space. So, eat what you can, and save the rest for later. Each new word, new thought, new paradigm is a seed planted in your subconscious mind that will spring into harvest when you become a vibrational match with the truth contained in the new idea. Ultimately, there are no new ideas, nothing new, only moments where we unearth truths that have been buried beneath years of conditioning and indoctrination. Let's go!

INTRODUCTION

Most of us are not big fans of change. Yet, we all change. However, we change at our own pace and in our own space. Change is the constant. The pace of change is the variable. No one can decide our pace or choose our space for us. Some of us are capable of emptying our cups, completely surrendering our egos and experiencing change at a quantum pace. Still others of us are a bit more reluctant and connected to a particular way of thinking, doing and being. There is not one route to change or even a required speed. Life will actually tell us what our speed of change should be. How? When the pain of remaining the same becomes more painful than the pain of change…we all decide to change…and change more quickly than we might have initially planned. Pain is a very powerful teacher that doesn't need our permission or ask for our consent in order to impart wisdom or share life lessons. And, for those of us who are not blessed with mentors or guides, pain is really the only teacher any of us need.

This book is designed to bring about positive change in your experience of life. The daily affirmations, teachings and prayers are all designed to challenge and stretch you. They are not intended to break you. Over the next 365 days I am going to offer you quite a bit of food. Much of it will be inspirational. Yet, some of the teachings may feel confrontational and are purposefully designed to make you think and reconsider. Some of it will taste familiar, while some of it may be new for you. So, eat what you want and what you can. If a specific day or idea trips you up, don't eat it. You don't have to eat all of your food at one time or consume everything you are offered. When you are full…stop eating, save it for later or simply throw it out if it doesn't taste right.

Religion tells you what to think. Spirituality teaches you how to think. In other words, religion sets a plate of food in front of you and tells you to eat, and eat all of it. Spirituality invites you to a restaurant and hands you a menu. Or, presents you with a buffet of food and then allows you to decide which type of food you want and how much. This is your life, your mind and your journey. Design it to fit you. There is no grade being earned and no diploma being handed out. The reward is peace, joy and learning to channel your power while refusing to give it away any longer. Transformation is a process. So be mindful, we are after progress, not perfection.

For most of my spiritual journey I struggled with questions like: "Is this accurate?" "Am I right or wrong?" "Who is correct?" These questions can never really be fully answered because life is not an exact science, or a "one size fits all" and radically varies from one perspective, one person and one place to another. What works for me may be destructive for you. Freedom may be the life giving element for one individual while freedom for others would quickly land them in bondage and enslavement.

The only question that really matters in life is this: IS IT WORKING FOR ME? All other questions are only feeding the ego, distracting from the real work that needs to be done and wasting valuable time and precious energy. Questions of right and wrong and arguments of accurate and inaccurate must all yield and give way to the truth of what works. And, what is working for one person may not be what works for another. Further, what worked for us during one leg of our journey may not work for us now. Consider each lesson. Ponder each idea. Chew on each bite. "Rightly divide the Word of Truth." Trust the Spirit of God within you to discern what is healthy for you, and what might be harmful. Let's walk together as we Challenge our Minds, Channel our Power, Change our Lives…and become Fully Awake!

A SUGGESTION

For each day of this journey, I want to encourage you to recite this Prayer of Surrender before you begin your daily affirmation and teaching. This is a simple invitation of truth that sets up the conditions for your soul to be fed and prepares the ground of your mind to be open and available for transformation.

PRAYER OF SURRENDER

> "Spirit of Truth, CARRY ME where You will, BRING TO ME what You will, TAKE FROM ME what You will, AWAKEN IN ME what You will. The Christ MAN is AROUND me. The Christ MIND is IN me. The Christ POWER flows THROUGH me. And, the Christ MYSTERY exists AS me. I believe it. I perceive it. And, now I receive it! I am surrendered. Amen."

365 AFFIRMATIONS
(dates based on 2023 calendar year)

January: LETTING GO
1 - Setting Goals and Making Resolutions (*New Year's Day*)
2 - The Power of Letting Go
3 - Dare to Lose Control
4 - Flying Above The Turbulence
5 - Stuck In The Middle With You
6 - Happiness Beyond the Death of a Loved One
7 - Attitude, Aptitude and Altitude
8 - God Gives You Nothing to Keep
9 - The Senility Prayer
10 - Little Victories
11 - The Divine Observer
12 - Getting Down to the Root
13 - Shifting Your Perception
14 - The Truth About Death
15 - Dealing With Stuck Emotions
16 - A Day On... Not A Day Off (*Martin Luther King Jr. Day*)
17 - Victim? Or Victor?
18 - Dying Daily
19 - A Flexible Faith
20 - Responding vs. Reacting
21 - Change is the Only Constant
22 - Let Me Be Spiritual
23 - Bless It Coming. Bless It Going.
24 - Feeling Hurt By Others
25 - Free FROM Sin and Free TO Sin
26 - Overcoming the Ego
27 - I Deserve Good
28 - The Blame Game
29 - It's OK
30 - Inclusion Conversion
31 - Nurse, Curse, Rehearse, Reverse

February: REDEFINING MY SPIRITUAL PRACTICE
1 - Rethinking Prayer
2 - Spirituality in a Pandemic Part I
3 - Spirituality in a Pandemic Part II
4 - Spirituality in a Pandemic Part III
5 - What's Your Why?
6 - Spiritual Maintenance
7 - Healthy Religion
8 - Communication With God is a Two-Way Street
9 - Just Like Me
10 - A Righteous Fast
11 - Start With the Basics
12 - The Process of Prayer
13 - Staying in Your Center
14 - The Experience of ME (*Valentine's Day*)
15 - Your Spiritual Journey Part I
16 - Your Spiritual Journey Part II
17 - Random Acts of Kindness (*Random Act of Kindness Day*)
18 - Polishing the Jewel
19 - Being Self-Ful
20 - Don't Ask... Declare
21 - The True Meaning of Spiritual Warfare
22 - Ho'oponopono
23 - Me First
24 - My Body is a Temple
25 - Working With Your Shadow
26 - Inside Out
27 - Step Out of the Boat
28 - Correcting Our Misperceptions
29 - Swaying in Place

March: THE POWER OF NOW
1 - Your Appointed Time
2 - Be Here Now
3 - Common Past. Uncommon Present.

4 - Happy For No Reason
5 - Temporary Containers
6 - You Have the Power
7 - Nothing New Under the Sun
8 - Sliding Door Moments
9 - Repent. Rethink. Renew.
10 - Always Divine
11 - The Eternal Me
12 - Get Happy, Stay Happy, Be Happy
13 - Iron Sharpens Iron
14 - The Power of Silence
15 - Politicians and the Savior Complex
16 - The WAY of Jesus
17 - St. Patrick's Day and a Break From Religion
18 - Telling Your Own Story
19 - Worshipping in Spirit and in Truth
20 - Springing Into Rest (*Spring Equinox*)
21 - Natural Mind vs. The Mind of Christ
22 - The Ever-Present Christ Presence
23 - The Power of Our Words
24 - Awake to my Time, Task, Treasure and Temple
25 - The Same…Yesterday, Today and Forever
26 - The Problem With Making Assumptions
27 - The Mind is Our Bridge
28 - Being in the Room
29 - I Can Only Create in the Present
30 - It's Your Birthday
31 - The Power of Resonance

April: TRANSFORMATION
1 - Loving Myself. Loving Others. Loving God.
2 - Agreeing With God (*Palm Sunday*)
3 - Say It. See It. Survey It. Shift It.
4 - Grace Abuse
5 - One Heart At A Time

6 - 4 Levels of Thought Progression
7 - My Triumphal Entry
8 - True Repentance
9 - The Same Spirit (*Easter Sunday*)
10 - Muscle Memory Part I
11 - Muscle Memory Part II
12 - The Gifts Of Imperfection
13 - Created, Creative and Creating
14 - Childlike vs. Childish
15 - At Peace With The God IN ME
16 - Old Dogs And New Tricks
17 - Fixing vs. Healing
18 - Matrix, Mind, Mouth, Manifestation
19 - Press Into It
20 - Be Ye Transformed
21 - Caring For The Earth
22 - Earth Day
23 - Send Me What I Need
24 - Water Magic
25 - Poison Or Promise?
26 - Break On Through
27 - Creating Good
28 - Spiritual Maturity
29 - Does God Need Praise?
30 - Heart Alchemy

May: I'M NOT IN TROUBLE. I'M IN TRANSITION.
1 - Generational Curses or Blessings?
2 - Just Say No!
3 - Ending With The Beginning In Mind
4 - Take Only What You Need
5 - Cinco de Mayo
6 - The Truth Of Self-Acceptance
7 - Get the Devil Out of Your Mind and Out of Your Mouth
8 - Generational Curses

9 - Set 'Em Up and Knock 'Em Down
10 - Spiritual Restoration
11 - From Chaos To Balance
12 - Get Back Up… Again
13 - Everybody's A Hero
14 - Love Has No Date (*Mother's Day*)
15 - Shaken. Not Stirred.
16 - Performance. Proving. Prerequisites.
17 - Jesus and John Wayne
18 - The Sacred Yes
19 - Like Water Off A Duck's Back
20 - Joy And Sorrow
21 - Joy And Happiness
22 - Count It All Joy
23 - Finding Stillness In The Chaos
24 - Victim of Chance? Or Agent of Change?
25 - Standing Up To Systems
26 - From The Pit To The Pinnacle
27 - Inspiration Or Desperation
28 - Right Livelihood
29 - Weathering The Storm
30 - When Two Halves Do Not Make A Whole
31 - Recognizing Destructive Patterns Quickly

June: RESPECTING THE JOURNEY OF OTHERS
1 - Get Off My Ship
2 - Are We There Yet?
3 - Let Others Be
4 - Don't Choose Sides. Choose Love.
5 - Saving Souls Or Revolutionizing Systems?
6 - Two Trees
7 - Living Above The Political Divide
8 - All Things To All People
9 - Looking Through The Lens Of Our Filters
10 - Christ Is All, and In All

11 - How We See Each Other
12 - Christ Outside Of Christianity
13 - Rock 'n' Roll Jesus
14 - High Vibes
15 - Father, Forgive Them…They Know Not
16 - Every Voice Matters
17 - Holding Space
18 - Casting Pearls Before Swine
19 - Freedom From The Past (*Juneteenth*)
20 - The Sin Of Jonah
21 - Learning To Share
22 - Out Of Many, One
123 - Healthy Mutts
24 - Agree Quickly With Adversaries
25 - Look Before You Leap
26 - Don't Fix It
27 - Love Is A Listening Ear
28 - One Blood
29 - Labels Are Lazy
30 - Walk A Mile In My Shoes

July: THE INNER KINGDOM
1 - The True Meaning of Living by Grace
2 - To Me. Around Me. Through Me. As Me. For Me.
3 - As Above, So Below
4 - Love is the Road to Freedom
5 - No Secret Thoughts
6 - Christ In Us
7 - Happy In My Own Clothes Part I
8 - Happy In My Own Clothes Part II
9 - Happy In My Own Clothes Part III
10 - Trusting Your Own Inner Voice
11 - Freedom From Form
12 - A Vision Of Love
13 - Why Do You Call Me Good?

14 - Is It Working For You?
15 - Sound Doctrine
16 - How To Clean Up Negative Self-Talk
17 - My Happy Place
18 - The Power Of I Am
19 - Dealing With Traffic
20 - Wielding Power Lightly
21 - Listen To Your Body
22 - Spiritual GPS…My Internal Navigation System
23 - It's In There
24 - Recognizing Happiness, Not Chasing After It
25 - Life's Changing Seasons
26 - We Don't Get What We Want. We Get Who We Are.
27 - Listen To The Still Small Voice
28 - Soul Prosperity
29 - The Difference Between Faith and Faithfulness
30 - The SPECK and the PLANK
31 - Why Is This Happening…Again?

August: THE BEGINNER'S MIND
1 - RenewING My Mind
2 - Become Like A Child
3 - The Beginner's Mind
4 - Taking On The Mind Of Christ
5 - Empty Your Cup
6 - A Prison Of Our Own Making
7 - I Am Not My Beliefs
8 - True Humility
9 - Eating The Question
10 - Spiritual Baking
11 - Dust In The Wind
12 - Saving By Playing Part I
13 - Saving By Playing Part II (Jesus At Play)
14 - Is It True? Is It Necessary? Is It Kind?
15 - The Beauty In Mystery

16 - Room to Grow
17 - God Wants US to be Happy
18 - Clearing Out Space
19 - Hitting The Reset Button
20 - The Sin Against The Holy Spirit
21 - The Optimist And The Pessimist
22 - I Am The Path To Happiness
23 - The Certainty Of Uncertainty
24 - Baby Steps
25 - No Male. No Female.
26 - Transactional vs. Unconditional
27 - Walking Your Talk On-Line
28 - The Higher Octave Part I
29 - The Higher Octave Part II
30 - To Be Poor In Spirit
31 - Not Knowing Why

September: TRUTH IS A JOURNEY, NOT A DESTINATION
1 - The Symbolism of 3
2 - The Dance Between Effort And Ease
3 - The Harmony Of Your Heart Space
4 - Finding A Rhythm…Not A Routine
5 - The Progression of Righteousness, Peace and Joy
6 - A Difficult Question
7 - The Beauty Of Duality
8 - The Middle Way
9 - God Honors Our Choices
10 - Don't Throw It All Away
11 - Avoiding the Trap of Literalism
12 - The Higher Octave Of Love
13 - Don't Get Distracted
14 - Literally?
15 - Love As Foundation And Filter
16 - Back And Forth… The Spiritual Journey
17 - The Spirit Gives Life

18 - 7 Universal Timeless Truths
19 - True Equality
20 - CHOOSING to Heal
21 - No Longer Children
22 - Aristotelian Happiness
23 - Unique Instead Of Special
24 - Freedom From Labels
25 - Doing Your Part
26 - Run Your Own Race
27 - Dominate Or Tend?
28 - Climb The Right Wall
29 - The IS-ness of God's Love
30 - Two For The Price Of One

October: NO FEAR
1 - No Fear
2 - The Knowledge of Good and Evil
3 - Don't Be Afraid Of The Dark
4 - Saved From God By Jesus?
5 - The Void Part I
6 - The Void Part II
7 - Fear: Friend or Foe?
8 - Divided By Language
9 - The Sacred No
10 - Protected By An Enemy
11 - Born To Stand Out
12 - Getting our Think, Say and Do in Harmony
13 - Learning Proportion
14 - Everything Is Spiritual
15 - Beyond The Reef
16 - Behind The Scenes
17 - The Treasure You Seek
18 - Who Created The Devil?
19 - Unexpected Vessels
20 - Focusing On The Good

21 - Don't Say It
22 - Effective Communication
23 - Saving And Spending
24 - Our Love Affair With The Supernatural
25 - Disappointments, Expectations, and Projections
26 - Daring To Do The Impossible
27 - Dealing With Loss
28 - Living In Integrity
29 - No Weapon
30 - Have The Conversation
31 - The Thing I Feared The Most (*Halloween*)

November: GRATITUDE
1 - The Pee-Pee Prayer
2 - The Butterfly Effect
3 - Honoring Our Ancestors
4 - What We Know Is What We Owe
5 - The Courage, Challenge, Charge, and Choice to Live Authentically Part I
6 - The Courage, Challenge, Charge, and Choice to Live Authentically Part II
7 - Living Our Love
8 - Flattery And Criticism
9 - Agape And Eros
10 - No Small Contributions
11 - To Each His Own
12 - The Righteous Pit
13 - Ask and You Shall Receive
14 - Divine Connections
15 - Walk Through The Door
16 - Learning Tolerance (*International Day For Tolerance*)
17 - What We Can Learn From Plants Part I
18 - What We Can Learn From Plants Part II
19 - The Walking Bible
20 - Heart Health

21 - Thank God My China Cabinet Is Clean
22 - Prodigal
23 - An Attitude of Gratitude (*Thanksgiving*)
24 - Pay It Forward
25 - Remember Who You Are
26 - Calling The Qualified? Or Qualifying The Called?
27 - The Purest Love
28 - Unguarded Moments
29 - A Double Portion
30 - Life As A TV Show

December: PURSUING PEACE
1 - Choose Peace. Seek Peace. Pursue Peace.
2 - The Peace of God and Your Piece of God
3 - Living Peaceably With All Men
4 - Pursuing Peace Without _____
5 - Single-Minded and Stable
6 - Gentleness Part I
7 - Gentleness Part II
8 - Guilty Peace
9 - Laughing In Difficult Moments
10 - Energy Management
11 - I Walk Down A Different Street
12 - The Power Of Choice
13 - Co-Existing Part I
14 - Co-Existing Part II
15 - At Peace With MY Faith Journey
16 - My Time And Energy Are Valuable
17 - Dealing With Stress
18 - At Peace With My Journey
19 - The Name Of God
20 - Good Tension
21 - The Shortest Day of the Year (*Winter Solstice*)
22 - Addicted To Stress
23 - The Best Gift: YOU!

24 - The Mad Rush (*Christmas Eve*)
25 - The Word Became Flesh (*Christmas Day*)
26 - Stillness Speaks
27 - I Don't Know Anything About That
28 - At Peace With Pain
29 - End The War
30 - Creating God In My Image
31 - Projecting Happiness Into The Future (*New Year's Eve*)

Excerpts and previews of D.E. Paulk's other books included...

FULLY AWAKE 365

*365 Days That Will Challenge Your Mind,
Channel Your Power and Change Your Life.*

D. E. Paulk and LaDonna Paulk Diaz

January 1

LETTING GO

Setting Goals and Making Resolutions

> *Affirmation*
> "Today, New Year's Day, I set only one goal. I make only one resolution: to REMAIN AWAKE. There is no need to wait for any person, any date, any event, or any time to create the life I want to experience. This day, and every day, is the day the Lord has made. Today, and every day, is the day of salvation."

I workout six days a week at several different gyms near my house and church. I have worked out for the last thirty-five years. I enjoy this time as it allows me a chance to unplug, relieve stress, listen to music and connect with my body temple. Admittedly, the month of January is my least favorite month to workout. Why? The parking lot is full, the gym is crowded, and the machines that I normally have easy access to have a sign-up sheet. January is the time everyone is going to get in shape and lose some weight.

Several years ago, I was approached in mid December by an individual who wanted me to train them. I responded with excitement, "Sure, let's begin tomorrow!" The individual replied, "No, let's wait and begin January 1st." What is the difference between these dates? Only the importance we ascribe to them. I knew then this individual would falter, making resolutions, and then projecting discipline and health into his idea of a future reality.

When we make resolutions on January 1st we many times break those resolutions by January 15th or even earlier! Projecting our best selves into the future, or being held captive by a calendar, is giving our power away. Now is the time! And, the time is always, eternally, inarguably NOW!

> **Prayer:** "God of the NOW, empower me to create my life now, not later. Be with me as I seize this day, honor this moment, and stay in the present. Amen."

LETTING GO

January 2

The Power of Letting Go

Affirmation
"Today I will learn to let go!"

Why do we hang on to things that hurt us? Things that make us suffer? Physically, it's against our nature to hold on to something that's causing us pain. What's your first, involuntary reaction when you grab something hot or sharp? You let it go!

When anything comes into contact with your body that makes you uncomfortable, what's your first instinct? *Get that away from me; or let me get away from that.* We literally have to force ourselves…we must use our will power in order to hold on to something that is hurting us physically.

So what does that tell us? That any time we hold on to something that is emotionally hurting us, it's a conscious choice we're making.

Of course it's unavoidable that we all go through painful experiences that we call "life lessons" - but once a lesson is learned, you're supposed to move on and incorporate whatever the lesson is into your life going forward - not stay in your pain until it becomes misery.

When you refuse to move on it's like filling your house with trash. You're choosing to live in the filth of your negative memories of pain because you have become stuck in the past. But the instant you decide to drop it - let it go and move forward - you become your eternal self because you are no longer holding that past version of yourself in place.

> **Prayer:** *"God of moving forward, help me to integrate the lesson my pain is teaching me rather than hold on to it and get stuck there. I am new every morning! Amen."*

Challenge Your Mind. Channel Your Power. Change Your Life.

January 3

LETTING GO

Dare to Lose Control

> ### Affirmation
> *"I am responsible for my life only. I will not pressure my loved ones to live life in the way I choose. I will allow them the freedom to choose for themselves."*

You have no control over anyone else's desires or what they want to try or what they choose. Please release yourself from that responsibility. We may understand the truth of this on an intellectual level, but it is no small task to live it out, especially when it comes to our children or other loved ones. It's only natural for us to think we know what's best for them. But ultimately, that's not helping them, nor is it loving them. It's only creating an attachment to them.

You could spend the rest of your life trying to understand the intricacies of what different people are creating for themselves and why, but you still couldn't - and shouldn't - because none of it is anyone's business except the one living out the experience.

You can worry about each and every possibility your mind presents to you and squander the joy that life is offering you because you're living in fear of something you don't want happening to someone you love, or you can decide to honor the choices they are making for themselves and trust they are creating the experiences that will help them grow and evolve.

Life becomes so much easier when you understand that you are the creator of your own life and so is everyone else!

> **Prayer:** *"Omniscient God, help me today to know that you see more than I ever can, especially regarding my loved ones. Help me relinquish any responsibility I feel to make choices for them. Let me show them love and leave them in your hands. Amen."*

LETTING GO

January 4

Flying Above the Turbulence

Affirmation
"Today, I will fly above the turbulence of lower thought. I will raise my vibration and watch as my thought life elevates me above the storms of small thinking and the strain of small-minded people. I consciously choose to create something new and different today!"

I have flown hundreds of times. Occasionally, I have flown through storms, some a little scarier than others. I remember the first time I flew, or rode nervously, through a storm. I looked out of the window nearest me and I could visibly see an immense storm ahead. Immediately, the plane began to shake and drop and I watched as the flight attendants found their seats very quickly. Suddenly, the pilot changed the trajectory and raised our altitude. The plane rose above the dark clouds, and amazingly, I could see the sun again. The shaking stopped, the plane stabilized and everyone on board breathed a sigh of relief as the flight attendants calmly brought them their peanuts and ginger ale.

There is always peace to be found. However, if we encounter, inherit or even create a storm, continuing to fly in the same way will not render us peace. The turbulence caused by gossip, worry, fear or any lower level of consciousness, cannot be overcome by continuing to create it. There must be a conscious decision to rise above and seek out a new altitude and attitude. When we fall into a pit, or even dig one ourselves, the absolute first choice to be made, if we want to get out of the pit, is to stop digging. Once we recognize the behavior and thought life that created turbulence, we can then rise above it and find the peace that has seemed so elusive. There is peace above the storm and even peace in the very eye of the storm. It can all be found by raising the level of our vibration and tapping into higher thoughts like love, trust, forgiveness, openness, flexibility and calmness.

Prayer: *"Calmer of the storm, give me the strength to rise above the turbulence created by lower thinking. Amen."*

Challenge Your Mind. Channel Your Power. Change Your Life.

January 5

LETTING GO

Stuck in the Middle With You

> **Affirmation**
> "Today I will focus on the power within me."

There's an old 1970's song that says: "*Clowns to the left of me, jokers to the right, here I am, stuck in the middle with you*" - obviously referring to being stuck between two groups of people. However, when any of us feel stuck between two things, what we're basically stuck with is making a choice.

When you've got a doughnut in front of you, what do you choose to look at - the doughnut or the hole? Meaning: if you only focus on the hole, you'll miss the fact that there's a doughnut sitting in front of you, which is much less fun than seeing it!

The way cult leaders get their members to give up their personal sovereignty, their money, and sometimes even their bodies is to get them to intensely focus on a tiny sliver of manipulated reality. That's the same way we all get stuck sometimes - by focusing too intensely on too small a sliver of reality, and perhaps one that's been manipulated by someone else.

Let's go back to our song lyrics: *stuck in the middle with you*. Which part of that phrase will you choose to focus on? The *stuck* part? Or the *you* part? If you get stuck on the word *stuck*, that's too small a focus, and you'll miss the bigger, more expansive part of the phrase, which is the word YOU.

The next time you feel stuck, focus on you and all the power within you rather than on the fact that you feel stuck. Don't focus on the hole and miss the doughnut!

> **Prayer:** "God of Freedom, help me to know I always have the power to choose what to focus on. Amen."

LETTING GO

January 6

Happiness Beyond the Death of a Loved One

Affirmation
"Being happy after the loss of a loved one is not betraying them."

The death of a loved one is never easy, but most of us believe it is ultimately a positive thing because they have now returned to the realm from which we all come. At the moment of their transition, they're good. They are instantly made whole and reunited with the source of pure love - the being we call God. And if they were in any pain, they are in it no longer.

So any sorrow we feel is actually not for them. It is for ourselves. And that's normal. But it's something we need to understand in order to process our grief. Because we are human, we're largely egocentric, whether we want to admit it or not. When someone we love dies, we are usually focused on how it is making *us* feel. Our sorrow comes from thinking about *our* lives here on this earthly plane without them.

Part of moving through our grief in a healthy way is not getting caught up in the feeling that we are somehow betraying them if we feel happiness after their death. Any loved one you have lost who truly loved you wants you to be happy after they're gone. Period.

It's hard for us to see it that way because we're still here, in this world of duality, and still having to deal with our egos. But once a person's spirit transcends this world, they don't think or feel like us anymore.

> ***Prayer:*** *"Source of Everlasting Life, help me today know that love is eternal and can never be lost; not even in death. My loved ones on the other side want me to be happy and at peace. Amen."*

Challenge Your Mind. Channel Your Power. Change Your Life.

January 7

LETTING GO

Attitude, Aptitude and Altitude

> **Affirmation**
> "My attitude, not just my aptitude, determines my altitude. I will protect my inner kingdom by maintaining my joy and by keeping my peace. No one can change my attitude but me. This week I will fly above the storm of worry and rise above the turbulence of anxiety. I will learn to let it go. I will raise the vibration of those around me by maintaining mine!"

I have often been amazed that the most successful people I have either met or studied are not always the most qualified. Many times these powerful leaders don't possess a high level of aptitude. However, they own a contagious positive attitude. The result is they reach great heights of altitude. My wife is a CPA and has worked for several Fortune 500 companies. During the interview process, she has discovered that the most qualified person doesn't always land the job. Many times the candidate hired is actually the most likeable, and carries an attitude that helps to foster a positive, productive and peaceful work environment.

Unfortunately, there are times when a person's qualifications disqualify them as they carry with them a "know it all" attitude. They smugly allow their higher aptitude to place them into a lower altitude. How many great athletes never reached the professional ranks because they were un-coachable? How many phenomenal musicians never reached their potential because no one could tolerate working with them? There is a healthy balance of being knowledgeable without becoming "a know it all."

There is an old church cliché, "God doesn't always call the qualified. Sometimes, God qualifies the called." We need to be qualified. But, more importantly, we need to maintain the right spirit.

> **Prayer:** "Mind of the Universe, I am willing to study, prepare and apply myself to acquire knowledge. As You grant me knowledge, I humbly ask for a spirit of wisdom in how to use this knowledge. Amen."

LETTING GO

January 8

God Gives You Nothing to Keep

Affirmation
"Today I am a willing vessel and open channel."

Famous gospel singer and composer, Dottie Rambo, once said, "God gives you nothing to keep." She then explained that the way it worked for her was that if she tried to hold on too tightly to a song God had given her the inspiration to write; if she was stingy with it, for whatever reason, or didn't think it was good enough and failed to share it immediately, she would cease being an open vessel through which her gift could flow.

According to spiritual teacher Gregg Braden, a growing body of scientific evidence now suggests that we do not hold memory, or even information, in the neurons within our bodies as was once thought. Instead, our neurons act like antennae that tune in and receive this information from a collective field that is accessible to anyone who wants to tap into it.

Ideas have their own energy and search for channels through which they can be expressed. They will knock on your door in the form of inspiration, but if you don't provide an open channel for them to flow through, they will find someone else to bring them into manifestation.

Both of these ideas are saying the same thing: share your gift, make your contribution, don't hide your light under a bushel - even if you think you, or it, is not quite ready. The fact that the inspiration came to you means the time is right for it to be shared!

> **Prayer:** *"God of Divine Timing, help me share whatever you give me without being afraid it's not good enough or I'm not ready. I trust the timing of your inspiration and I will let my gift flow freely. Amen."*

Challenge Your Mind. Channel Your Power. Change Your Life.

January 9

LETTING GO

The Senility Prayer

> ***Affirmation***
> *"God, grant me the senility to forget the people I never liked anyway, the good fortune to run into the ones that I do, and the eyesight to tell the difference."*

Most people have heard of the Serenity Prayer. Have you ever experienced the Senility Prayer? Although it is obviously humorous, there is an amazing amount of wisdom in this silly prayer. Jesus said, *"Agree quickly with your adversary while you are in the way with him"* (Matthew 5:25). Jesus and Luke give us a great avoidance plan that when someone doesn't like you or accept you, simply stay away from them and *"shake the dust off your feet"* (Matthew 10:14; Mark 6:11; Luke 9:5; Acts 13:51).

One of the most painful lessons of adolescence is when we learn that everyone is not our friend. To say it positively, all of us will eventually find our tribe. How many years have we wasted trying to fit in with a certain crowd or win a specific person over? Eventually, either by frustration, exhaustion, or by default, we shake the dust of rejection off of our feet and move on to a place or acceptance and inclusion.

Similar to society, the Body of Christ is made up of many different parts and expressions. I don't have to hang out with the parts that are not on my vibratory level to appreciate that this diversity brings about a necessary balance. Many people are born into families that don't understand or celebrate them. As much as they strive for approval and affirmation it may never happen. For survival, they may have to remain in an environment of tolerance until they are self-sufficient. Inevitably, the day will come when they will choose to be celebrated, not tolerated. Maybe this is that day?

> **Prayer:** *"God of Wisdom, in my heart I know I deserve to be loved and accepted. Give me the strength to walk toward celebration and away from toleration. Amen."*

LETTING GO

January 10

Little Victories

Affirmation
"Although change is constant and consistent throughout the universe, change can be a challenge in my life. As I embark on the journey of creating change and manifesting the life I want to experience, I am aware it will not happen all at once or overnight. I am looking for progress, not perfection. And, until I arrive at my destination, I will learn to celebrate the little victories along the way."

Before David faced Goliath, King Saul had a conversation with David trying to offer him advice as he faced this seemingly impossible mission. Surprising to Saul, David came across as very confident and prepared. Saul asked David why he felt he would experience victory against this giant. David let Saul know that this was not his first fight. David informed Saul that a lion had attacked his flock and that God gave him victory over the lion. Similarly, David shared a story about a bear attacking his flock and God had enabled him once again to overcome the bear. Finally, David lets Saul know that the same God who gave him power over a lion and a bear, would give him the victory over Goliath. David had learned to celebrate little victories along the way that gave him the courage and confidence to face a larger challenge in his life.

The prophet Elijah offers us a similar example. In Elijah's day, there was a severe drought. Elijah began to send out his servant to see if there was any rain on the horizon. Time after time, his servant came back with the report that there was no rain, and not even a cloud. Finally, on the seventh time, Elijah's servant comes back and tells him he saw a very small cloud about the size of a man's hand. Elijah celebrates this little victory and begins to declare that he hears *"the sound of abundant rain."* Celebrate little victories today. They have a way of becoming bigger victories!

Prayer: *"Victorious God, today I give thanks for little victories and I trust You are able to turn little victories into big victories. You have delivered me in the past. I know You can do it again! Amen."*

Challenge Your Mind. Channel Your Power. Change Your Life.

January 11

LETTING GO

The Divine Observer

> **Affirmation**
> *"I am not getting older. I am growing wiser! I am not broke. I am learning to be faithful over a little as God is making me ruler over much! I am not lonely. I am learning to love myself! I have never failed at anything, but I have started over again many times with more wisdom! I am not a sinner or sinning. I am only learning how to navigate my Innate God-given Divine Creativity. And, I can re-create my life anytime I desire a new existence. I am not my experiences. I am the Divine Observer of these experiences."*

We chose to come here, to earth, from a spiritual dimension, to experience temporary situations and even painful difficulties, for the evolution of our eternal spirits. This mystical idea is beginning to gain quite a bit of popularity in many circles. Whether it is true or not…I really can't say. I am learning that I don't necessarily believe everything I consider. However, if there is something of truth or even anything helpful, I will continue to consider it as long as it brings me to a higher awareness of my divine self and soul. The Bible speaks of God knowing us before we were formed in our mother's wombs. Jesus, chose to come to earth for a higher purpose. Scripture speaks of us being predestined for a purpose and that certain good works were already put in place for us "beforehand."

If this idea is true, then when bad things happen to us or even through us, we can step away from the event itself, and look at it as a Divine Observer. In this context, the event happening "to us" is not personal or even permanent. It is designed to teach us or help us learn how to better navigate our Divine Creativity to manifest the reality we desire to experience. Can you step back from past experiences and see the learning without being overwhelmed by the pain? Try it. You might outgrow the pain.

> **Prayer:** *"God before time, I am not what happens to me. Today, I declare nothing has or is happening TO ME. All life is happening THROUGH ME, FOR ME and AS ME! I am here to observe, grow, evolve and create. Amen."*

FULLY AWAKE 365

LETTING GO

January 12

Getting Down to the Root

Affirmation
"Today I will learn to discern between the root emotions of love and fear. I will work on increasing the thoughts and activities that result in love and decrease those that result in fear."

There are only two foundational emotions from which all other emotions spring - love and fear. Love is the foundation of all positive emotions, and fear is the foundation of all negative ones. Every other emotion can be boiled down or traced back to one of these two.

So when you're mentally identifying your feelings, it's important to get to the root emotion. This makes it easier to deal with. Once you've determined which of the two foundational emotions is at the base of what your secondary emotion is you can start seeing your personal emotional patterns.

If the root emotion of a particular activity or thought is fear, you can make the appropriate adjustments to decrease it and eventually cut it out of your routine entirely. If the root emotion of a particular activity or thought is love, then that is something you can promote, expand and put more focus on in your life.

Prayer: *"Loving God, help me today to know myself better by identifying my own emotions and actively pursuing the things in my life that result in love. Amen."*

Challenge Your Mind. Channel Your Power. Change Your Life.

January 13

LETTING GO

Shifting Your Perception

Affirmation
"I have the power to choose my level of consciousness. I can do this by shifting my perception and changing my thoughts."

We all have the ability to choose what level of consciousness we want to live on and operate from. That begins with our thoughts. The first thing we can do is learn how to shift our perception. When you find your perception needs adjusting, there are three fairly easy ways to do it. You can do all three, but usually just shifting one will be enough to make a positive change.

1. You can change your perception about a thing, a situation, an event, an object or a principle. You can look at it from a different angle entirely.

2. You can change the way you think about another person. If you're not having good thoughts about them, dig a little deeper and try to find out why. Then see if you can put yourself in their shoes or see it from their perspective instead of just dismissing them.

3. You can change the way you are thinking about yourself. Sometimes it's easy to get stuck in our own thoughts about ourselves. It's easy to begin sentences - even if it's only in your head to yourself - with phrases like: "I could never" or "I always." If you can shift that just a little and say, "Maybe I could" or "I am capable of changing this about myself" - then a whole new world of possibilities will open up to you!

Prayer: *"God of Truth, help me to know I have the power to change how I perceive things. Help me to choose the highest thoughts available to me. Amen."*

LETTING GO

January 14

The Truth About Death

Affirmation
*"Today I know that eternity does not begin when I die.
I am living in it now."*

Most of us associate death with suffering, loss, and sorrow. Because of this, it is an uncomfortable subject to discuss or even to think about. But we need to talk about those things that make us uncomfortable so that we can get ourselves to a place of peace with them instead of running from or resisting them.

Death is not the opposite of birth. They are merely two events in the totality that is our life - equally a part of the life cycle - yet we celebrate one and dread the other. What does that say about us and what we believe?

Most of us say we believe we existed in spirit form before our birth, and that our spirit will live on in some other realm after our physical body dies where we will be reunited with God and our loved ones. So what we fear is not really the experience of death, but our inability to know exactly what it will be like. What we fear is the uncertainty of it; how it will happen and when, and whether or not it will be painful.

But we will not be able to know this until the experience comes to us. And no amount of worry or dread will change that. So, the best thing we can do in the meantime is live our lives to the fullest while we're here, trusting in the perfection of love, for where perfect love is, there can be no fear.

> **Prayer:** *"Eternal God, help me live in such perfect love that I no longer fear the dimensional transition known as death. Amen."*

Challenge Your Mind. Channel Your Power. Change Your Life.

January 15

LETTING GO

Dealing With Stuck Emotions

> ***Affirmation***
> *"Today I will be aware of the importance of dealing with stuck emotions before they begin to cause problems in my life."*

Have you ever noticed that it's not our positive emotions that tend to get stuck in us? They make us generous. When we're happy and full of joy, it's easy for that to spill over onto those around us - for us to let it flow through us to others. Positive emotions don't often hang around unprocessed.

It's the negative ones that are hard to deal with, but as much as we might hope to, we can't completely escape them no matter how hard we try. We don't get to decide which emotions rise up within us, but we do get to decide what to do with them once they're there.

If anger comes up, are you going to push it down? Ignore it? Act like you're not angry? Or will you go in the other direction and let it cause you to lash out at someone else in a hurtful way? A better option is to release it in a healthy way, perhaps by channeling it into a physical activity like exercise. Some people kickbox, hit a punching bag - or even a pillow.

Others have different methods. There are literally hundreds of them. The main objective should be to become aware when you have allowed an unprocessed emotion to get stuck and then work on it in whatever way you choose.

> ***Prayer:*** *"Source of Energy, help me understand today that emotions are just energy and that it is always my choice how to deal with them. Show me healthy ways to keep my channel clear for your energy to flow through easily and unhindered. Amen."*

LETTING GO

January 16

A Day On... Not A Day Off

Affirmation
"Today, I will honor those who gave their lives for my freedoms by being personally mindful of little ways that I can impact positive change. I may not be a recognizable, famous Civil Rights hero or Human Rights shero. However, I can be a change agent who seasons the minds of those within my sphere of influence."

The third Monday of January is celebrated as a national and international holiday in the U. S. and in countries around the globe. It is a day that we honor the life and legacy of Dr. Martin Luther King, Jr. It is also a day to celebrate many Civil and Human Rights leaders who have endeavored to speak truth to power and create a more egalitarian society that works for all of the human family. I have attended and participated in many MLK day gatherings. One of the mottos that we hear regarding this day is "A Day On…Not A Day Off." This saying is designed to encourage people everywhere not to merely enjoy a day off from work, but rather to do something productive in the community to help realize change.

All of us may not lead a march or deliver a speech to elected officials. Yet, we can all be change agents within our own circles. We can challenge family and friends to think on higher planes of consciousness, recount the history of the struggle for equality to our children, and be aware of current issues that need our support as voters and socially engaged active citizens. This January 16th, in your own way, *"be the change you want to see in the world."* ~ Mahatma Gandhi

Prayer: *"Unchanging Ever-Present Spirit, embolden me to be an agent for positive change wherever my feet trod. Amen."*

Challenge Your Mind. Channel Your Power. Change Your Life.

January 17

LETTING GO

Victim? Or Victor?

> **Affirmation**
> *"I am not a victim. I am a victor! I am not bitter. I am better! I am not what people call me. I am what I answer to. Your 'YOU ARE' will never be as powerful as my 'I AM!' Today, I will only answer to righteousness, peace and joy."*

The first name we have for God in the Bible is simply *"I Am."* God begins a conversation with Moses and instructs him to go speak certain things to a very powerful Pharaoh. Moses asks God, *"who should I say sent me?"* God replies, *"tell them I Am that I Am sent you."* Seems awfully vague and abstract. Doesn't it? Yet, this is possibly the most brilliant answer ever given. God would not say a specific name because that would be a limiting decision. *"I Am that I Am"* leaves an entire universe open to possibilities. In other words, I am not what you say I am. I Am who I say I Am! A wise man once told me "Once people can define you they will disqualify you."

Many people in our lives use the two words "you are" to describe what they think of us. Nevertheless, "you are" has absolutely no power over us. The power is in the "I Am!" The only way "you are" impacts us is if we allow someone else's "you are" to become our "I am." Never allow anyone's "you are" to become your "I Am!"

Only what you say after "I am" really matters. I am not a victim of anything that anyone has done to me. I am a victor who has overcome. I am not a survivor. I am thriving and what didn't kill me made me stronger. What didn't break me made more flexible. And, my mistakes have only made me wiser.

> **Prayer:** *"Infinite I Am that I Am, I give thanks today that my 'I am' is stronger than anyone's 'you are.' I am grateful that life and death are in the power of my tongue…not anyone else's. Grant me the strength today to speak from the power of I am. Amen."*

LETTING GO

January 18

Dying Daily

Affirmation
"Today I understand that physical death is but a transition from one form into another; a graduation to my next level of existence."

Whether you personally believe in reincarnation or not, you can still view death as part of a circular life cycle where your physical death here on earth is just your birth into the heavenly realm. Another way to look at it is that we die many smaller deaths throughout our lifetime.

Christianity encourages this. The Apostle Paul speaks of dying to himself daily, which we understand as him dying to his flesh, or lower nature, so that his spirit, or higher nature, can emerge.

If you learn to practice these smaller deaths as a lifestyle, then when physical death comes, you will view it more as a graduation to the next level of your existence because you've learned to see every other "death" you've experienced as just the beginning of a new and better version of you.

Learn to face death well before the day you die by learning what things you should die to during this life, for instance, those beliefs and behaviors that no longer serve you or keep you from relating properly to your fellow man.

Die to any cultural conditioning that tells you who you must be in order to be accepted. Die to your need to be right all the time. Die to your desire to compare your life to that of others or to judge others and treat them in a way you would not want to be treated yourself.

Most importantly, die to your fear of death, because in doing so, you will graduate into your greatest life!

Prayer: *"Life giving Spirit, help me die daily to all in me that does not reflect you. Amen."*

Challenge Your Mind. Channel Your Power. Change Your Life.

January 19

LETTING GO

A Flexible Faith

> **Affirmation**
> *"My faith is NOT fragile. My faith is FLEXIBLE. I am willing to shift so that I will not be shattered. Religion breeds rigidity. And, rigidity breeds weakness. I am NOT religious, rigid or weak! I am flexible, strong, open and available for Spirit to guide me into all truth. As I journey from glory to glory, I will keep an open mind and maintain a young spirit."*

One of my favorite preachers would say, "Blessed are the flexible, for they shall not be broken." How powerful! Strength lies in flexibility, not in rigidity. The tallest skyscrapers are designed to sway with the wind so they don't collapse and crumble. Only the trees that bend in a heavy storm survive. Can this principle of flexibility be applied to our spiritual lives? "Mighty fortresses," "strong towers," "solid rocks" are fairly common lyrics and phrases in the religious world. Strength seems to always be parallel with a rigid regimen of changelessness. Yet, we are encouraged to go from glory to glory; to advance from one precept to another precept; to be changed, renewed, transformed. God feeds us with manna (mystery), Daily Bread (daily word), Living Water (organic spirituality), Living Wells (new avenues) and Green Pastures (fresh places). Organic spirituality demands flexibility and openness. Perhaps this is why Jesus repeatedly said *"you have heard of old, but I say"* as a challenge to those who were stuck in a religious rut?

Jesus spent a great deal of His ministry dealing with religious rigidity. Unbending, unopen, unteachable religious orders of sincere men who lacked flexibility of mind. Jesus is so complex and challenging that rigidity of thought will inevitably lead to theological crisis. In order to follow Jesus, and be led by the Holy Spirit into new truth, there must be a flexibility of thought and openness to progress. Resistance and rigidity will only detour us directly to ignorance, irrelevance, denial…and eventually to collapse.

> **Prayer:** *"God of Strength, empower me to bend and not break; shift and not be shattered; to sway, grow, unfold and evolve. Amen."*

LETTING GO

January 20

Responding vs. Reacting

Affirmation
"Today I will strive to respond rather than react."

Some people use the terms *responding* and *reacting* interchangeably, but there is a world of difference. A reaction is instant and is driven by the beliefs, biases, and prejudices of the unconscious mind. A response, on the other hand, usually comes more slowly. It's based on information from both the conscious and unconscious mind and takes into consideration the well-being and long term effects on you as well as others.

A response is always more effective, and the reasons to respond rather than react can be remembered by a string of "r" words.

When you find yourself faced with some sort of stimulus that's going to elicit a reaction or a response, the first thing to remember is that you can **Reach** for either. You always have a choice.

Reaching for a reaction leads to one of two things: you will **Recoil** from the situation (run away and avoid) or **Resist** (fight) what is, which only serves to create more of it or hold it in place. Both of these lead you to **Return** to old habits and patterns from the past, which didn't work then and won't work now; the end **Result** being to **Repeat** the cycle of something you don't want.

If instead you respond, you will be able to **Review** (remember how reacting in the past worked out) and **Realize** you have an opportunity to make a decision more in line with your core values. **Reforming** your ideas about the way you should behave in this situation will **Result** in **Resolving** to go in a different direction this time.

> **Prayer:** *"Redemptive God, thank you for giving me opportunities to refine the way I respond to situations as I grow and mature. Amen."*

Challenge Your Mind. Channel Your Power. Change Your Life.

January 21

LETTING GO

Change is the Only Constant

Affirmation

"Change is the only constant in my life. As my divinity continues to unfold I will progress from one season to the next. Friends will come and go. And, as they do, I will not live in bitterness or un-forgiveness. On the contrary, I will remain open and give thanks for each new level of understanding and the newness it brings. I am not what I have, do, believe or what others think of me. I am…"

Change is the only constant in the universe. The universe continues to expand. Animals, and humans, continue to evolve and adapt. And, our ideas, philosophies, theologies, opinions and perspectives will change until the moment we make our transition back to Spirit. As we continually change, we will make new friends and lose touch with old friends. One of my mentors told me that every person only gets five lifetime friends. I don't believe this means we are all negligent and unfaithful as friends. On a deeper level, we are all unfolding and growing spiritually at our own pace and in our own space. When one friend's growth or pace of change is slower, there will be a natural distancing. We are all vibrational beings in a vibrational universe. When our vibration no longer matches the vibration of our friends, there will be an unseen force pushing us away from some friends and attracting others to us who share our same vibration. This is not just spiritual. Scientifically, this is an understanding of magnetism.

With this knowledge, we can feel less bitter about friends failing to keep in touch and also feel better about not keeping in touch with old friends. It is not simply that "life happens." Change and vibration happen. Bless people as they vibrate away and leave your life. Welcome new friends as they vibrate toward and are attracted to you. This way, you keep your mind open to new growth and your heart free from bitterness.

Prayer: *"Original Vibration, I am awake to the laws of attracting to and vibrating away. I release what goes and welcome what comes. Amen."*

LETTING GO

January 22

Let Me Be Spiritual

Affirmation
"Today I set my intention to make the main thing the main thing. I will not get lost in the smallness of rules, clothes, prayers or symbolism. I am an intelligent, awakened and self-aware spirit-being with the capacity and courage to see what is beneath the surface. I do not need a title, a reserved seat, a special parking space or a fancy robe to be spiritual. I AM created in the image and likeness of God and Good. And, tapping into my God-given Divinity is the most spiritual thing I will ever do!"

Rules. Regulations. Rituals. Restrictions. Regimens… Religion. Somewhere in the minutia of this mad monotony we lose sight of the main thing while desperately chasing a passing grade. Religion has a slow and subtle way of succeeding in attracting our attention to everything but the main thing. Jesus described this syndrome as *"straining at a gnat but swallowing a camel."* In other words, focusing on the things that really don't matter while forgetting and neglecting the things that do. Special diets, sacred days, sanctimonious robes, solemn symbols…all very important and unique to religious culture and expression. But, by no means the main thing.

Several years ago I spoke at a New Thought church for the first time. I was excited to have a new "spiritual" worship experience outside my religious norm. I was weary with religious literalism, predictable protocols and pretentious pageantry. At this New Thought Church, we were going to practice meditation. We were instructed how to hold our hands, breathe, etc. Yet, I did it a bit differently as my own way of connecting to God. I was told by a congregant I was doing it wrong. I politely explained I had enough religion and wanted to be spiritual. I believe she missed the point. Everyone worships, connects to Spirit their own way. Don't get lost in details or people's projections. Make the main thing the main thing. And, keep it that way.

Prayer: *"Common Sense, I desire to be spiritually free, not religiously restricted. Enable me to make the main thing love, peace and joy. Amen."*

Challenge Your Mind. Channel Your Power. Change Your Life.

January 23

LETTING GO

Bless It Coming. Bless It Going.

> **Affirmation**
> *"Today, I will remember not to block any blessing coming my way by closing my heart or my hands. I will allow blessings to flow to me and then through me. My mind is the channel through which good things come to me. As good things flow to me, I will hold them loosely, enjoy them as long as they are positive, purposeful and productive, and then know when to graciously release them. I am confident that the same Source who sent one blessing my way has many more in store."*

The musical group 38 Special wrote a song entitled *"Hold on Loosely."* The lyrics hold quite a wealth of wisdom, *"Just hold on loosely, but don't let go. If you cling too tightly, you're gonna lose control."* I resonate with most of this philosophy. When we cling too tightly, to money, to relationships, to things and become overly possessive or hyper protective, we unconsciously operate in a vibration of lack and a spirit of fear.

Sometimes we have to let go, release and rest assured that just as we celebrate new friends who come into our lives we may have to release them at some point. When we learn to bless and release we safeguard our minds against any bitterness that may clog up the conduit through which other blessings are trying to flow to us and through us. Friends, jobs, things, even thoughts…bless them all coming and going. Our minds are channels, portals, receptors. And, we can either keep our pipes clean and our plumbing clear or we can allow them to get stopped up with fear and backed up with resentment. How we end or release one season determines how we begin the next season. All highways connect to another. Streams flow to rivers and rivers connect to the ocean. And, one season of our lives is connected to the next. When a new season arrives, bless it. When it fades, release it. And, watch what happens when you remain open.

> **Prayer:** *"Ever-Flowing Source, today I will celebrate new blessings and gladly release them knowing they flow to me and through me. Amen."*

LETTING GO

January 24

Feeling Hurt by Others

Affirmation
"I will stop and think before reacting to hurtful comments or actions."

When you feel you've been hurt, it usually involves an interaction with another person and you frame it like this: *They* did or said something that hurt *me*. The first thing to do is to stop and ask yourself, "Is this true?" You already know it *feels* true for you, or it wouldn't have hurt. But is it true for them? To figure that out, you have to have a little conversation with yourself by putting yourself in their shoes and trying to see it from their perspective.

For someone you know well, this will be easy. Or, you might want to have an actual conversation with them about it.

For those you don't know very well, the problem is solved pretty quickly because not knowing their past or what issues they might be currently struggling with, you can't know exactly what caused them to say or do this thing that you've allowed to hurt you.

Secondly, if you don't know them well, ask yourself why you are letting their opinion bother you? Does it really matter to you? Or did it just trigger something inside you that you actually feel about yourself?

If this is the case, you'll know there's an issue that needs to be dealt with, but it is no longer between you and them; it's now between you and you - and your own thoughts about yourself that whatever they said or did only brought to the surface.

Prayer: *"Comforting Spirit, help me understand that some things I react to that I think are coming from others, are actually just things I think about myself that I need to deal with. Help me do so lovingly today. Amen."*

Challenge Your Mind. Channel Your Power. Change Your Life.

January 25

LETTING GO

Free FROM Sin and Free TO Sin

> *Affirmation*
> *"In the Christ Reality, I am free from sin, even if my mind does not perceive it yet. I cannot offend God. I can only miss the mark of my own divinity. In other words, I can only sin against myself. Today, I am free FROM sin. And, I am free TO sin. However, that doesn't mean I will create hell for myself. I will ask for wisdom from God concerning how to utilize my divine creativity to create the abundant life I want to experience."*

While baptizing one day, John suddenly looked up and saw his cousin Jesus. Describing Jesus, John said, *"Behold the Lamb of God who takes away the sin of the world"* (John 1:29). The word sin in this verse is actually the Greek word *hamartia* which means "to offend God." Jesus, the Lamb of God, has taken away the world's ability to offend God. Wow! So, if we no longer offend God, how do we sin? In the first epistle of John we find out that we do sin, but in a different way and against a different entity. *"My little children, these things I write to you, so that you may not sin. And if anyone sins, we have an Advocate"* (1 John 2:1). The use of sin here is the Greek word *hamartano* which means "to miss the mark." So, when we sin now, it no longer offends God. However, it is a missing of the mark. What mark? And, whose mark? And, who are we sinning against if God is not offended? We are sinning against ourselves. And, we are missing the mark of our own divinity by falling beneath our own godlikeness.

The Apostle Paul received a revelation of this when he declared *"all things were lawful"* for him, but all things were not helpful and did not edify (1 Corinthians 6:12; 10:23). Paul also declared that although he was free to do all things, he did not want to be *"brought under the control"* of anything. So, we are free from sin and free to sin, and still be loved by God. Yet, we are encouraged to not miss the mark by creating hell for ourselves or for others.

> **Prayer:** *"Lamb of God, thank you for taking away the offense. Today, empower me not to miss the mark. Amen."*

LETTING GO

January 26

Overcoming the Ego

Affirmation
"I am not what I have, do, or what others think of me. I am not separate from others or from God. And, I am not separate from what's missing in my life! I am the artist painting and sculpting the masterpiece of my life. My thoughts are like seeds. And today, I choose to grow flowers…not weeds!"

Immediately after His baptism, Jesus spent 40 days in the wilderness being tempted by the Devil. After a closer look, we find that Jesus was actually *"driven by the Spirit to the wilderness to be tempted by the Devil"* (Matthew 4:1). Why would the Spirit drive Jesus to the Devil? When we research the nature of these temptations, we can clearly see Jesus is being forced to deal with His ego and face His lower human nature. During this testing, Jesus would face issues like identity, desire for fame and possessions. This process of Jesus overcoming His ego corresponds with how Dr. Wayne Dyer described the ego. Dr. Dyer defined the ego this way: *"I am what I have. I am what I do. I am what others think of me."* So, overcoming the ego is a process of retraining how we see ourselves. It might be helpful to turn it around: I am not what I have. I am not what I do. And, I am not what others think of me.

When we are able to see ourselves minus the dependency on our possessions, without the blinding glare of our career or calling and separate from the inordinate attachment to other people's opinions of us, we find it easier to clear our minds of expectations and judgments. Then, we find new ways of defining success. We experience victory over criticism. And, we discover an immunity to flattery. With this new clarity, we are able to create life without the constant interference of the ego. In essence, we can plant new seeds without the threat of old weeds. When the weeds of ego are gone all that remains is Spirit. You are bigger than anyone's definition of you…even your own.

Prayer: *"God above definition, enable me to create my life from a clear mind, without judgment, void of criticism and free of ego. Amen."*

Challenge Your Mind. Channel Your Power. Change Your Life.

January 27

LETTING GO

I Deserve Good

> **Affirmation**
> "Today I am finally aware, and fully awake to the truth, that I create my life experience by my thoughts, words and choices. However, I am also aware that I don't deserve some of the things I have created. I can even completely own the negative things I create without being convinced that I deserve anything negative in my life. Because I am created from love and by a loving Creator, I know that I deserve love, peace, joy and happiness! Anything and anyone who tells me differently must be silenced!"

Many people, even entire families, have a long history of reaping difficult consequences associated with poor choices and negative thinking. When this vicious cycle repeats, often times people begin to believe there is no existence other than what they are experiencing. Even worse, people accept a false reality that somehow they don't deserve anything better. The pain and disappointment they have grown accustomed to just becomes their "plight" in life. And the most dysfunctional, destructive mindset is convinced that somehow this perpetual suffering is God's will and ultimately unalterable.

Bad things happen to good people…to all people. Sometimes it is entirely coincidence. Other times people think, speak, believe and then manifest bad things unknowingly and subconsciously via ignorance to their divine creative capacity. Whatever the case, we all deserve good things. If you create peace by consciously creating it, you deserve peace. If you plant seeds of drama and pain, you will reap the harvest of your creation. This doesn't mean you deserve it. Sowing and reaping, action and reaction, give and take, what goes around comes around, karma, are universal laws operating as exact sciences. We reap what we sow! Nonetheless, your Creator desires for you to be at peace and live in prosperity. Don't convince yourself you don't deserve good things. You do! Start creating good today!

> **Prayer:** "Ultimate Good, I know the plans You have for me and that You desire good things for me. Help me to accept that I deserve them. Amen."

LETTING GO

January 28

The Blame Game

Affirmation
"Blame is the subtle way I give my power away. Shame is the way I forbid my power from returning. I will not play the blame game or allow shame to keep me from re-creating my life. I will own, harness and learn to navigate the use of my divine creative capacity without any connection to blame or shame."

In the Garden of Eden metaphor, Adam and Eve are only forbidden one thing…not to eat of *"the tree of the knowledge of good and evil."* After they make the decision to eat or learn of this knowledge, they realize they are naked and attempt to cover and hide themselves. God descends to them in the garden and asks Adam why he has done this. Adam responds by saying *"It was the woman You gave me."* In Adam's response, we find two separate blames. Adam blames the woman, Eve. And, Adam indirectly blames God for giving him this woman. God then asks Eve why she has done this. Eve responds, *"it was the serpent."* So, Eve has blamed the serpent (or the devil) for making her do this. Adam nor Eve take any responsibility for their choice. In this case, shame leads to blame. And ultimately, shame and blame lead Adam and Eve away from God's Presence and keep them from waking up to their divine creative power.

This process exists all around us. One political party blames the other. One race blames all others. Churchgoers blame the devil (and occasionally God). Spouses blame spouses. Parents blame children. Children blame parents (even adult children blame parents). Sometimes people other than us are actually guilty and blameful. However, mostly we are directly involved with the realities we experience. In either case, when someone or something outside of us is always to be blamed, we are admitting that we have no power and continue to unconsciously give our power away. Reclaim your power today by refusing to give it away via shame and blame.

Prayer: *"Giver of Power, thank you for giving me power. Help me reclaim my divine power by not giving it away to anything outside of myself. Amen."*

Challenge Your Mind. Channel Your Power. Change Your Life.

January 29

LETTING GO

It's Ok

Affirmation
"Today I will remember: it's ok."

When you go through something that is difficult, it's ok and even necessary to be able to hold different emotions at the same time. It's good to feel strong and positive in the face of bad news and to encourage yourself and believe you have the strength to overcome whatever the obstacle may be. But it's also ok to feel a little scared and overwhelmed at the same time. That's not wrong. That's being human.

Feeling overwhelmed doesn't mean you have failed or that you have lost your faith. When you're struggling with something painful, you're going to have some good days and some not so good days. And on the not so good days, it's ok to ask for help and to let others be your strength during those times. That's one of the purposes of spiritual community.

Unfortunately, a certain degree of pain comes along with the whole human experience. But you must make the decision to trust God and know everything is working for your good. And not just once, but make that decision over and over on a daily basis whether you're on top of the world and feeling blessed or you feel like everything in your life is being shaken.

During times of shaking, whatever is inside you - all the things you have put there through your spiritual practice during calmer times - is what's going to come out. Learn to put good things in regularly, so they will be there when you need them.

Prayer: *"God of the Difficult Times, help me to learn how to trust you always and to know it's ok to lean on my brothers and sisters when I am feeling overwhelmed. Thank you for providing me with a spiritual community. Amen."*

LETTING GO

January 30

Inclusion Conversion

Affirmation

"As I ascend to new levels of consciousness and spirituality I will celebrate where I am, where I have been and where I am going. However, I will not project my individual journey onto others. Everyone changes. But, they change at their own pace and in their own space. I will trust that the same Spirit working in me is also working in others and in all of creation. I will surrender to the idea that spirituality is not a 'one size fits all.' I will remember that what works for me may not work for everyone. If the opportunity presents itself, I will gladly and respectfully share the beauty of my awakening without forcing it on anyone."

I was raised in an Evangelical Christian environment. This means many things. But, for the sake of today's affirmation, it meant we were commissioned to convert other people, actually all people everywhere, to think and believe like us. People from other religions, and atheists of no religion, were the potential "harvest." And, our job was to get out there into the "highways and hedges," into "the systems of the world," into the "field," and reap the harvest by successfully converting them to our religion…even to the specific denominational and doctrinal expression of our religion.

As I journeyed through my religious experience, I began to undergo a steady, and occasionally quantum, transformation. My theology evolved. My understanding of the nature and character of God changed. I became much more inclusive in my approach and much more expansive in my thought and theology. Everything about my understanding of God and the universe shifted. However, I unconsciously drug my Evangelical practice of conversion into my new way of seeing God. I no longer sought to get anyone saved. But, I did pressure people to see and accept my new understanding as their own. I was attempting to convert the world to inclusion. I recognized it, shifted and gave it to God.

Prayer: *"Inclusive Love, thank You for shifting me, shaping me and sharing with me. I trust You are doing this with all of Your children. Amen."*

Challenge Your Mind. Channel Your Power. Change Your Life.

January 31

LETTING GO

Nurse, Curse, Rehearse, Reverse

> **Affirmation**
> *"I recognize that I have been betrayed, lied about, falsely accused, rejected, abandoned, hurt and have experienced pain throughout my life. I am also aware that I cannot live in this hurt forever or allow this pain to become a filter through which I see and create life. Today, I make the conscious decision not to Nurse It, Curse It, or Rehearse It, and I know God will Reverse It."*

Today involves a subject that will require a little more time as we are going to dissect a very powerful biblical story together. This devotional is going to be longer than any other day. But, it will be worth it. And, it will be a moment of clarity and mental healing for all of us.

The three Hebrew children (Shadrach, Meshach and Abed-Nego) are in a situation where the king (Nebuchadnezzar) is attempting to force them to worship his god, his way. The three Hebrew children refuse and it angers the king. The king decides to put them to death in a fiery furnace. Let's walk through this process as we learn the valuable lesson not to Nurse It, Curse It, or Rehearse It, and then watch God Reverse It.

> *"He spoke and commanded that they heat the furnace seven times more than it was usually heated. And he commanded certain mighty men of valor who were in his army to bind Shadrach, Meshach, and Abed-Nego, and cast them into the burning fiery furnace"* (Daniel 3:19-20).

Notice here, the king orders the furnace to be heated 7 times hotter than normal. In biblical symbology, 7 is always a day of completion and rest, meaning, this furnace is not designed to kill them. This situation is designed to perfect them. Also, be aware that the soldiers who put them into the furnace, at the king's command, were *"mighty men of valor."* This will be important later.

LETTING GO

> *"Then these men were bound in their coats, their trousers, their turbans, and their other garments, and were cast into the midst of the burning fiery furnace"* (Daniel 3:21).

The important piece here is that the three Hebrew children went into the fire bound. But, they are about to come out free.

> *"...the flame of the fire killed those men who took up Shadrach, Meshach, and Abed-Nego"* (Daniel 3:22).

Remember the *"mighty men of valor"* who put the three Hebrew children into the furnace? The fire actually killed them. So, we can see two aspects of wisdom here. One, when people set traps for you, be at peace. When you keep your mind right and spirit free from lower thinking, the trap they set for you will actually ensnare them. Second, these seemingly good, trustworthy, powerful men of valor, entered into the king's offense. Yet, the king survived this situation while they were killed. The lesson is this: Don't enter into other people's hurts. We are here to heal the room, to help people grow past their hurts, not to enter into their offenses with them.

> *"Look!"* he answered, *"I see four men loose, walking in the midst of the fire; and they are not hurt, and the form of the fourth is like the Son of God"* (Daniel 3:25).

Because of their attitude in this difficult situation, the three Hebrew children are not hurt by this unfair and unjust situation. They went in bound. They came out free from bondage. And, in the midst of their most trying time, there is a fourth Man in the fire, who looks like the Son of God! We are never alone in painful moments. We can confidently rest in the knowledge that in the darkest seasons of our lives, the Spirit of Christ walks with us.

> *"...on whose bodies the fire had no power; the hair of their head was not singed nor were their garments affected, and the smell of fire was not on them"* (Daniel 3:27).

Wow! This heated situation has not harmed them. Their bodies, their possessions, and most importantly, their spirits, are not affected. The smell of fire or smoke was not on them. So many times, I have witnessed people survive very stressful, trying, unfair and painful seasons. Survive is an

---

Challenge Your Mind. Channel Your Power. Change Your Life.

accurate word because they smell like a survivor. The pain, the anger, the bitterness all seem to be a lingering stink they wear for the rest of their lives. When you come out…let it go…let God…laugh, love, live…and forgive. Refuse to smell like pain. Resist the stink of bitterness. Reject the stench of anger. And, receive the reward of righteousness, peace and joy!

> *"Then the king promoted Shadrach, Meshach, and Abed-Nego in the province of Babylon"* (Daniel 3:30).

This story ends with Shadrach, Meshach and Abed-Nego being promoted in a strange land, finding favor with the king who tried to destroy them and influencing the king to have a new openness to their way of connecting with God. When we maintain a high vibration, even in moments of stress and strain, we influence people's lives for good, and for God. And, even turn enemies into allies.

> **Prayer:** *"Fourth Man in the Fire, thank You for walking with me and for delivering me out of the fires that were designed to destroy me. Help me to not smell like smoke, or the pain of my past, for one more day. Allow my example of love, openness and forgiveness to bring peace to volatile situations. As I keep my peace, I trust You to defend me and promote me. Today, I will not Nurse It, Curse It, or Rehearse It. And, I will watch as You Reverse It! Amen."*

REDEFINING MY SPIRITUAL PRACTICE

February 1

Rethinking Prayer

Affirmation
"Today I recognize that all is sacred. As such it is possible for me to pray without ceasing. Prayer is not an action, but rather a way of life."

The Bible instructs us to pray without ceasing, which is a next to impossible task, especially when thinking of prayer as we have come to in Western Culture - something we do for a few moments in time - we interrupt our "regular" activities in order to have the spiritual experience of prayer, and then return to our normal routine. This is the result of our separating between what we feel is sacred in our lives and what we think of as secular, or non-spiritual.

Prayer, however, should be something we live at all times, not just something we do at certain prescribed times. When we shift our perspective and see every action we take and every thought we think as sacred, we can fulfill this biblical instruction.

We no longer think of prayer as being the action of getting on our knees, closing our eyes and saying a few words, but rather as being a feeling and an attitude that we hold in our hearts from moment to moment, being mindful of how our every thought and action create for us either a life that is working for us or against us.

Prayer: *"God of unceasing prayer, help me to make my entire life a prayer to you by no longer distinguishing between what is secular and what is sacred. Amen."*

Challenge Your Mind. Channel Your Power. Change Your Life.

February 2

REDEFINING MY SPIRITUAL PRACTICE

Spirituality in a Pandemic Part I

In 2022, at 49 years of age, I graduated from Emory University with a Master of Theological Studies degree. While taking a Contemporary Spirituality class, I was required to write a blog.* The piece I wrote was posted to the Emory Scholar's website. I present it to you over the next two devotions: In this blog I would like to speak to several ideas. One, the silver lining of the pandemic. Two, creative ways to reimagine communal spiritual practice when social distancing is needed. And three, I would like to offer a new perspective of sabbath.

A Silver Lining In A Dark Moment

While the pandemic has caused chaos, there is a hidden, subtle, creative potential being presented to faith communities and people who care about spiritual life. I find a silver lining in this storm. This is a space full of both fear and possibility. And, here it is. The spiritual well-being for believers and atheists alike is paramount during the pandemic. Spiritual communities have responded in diverse ways to the pandemic. When I speak of spiritual communities I include our agnostic and atheist brothers and sister as a spiritual community. Being raised as a Christian, anyone who did not believe like us, or who did not believe in God, was labeled as an "unbeliever." How broad this term is. If someone does not believe like us does this mean they do not believe? Non-religious does not necessarily mean non-believer. I find many who do not have a specific belief in the Divine to be very strong believers. Atheists and Agnostics alike believe in love, humanity, community, cooperation, interconnectedness. From an interconnected consciousness, we can see the human family is desirous of peace and connection in crisis, regardless of belief. Many are exhausted in the midst of dealing with the challenges of the pandemic. Perhaps the ideologies that separate us might also suffer exhaustion during this time of crisis?

A New Day Demands A New Way

As we find ourselves in a transitional space of liminality and uncertainty, the religious practices and rituals that enjoy concrete and absolute expression have begun to consider a more flexible approach. Religion tends to demand certainty. Spirituality is unafraid of entertaining questions and invites abstract thinking. Spirituality celebrates the unending journey toward truth, awakening, and unfoldment. Religion seems to hold dogma and doctrine as some sort of final destination.

---
*   Pui Lan, Dr. Kwok (PhD. Harvard Divinity). Special Topics in Systematic Theology: Spirituality for the Contemporary World. Emory University, Candler School of Theology.

REDEFINING MY SPIRITUAL PRACTICE

February 3

Spirituality in a Pandemic Part II

A New Day Demands A New Way (continued)

Resistance to change, and resentment of the unfamiliar, liminal spaces of darkness can sentence us to a lifelong wilderness of transition. Spirituality implores a mindful awareness of the truth that nothing is born, or even incubated, in the light. And, in this surrender, the liminal spaces go as quickly as they come. As my spiritual community has reimagined our rituals of gathering, worship and connection, we have uncovered new ways to worship. Sacred laughter, observing nature, stillness and mindfulness have all become new rituals that provide strength and connection. This may seem lewd, but I have learned to live in and practice gratitude for daily mundane obligations. When I awake in the morning, I immediately need to relieve my bladder. As I do, I give thanks for my bladder, kidneys, and digestive system working properly. This silly moment of gratitude has become known in my community as the "Pee-Pee Prayer!" And, in this morning ritual that we all share as humans, we find gratitude, interconnection, sacred laughter and higher vibration. Wow!!! Reimagining connection with the Divine as nature, laughter and urination. Blessed are the flexible, for they shall not be broken…not even in the midst of a global pandemic. Worship does not have to be seen as monolithic. It is all worship. It is all good. It is all God.

To Fast Fasting

Growing up Christian, we honored the sabbath with church attendance. And, I mean all day church. I attended three Sunday morning services and then a Sunday evening service (not to mention Monday night youth group meeting, Tuesday morning prayer meeting, Wednesday night Bible study, Thursday choir rehearsal and Saturday discipleship meeting). I even recall my mother not allowing me to run to the grocery store on a Sunday because it might be profaning the Sabbath. Presently, I sabbath or "cease" in new and diverse ways. I cease from seriousness and allow myself to fully embody joy. I cease from, or sabbath from, worry and from projecting my happiness into the future by fully embracing the present moment. I sabbath from guilt and shame, knowing that I will continually encounter mistakes and missteps in my journey of learning to navigate my divine creative power in a way that brings more joy than pain. I also have ceased from fasting. I fast fasting! And, instead of not doing something I do something. I connect with God more deeply through reaching out to a hurting soul than by refusing food. Is my hunger pleasing to God more than my love for humanity?

Challenge Your Mind. Channel Your Power. Change Your Life.

February 4

REDEFINING MY SPIRITUAL PRACTICE

Spirituality in a Pandemic Part III

Affirmation
"My spiritual practice is not based on a physical building or social gathering. Today, I am awake to the truth that I am the church. I am the Body of Christ. And, wherever I am, there God is."

So many of us think of buildings and gathering spaces when we think of church. So, what happens to "the Church" when the physical doors close during a global pandemic? I will admit, as the senior pastor of a local church that gathers physically each week, that I was in a state of panic when the pandemic forced us to stop in-person services. For almost an entire year we only met virtually. However, there was a gift of imperfection that surfaced in the midst of the chaos.

What we found is that the church is not buildings. The church is the mission, message and mandate of modeling love, inclusion and the kingdom of God on earth as it is in heaven. Furthermore, we realized the church really is the people who are connected to the mission, message and mandate. Our older members learned how to connect virtually through Zoom, Livestream, YouTube and Facebook. Outreach to the community continued. And bizarrely, our virtual attendance for Sunday, Tuesday and Wednesday services actually increased! We began a daily morning devotion that was well attended and celebrated by the entire church. What looked like a curse unveiled itself as a blessing. Can we agree to always be open to changes that come our way and be receptive to the shifts that carry the potential for greater unfoldment?

Prayer: *"God outside the four walls of the church, today I give thanks that the church is not a building, but a people and a purpose! Amen."*

REDEFINING MY SPIRITUAL PRACTICE

February 5

What's Your Why?

Affirmation
"Today I will not be swayed by negative voices outside myself. I will remember why I set out to accomplish certain goals and I will make my dreams a priority."

All of us have dreams and goals - things we want to accomplish. All of us also encounter obstacles to these dreams and goals, often on a daily basis. Sometimes we hear *no* over and over again instead of the *yes* we long for. When this happens, it's easy to get discouraged, sometimes to the point where we give up. This is a good time to remember WHY you set that goal and had that dream to begin with, and then refocus your energy. It helps greatly when you have a bigger yes burning inside you than all the no's you are hearing externally.

Once you decide what you want to do, put all of your positive energy toward it and cut out everything that is not essential (including the negative voices of others) to achieving that goal. Whether you are criticized, made fun of. . . whether you have major setbacks professionally or problems personally, decide not to tell a story of defeat and victimhood.

Remember that you are the creator of your own reality. The author of your own life. Dare to rewrite your story and give it the ending you want.

Prayer: *"God of the Sacred Yes, I say yes today to the dreams and goals in my heart of hearts and I ask that you help me prioritize my schedule, my energy, my resources and my focus in the way that will best to accomplish them. Amen."*

Challenge Your Mind. Channel Your Power. Change Your Life.

February 6

REDEFINING MY SPIRITUAL PRACTICE

Spiritual Maintenance

> *Affirmation*
> *"Today I recognize the importance of a spiritual practice. I know no one else is responsible for creating or maintaining it for me. I will do so for myself in order to keep my sense of joy and peace as stable as possible."*

In the biblical book The Song of Solomon, the author warns about little foxes that come and ruin the vineyards by stealing the grapes. Metaphorically, we understand this to mean small problems or issues that pile up on us and threaten to steal our joy and our peace.

It's important to learn how to avoid letting these minor situations turn into big monsters. So, how do we catch or chase away the little foxes as soon as we become aware of them? The same way we take care of anything in our lives - regular maintenance.

When you have a daily spiritual practice you don't have to run around in a panic trying to get all the things you need at the last minute. It's like putting money in the bank to be withdrawn when needed, or taking 200 practice free throws every night in the driveway so you'll be ready when game time comes.

No one can tell you what this practice should be, in fact, beware of anyone who tries to. Rigidly specific rules about how and when you should meditate or pray, etc. is not a spiritual practice. That's religious dogma. There are limitless ways to commune with God. It doesn't really matter how you do it, just that you do it.

> **Prayer:** *"Consistent Source, help me to create and maintain a regular beneficial practice of communing with you. Amen."*

REDEFINING MY SPIRITUAL PRACTICE

February 7

Healthy Religion

Affirmation
"Today, I set my intention to practice Healthy Religion. The hurt caused by my past religious experiences and expressions can serve to open my eyes to a bigger and better vision and version of the awesomeness of God, and of me! If fear, shame, intolerance and inflexibility have not produced a harvest of peace, joy and love in my life, I am willing to let go of unhealthy thoughts and unhealthy religion. I have received new wine. I will not put it into an old wineskin. Today I will begin the journey of creating a healthy religion, healthy mind, healthy thoughts, healthy body and healthy relationships."

In almost 30 years of full time ministry I have heard countless stories of how positive, and negative, the effects of religion have been on many people's lives. I have encountered amazing stories of the beauty of worship and God's presence. Conversely, I have endured tearful accounts of condemnation and manipulation in the name of God.

The tendency is to either buy it all or reject it all. So many people hold to the idea that it's either all true or it's all a lie. In my study of all the major world religions I have discovered profound truth and also uncovered ridiculous fallacies. I have been overwhelmed with timeless wisdom and been shocked by cultural craziness. There is an old saying, "Don't throw the baby out with the bathwater." Seek to find a healthy balance where you are open to truth contained in religion, but also vigilant and watchful not to be deceived by man's devising.

> **Prayer:** *"Eternal God, today I purpose in my heart to practice healthy religion. I have been helped and hurt by religion. My soul is thirsty for a path that cultivates a spiritual awakening and an ever-expanding consciousness. Grant me the wisdom to receive what is healthy for me. And, bless me with discernment to know what is harmful. Amen!"*

Challenge Your Mind. Channel Your Power. Change Your Life.

February 8 — REDEFINING MY SPIRITUAL PRACTICE

Communication With God is a Two-Way Street

Affirmation
"Let the words of my mouth and the meditation of my heart be acceptable in Thy sight, oh Lord."

We are a culture obsessed with speaking, but communication is a two-way street. Speaking is only half of the equation. The other half, and the only way communication is complete, is through both speaking AND listening.

We are also an incredibly distracted culture. We highly value the ability to multitask, but often to our own detriment because, as a result, our minds are usually far too noisy to really listen well.

Have you ever noticed that the words silent and listen are made up of the exact same letters, just arranged in a different order? You can't really listen to someone until you become completely silent. There is a distinction between being quiet and being silent. You can whisper quietly. You can physically not be talking but still have words running constantly through your mind. Silence is when both your mouth and your mind are still.

There is also a distinction between prayer and meditation. It helps me to think of prayer as talking to God and of meditation as listening to God. Sometimes we don't get an answer to our prayer simply because we don't wait long enough to hear the answer. We say, "God give me… God help me… God bless me." And then we get up and walk away.

We must learn to listen as well as to speak when communicating with God.

Prayer: *"God of Stillness, help me listen as much as I speak, especially when communicating with you. Amen."*

REDEFINING MY SPIRITUAL PRACTICE

February 9

Just Like Me

Affirmation
"Today I will add 3 words to every judgmental statement I make."

As humans, we are constantly making judgments about everything in our environment. But what each of us must remember is that our world is just a mirror reflecting "us back to us."

Judgment is not wrong in and of itself. In fact, it can be used as a tool to help us evaluate ourselves once we learn to apply it appropriately. There is such a thing as "good judgment" - we use that phrase as a compliment all the time. Judgment is just a process of either separation or inclusion, and the difference between those two is just three little words.

Here's an example: You make a judgment and say something like "She is so stupid" or "He is so pushy." Those statements create separation because the implication is that you would never be either of these things. But statements like "She is so beautiful" or "He is so kind" - although positive, can also create separation if the implication is that those are attributes you feel you do not have.

Add the words "just like me" to each of those statements, and the separation is gone!

She is so stupid - just like me.   He is so pushy - just like me.
She is so beautiful - just like me.   He is so kind - just like me.

These three words are the difference between judgment that separates you from others and judgment that includes yourself with them.

You can't stop yourself from making judgments, but when you add these three words, it becomes a different world.

Prayer: *"God of Inclusion, help me not to separate myself from my brothers and sisters through judgment, but instead use the tool of judgment to evaluate and better myself. Amen."*

Challenge Your Mind. Channel Your Power. Change Your Life.

February 10

REDEFINING MY SPIRITUAL PRACTICE

A Righteous Fast

> ***Affirmation***
> *"God takes no pleasure in my suffering. God takes delight in my prosperity. God does not need to see me in pain in order for me to prove the depth of my love or the level of my commitment. I am capable of shifting my paradigm about fasting. I am not anointed NOT TO DO. I am appointed TO DO! I will not live a life founded on what I keep from doing. I will spend my energy focusing on what I can do. I will create joy. I will pursue peace. I will heal the hurting. I will be inclusive of those who have been left out. This week, I will be conscious of the truth that what I DO is so much more powerful than what I DON'T DO!"*

I grew up around the discipline of fasting… fasting food, chocolate, soda, meat, television, radio. We fasted 40 days during Lenten and then every Friday of the year. We fasted when we wanted God to answer a prayer, change His mind or share His mind with us. I used to think many of our church members fasted smiling and laughing because they were so serious all the time…especially when fasting! Fasting was just a vital part of my religious experience and expression. Somehow we believed that suffering would get God's attention or at least prove to God how much we loved Him.

My tradition's fasting consciousness subtly conditioned us to believe God enjoyed our pain and suffering. Consequently, we focused more on what we couldn't do than on what we could do or should be doing. The prophet Isaiah gives us a beautiful alternative to religion's traditional view of fasting (Isaiah 58:6-7). Isaiah instructs us to DO something, not keep from doing something. Set the oppressed free. Feed the hungry. Include the outcast. This is the fast God has ordained. Ironically, Isaiah tells us to fast fasting.

> **Prayer:** *"Spirit of Truth, today I will begin a new fast. Empower me to help others by what I DO…not by what I keep from doing. I know You are more pleased when I love my neighbor than when I starve myself. Today, I choose the fast You have ordained. Amen."*

REDEFINING MY SPIRITUAL PRACTICE

February 11

Start With the Basics

Affirmation
"Today I will make dealing with my physical and soul-level needs a priority."

When something is wrong with your car and you take it to a mechanic, if they're good, they'll always start with the simplest and least expensive solution first. Then, if that doesn't completely resolve the problem, they will move on to the more complicated, more expensive solutions. But why spend a lot of money if the problem can be fixed in less time for less money?

Sometimes we are too quick to think we have a spiritual problem when actually, we just need to check the more foundational aspects of our lives.

First, take a look at yourself on the physical level. Are you taking care of your body? Getting enough rest? Exercise? Eating properly? Getting those things in balance will solve a multitude of issues that might be presenting themselves in the form of a bad attitude, depression, lack of energy, etc.

Next, check your soul. What's the status of your relationships? How are you getting along with the people in your life? Do you enjoy your job? Do you have a lot of issues from the past still needing to be processed? Do you have goals you are actively working toward? What's the balance between how much you're giving and how much you're receiving?

You can't even give your spiritual life your full attention until these foundational things are made right. But once they are dealt with, your spiritual life can't help but be enhanced.

Prayer: *"God of Clear Vision, help me to see clearly the areas that need to be taken care of in my life on a physical and soul level so that I may concentrate more fully on my spiritual life. Amen."*

Challenge Your Mind. Channel Your Power. Change Your Life.

February 12

REDEFINING MY SPIRITUAL PRACTICE

The Process of Prayer

> *Affirmation*
> *"Today I will follow the example of Jesus, the Christ, and pray the same prayer he prayed in the garden: Thy will be done."*

According to Catherine Ponder's book *The Dynamic Laws of Prayer*, the most effective way to pray is by using this 3-step process:

- **Purification** - forgiving others as well as yourself, clearing out all the negative stuff that blocks your channel so that the energy of God can now move through freely.
- **Illumination** - asking Spirit to show us the truth of any situation from the perspective of our higher self and then allowing Spirit to carry us where it will, bring to us what it will, take from us what it will, and awaken in us what it will.
- **Union** - surrendering our small, individual, unconnected to Source will to the Divine Will, which is permanently perfect.

This is a very different view of prayer than most of us were taught, which is asking a Santa Claus-like figure, far away somewhere up in the sky, to give us things or fix things for us or get us out of sticky situations.

Once we have received what the book refers to as illuminative guidance, we are under no obligation to follow it. We always retain the free will God gave us. But when we understand that what we have been shown will put us on the most productive path, it is easier to let our own will and plans for our life go.

> **Prayer:** *"God of Illumination, help me see today the value of coming to you in prayer through purification, allowing you to illuminate the most productive path for my life, and then coming into union with your Divine Will. Amen."*

REDEFINING MY SPIRITUAL PRACTICE

February 13

Staying in Your Center

Affirmation
"Today I will stay in tune with my fellow man by staying in tune with the Christ in me."

Often, before an orchestra begins to play, the pianist will hit one note so all the other instruments can tune themselves to that note. If each instrument tried to tune themselves to the instrument beside them, it would never work. But if each individual instrument is tuned to the piano, they will automatically also be tuned to each other.

Some of us spend far too much time, effort and energy trying to get along with each other. It's exhausting having to bi-laterally work things out with each person you have a relationship with.

Sometimes it feels as if you have just put one emotional fire out when another pops up somewhere else needing to be doused. It's literally impossible to keep your life in balance and to stay in your center that way.

It's so much easier and more effective to never leave your center by tuning your instrument to the piano as it were. The Christ Consciousness inside you is that one steady note. In the Bible, Paul says that if there be anything good, we should think on those things.

The more focus you place on your own Christ nature, the more good there is inside you; and whatever you have the most of inside is what will come spilling out when someone or some situation threatens to throw you off balance.

Constantly tuning yourself to your Christ nature keeps you in your center, and in turn, in tune with your fellow man as well.

Prayer: *"Christ Consciousness, help me recognize, connect with and focus on the Christ nature that is within me today and every day. Amen."*

Challenge Your Mind. Channel Your Power. Change Your Life.

February 14 — REDEFINING MY SPIRITUAL PRACTICE

The Experience of Me

> ***Affirmation***
> *"Today, whether I am married, dating or single, I will allow myself the experience of loving who I am. Where I go, and who I am with, may change over my life's journey. Yet, I will always be with me. This Valentine's Day, I choose to experience the highest version and best expression of me!"*

Several years ago, I was driving with a dear friend and mentor. We flowed effortlessly and seamlessly from riotous laughter, to deep sorrow, to taboo biblical and philosophical mysteries. In the midst of this safe, sacred space, I said to him, "I want you to know how much I honor and love you." He replied to me, "You know, you really don't love me. You love the part of yourself that you experience when you are with me." To tell the truth, I was a bit offended. I thought he might respond differently. Yet, after several sessions of soul searching, I had to admit to myself that he had made a powerful point.

How is it that we can fall deeply in love with someone, fall out of love with them, and then move on to new and different person with whom we fall in love? Could it be that we are in love with being in love? Or in love with the feeling of love that tends to remain hidden away deep inside of us? People love vacation destinations, television shows, outfits, churches, trainers, restaurants, leaders, friends, and then one day realize these people, places and things are no longer pieces of their reality. This Valentine's Day, fall in love with someone, with Paris, with an elegant restaurant. But, most of all, fall in love with yourself, the one and only constant that will never leave you.

> ***Prayer:*** *"Manifest Love, on this day I pray to fall in love with the divine, perfect, beautiful creature You breathed into existence. I have fallen in love with me and I will never fall out! Amen."*

REDEFINING MY SPIRITUAL PRACTICE

February 15

Your Spiritual Journey Part I

Affirmation
"Today I accept I am a uniquely created being who will experience God differently than anyone else. My relationship with God is personal."

People can describe to you, in great detail even, an experience they've had and you can get an idea of what it feels like, or more accurately, what it felt like *for them*. But you'll never know how it feels for you until you have the experience for yourself. Because we're all unique, we will experience things differently, and that includes our relationship with God, which won't be, and shouldn't be like anyone else's.

Even when a pastor or spiritual leader speaks from their heart to a congregation what they believe is a divine revelation from God in the form of a sermon, it's still very personal to *them*. It's still coming through their lens.

The people listening then have the opportunity to say either: *Yes, this resonates with me and this information is helpful to my spiritual walk.* Or: *I interpret or experience that a little differently than they do.*

The point is, there is no greater experience than direct personal experience. That, among other things, is one reason we shouldn't compare our spiritual journey to that of others, and also why we should never judge another's spiritual journey.

Any time you find yourself wanting to defend your personal experience with God or a particular spiritual practice that resonates with you - stop - and realize that's dogma at work. A spiritual experience should largely be about what *you* get from it personally, and not how well you can convince others of it after the fact.

Prayer: *"God of my Individual Nature, help me today create my own personal relationship with you and not depend on others to do it for me. Amen."*

Challenge Your Mind. Channel Your Power. Change Your Life.

February 16

REDEFINING MY SPIRITUAL PRACTICE

Your Spiritual Journey Part II

> ***Affirmation***
> *"Today I know that everyone's spiritual journey is unique to them and it is not my job to convert anyone to any particular path."*

It's very tempting, when you've had a wonderful experience, spiritual or otherwise, to want to share it with others, and that's fine. However, it's important to remember that no two people ever experience something exactly the same way; perhaps similarly, but not exactly.

So don't expect others to be as excited about your experience as you are and don't get disappointed, or worse, upset and angry, when they're not. Just let the experience be what it is to you and let them have their own. Appreciate every lens.

Also, it's not your job to be out converting people to Christianity or any other spiritual path in the first place. It's only your job to connect with God however you feel is most comfortable for you. Frankly, other people's spiritual experience is none of your business.

Learn how to use your valuable time and energy on something more important and positive than arguing with other people about how your particular way of relating to God is better than theirs. You can never go wrong with just loving them and letting them be. Be content in your own experience. This gives everyone around you permission to do the same.

> **Prayer:** *"God of All Faiths, help me today connect with you in the way that makes me comfortable. And let me be comfortable letting others have their own unique experience with you. Amen."*

REDEFINING MY SPIRITUAL PRACTICE

February 17

Random Acts Of Kindness

Affirmation
"Today, I will be kind to those I know and love and to strangers. As I do so, I am helping to raise the collective consciousness and elevating the corporate vibration of the human family."

Mahatma Gandhi encouraged us to *"be the change"* we want to see in the world. Gandhi battled oppressive systems, led millions in non-violent protest, and was so successful in affecting change that Dr. Martin Luther King, Jr. actually patterned the American Civil Rights movement and non-violent resistance strategy after Gandhi's work. Amazing! Yet, all of us will not lead millions or challenge empires. So, what can we do?

A simple random act of kindness is something all of us can do every day. Help a senior citizen load groceries into their car. Speak a word of encouragement to someone having a rough day. Relocate a mama turtle from the street and back into a safe habitat. Comparing our work, and our societal impact, with others subtly sets up a system of competitiveness. Kindness is not a competition but it can be contagious. Offering a genuine smile, picking up someone who has fallen or granting grace and patience to someone under stress can radically change the vibration of your environment. Begin today!

Practice the religion of kindness. ~ Dalai Lama

Prayer: *"Spirit of Kindness, today I am grateful that I do not need a temple or complicated philosophy. My heart is the temple. And, Kindness is the philosophy. Amen."*

Challenge Your Mind. Channel Your Power. Change Your Life.

February 18

REDEFINING MY SPIRITUAL PRACTICE

Polishing the Jewel

> ***Affirmation***
> *"Because we are all connected, the more I work on myself, the clearer a mirror I become for others, and the more light I project into the universal field."*

There is a concept in many spiritual traditions called polishing the jewel which comes from the story of a net hanging over the entire world similar to a spider web. At each place where the net connects, there is a beautiful, multi-faceted jewel.

This metaphor is used to describe our interconnectedness with each other and with the universe. Every jewel represents a separate consciousness, yet all are connected by a universal thread and serve as reflections of one another like millions of tiny mirrors.

What this means is that when any one of us, as an individual consciousness, chooses to self-reflect, see our shadow self (or dark side), and then work on ourselves in that area in order to be better, we are polishing the jewel that is us, and in doing so we make ourselves shine brighter, projecting that much more light out into the universal field. This also provides for the other jewels a clearer surface in which to see their own reflection - much like cleaning a mirror.

The end result is that the entire universe lights up brighter and brighter the more that we, as individuals, polish the jewel that we are.

> ***Prayer:*** *"Creator of Beauty, help me to see myself as a precious jewel connected to other jewels for whom I am a reflection. Help me to shine as brightly as I can today. Amen."*

REDEFINING MY SPIRITUAL PRACTICE

February 19

Being Self-Ful

Affirmation
"I will take care of myself by being self-ful, not selfish."

I heard someone say the other day that she no longer uses the word selfish, but has replaced it with the word *self-ful*, which means being fully yourself - full of love, full of confidence, full of energy - just *full*. That's your first responsibility; to take care of your *self* so that taking care of you doesn't become someone else's responsibility - physically or emotionally.

There's a scripture in the Bible that says, *"Foxes have holes. The birds of the air have their nests. But the son of man has no place to lay his head."* (Luke 9:58) I think that's referring to our thoughts. At the end of each day, when it's time to rest, the animals all know where they belong because they live in total cooperation with nature and follow their instincts. But we've forgotten how to do that, so it's difficult sometimes for us to mentally shut down.

Before you go to sleep, take a few moments and look back over your day. Know that you've done the best you could. And if you haven't, resolve to do better tomorrow. In any case, own what you're feeling and let go of anything - any anger, disappointment, or sadness - that's not serving you.

When we hang on to painful emotions and continue to nurse past hurts, that's not self-care. That's not self-love. That's not being *self-ful*. Remember that you can't love others unconditionally until you first extend unconditional love to your *self*. Finding a peaceful place to *lay your head*, to let go of your negative thoughts, is the ultimate self-care.

> **Prayer:** *"Loving God, help me find rest each night not only physically but within my thought life. Amen."*

Challenge Your Mind. Channel Your Power. Change Your Life.

February 20
REDEFINING MY SPIRITUAL PRACTICE

Don't Ask... Declare!

> ***Affirmation***
> *"Today, I will not ask. I will declare! I will not speak that I lack anything. On the converse, I will give thanks in advance! Instead of asking for anything, I will be open and available for Spirit to reveal to me what I already have."*

Asking for something is a very subtle admission that you don't have it. This is why Jesus said, *"when you pray, believe you already have what you're asking for"* (Mark 11:24). God does not desire to be begged for anything. God especially doesn't want us to grab onto the horns of the altar and refuse to let go until we somehow successfully persuade God by relentless begging and groveling. God takes pleasure in our prosperity. God's desire is to give us the kingdom. God wants us to have long life. Furthermore, God has already *"given us all things pertaining to life"* (2 Peter 1:3). Why would we ask for something we already have?

So, our approach must line up with these powerful truths. We must awaken to the revelation that we can approach the throne of grace boldly. King Solomon shares some wisdom with us that *"as we think, so are we"* (Proverbs 23:7). If we perceive we are lacking, then that is what we will create. We must begin to speak from power, being confident that God is good, that all good flows from God and that God would not keep any good thing from us. Instead of asking for something and making a declaration of lack, declare that you already have it. If you ask for anything simply ask that God reveal to you what you already have.

Jesus trusts us with a powerful truth. We don't have to ask for anything. All we must do is *"seek first the Kingdom of God, and all these things will be added to us"* (Matthew 6:33).

> ***Prayer:*** *"Divine Creator, today I give thanks that I have all things pertaining to life and that I need not ask or beg for anything. I only ask that You allow me to see what You have already given to me. Amen."*

REDEFINING MY SPIRITUAL PRACTICE

February 21

The True Meaning of Spiritual Warfare

Affirmation
"I wrestle not against flesh and blood."

Those of us raised in traditional Christianity are familiar with the term *spiritual warfare* and the concept of being a *spiritual warrior*, which meant we were always fighting something external, but invisible - the powers of darkness, or, more specifically, Satan.

We think of a *regular* warrior as someone who physically battles another human who he has decided is "the enemy," and that's what the idea of a spiritual warrior is based on - "the enemy" just shifted from an actual human we could see to an invisible force we labeled "the devil."

But here's a different perspective on that. If we believe that God, Jesus and the Holy Spirit are three aspects of the same entity, as the doctrine of the Trinity suggests, then in the biblical accounts of Jesus, both in the wilderness and in the Garden of Gethsemane, who is he speaking to?

From our human, dualistic perspective, we tend to view these as conversations with an external presence (Satan in the wilderness, and God, the Father in the garden). But there's a pretty good case to be made, in both instances, that he is actually speaking to and struggling with - himself - his human nature vs. his Christ nature.

Similarly, the only spiritual warfare we ever really engage in is with ourselves. When we understand this, our whole concept of it changes. None of us are battling other people, or even invisible forces of darkness. We are all struggling within ourselves for our Christ nature to be stronger than our human nature.

Prayer: *"Christ Consciousness, help me to know today that the only battle I ever have to fight is within myself. And help me to always let my Christ nature prevail. Amen."*

Challenge Your Mind. Channel Your Power. Change Your Life.

February 22

REDEFINING MY SPIRITUAL PRACTICE

Ho'oponopono

Affirmation
"I Am All."

In the Hawaiian tradition there is a practice called Ho'oponopono which is a process of letting go of the toxic energies within you, allowing your wider surroundings to be divinely impacted.

The basic premise is that peace in your life and in your environment is your responsibility - the creation as well as the maintaining of it. Once peace is lost, it doesn't matter where you believe the problem or breakdown came from - an external or internal source - it becomes yours to deal with and you blame no one else for it.

No matter the cause, you have the choice to continue to engage with a less than peaceful state of being and let it keep replaying in your consciousness, which only reinforces it in the collective consciousness. Or, you can ask God to transmute it INSIDE YOU, which miraculously also heals it in your outer experience.

As you cleanse yourself with this simple 4 sentence prayer: *"I'm sorry. Please forgive me. Thank you. I love you,"* the world around you is also cleansed because you are integrally connected to everything and everyone in it.

By praying in this way you take 100% responsibility for any part you, personally, had in creating the environment where the breakdown occurred whether it was directly your fault or not. You are taking it upon yourself to energetically heal and make right something on behalf of the collective.

You heal others by healing yourself and cleaning up your own energy. This works because at the deepest level we are all connected by our inner divinity. When you deal with your inner world, your outer world, and all who are in it, can't help but reflect that change.

Prayer: *"Divine Healer, I'm sorry. Please forgive me. Thank you. I love you."*

REDEFINING MY SPIRITUAL PRACTICE

February 23

Me First

Affirmation
"Everything in my life begins with me."

A common philosophy most of us are taught by traditional Christianity is: *God first, others second, me last.* There's only one problem with it. It doesn't work very well. If it did, we wouldn't be having the problems in our world right now that we're having.

You see as humans, we're not very good at understanding abstract concepts without something concrete to base them on. Loving a God you can't see is an abstract concept. Similarly, if you have no love for yourself (the only vehicle you have through which to experience anything in this earthly life), there is no foundation from which to love others.

Everything in your life begins with you. There are no exceptions. Even love, as you experience it here on earth, must begin with you. God first, others second, me last is a vertical hierarchy - top to bottom, highest to lowest.

It might be more helpful to visualize this concept horizontally. When you begin with self-love as the center, it's more like a circle that expands outward, including more love as it grows.

I love and honor myself as a divine creation first, which allows me to love others the same way as I love myself, which then expands into the highest and greatest expression of love there is - God.

This order puts all the power back in your hands - no longer far away from you with a God you cannot see, or with others whose behavior you cannot control. When you love yourself first, you are able to expand that love to include others, then God who is all and is in all - The Alpha and Omega. But it all begins with you.

Prayer: *"Unseen God, help me to love myself first today. Amen."*

Challenge Your Mind. Channel Your Power. Change Your Life.

February 24

REDEFINING MY SPIRITUAL PRACTICE

My Body is a Temple

> ***Affirmation***
> *"Today, I am aware that my body is the temple of the Holy Spirit. This temporary physical body houses my eternal spiritual self and soul. My physical body temple may not last forever. However, while I am in it, I will honor and respect it while it helps to facilitate my purpose and impact on the world and on those around me. Today, I choose to be aware of both unhealthy patterns and healthy alternatives. Today, I choose divine health over divine healing. Today, I choose to do my part in creating a long, happy and healthy life."*

Healing evangelists and miracle services were not uncommon in the church where I was raised. Occasionally, I did witness some divine moments of healing taking place for others and even in myself. In this atmosphere and culture of the miraculous I noticed a subtle, dangerous line of thinking. I watched as many sincere believers began leaning toward divine healing, not divine health. I observed levelheaded, good-hearted people choose a practice of treatment rather than creating a pattern of prevention. To be plain, I watched people neglect their physical health and then ask God to heal them when their bodies reacted to this poor treatment.

I believe in divine healing and in God's power! But, I also believe we have a responsibility to care for our body temples and respect its function of carrying our spirits and facilitating our earthly purposes. All of us are genetically predisposed both to certain physical strengths and health risks. We may not be able to change our genetic codes. Yet, we can do the best with what we are given. Make the choice today to exercise, eat, rest and live in such a way that your physical body temple will fulfill its destiny of carrying your spirit until it makes its transition back to God.

> **Prayer:** *"Divine Healer, give me the discipline to choose divine health. Empower me to respect my body as the temple of the Holy Spirit. Fill my stomach with healthy food and my mind with healthy thoughts. Amen."*

REDEFINING MY SPIRITUAL PRACTICE

February 25

Working With Your Shadow

Affirmation
"By embracing my darkness, I make it a friend and take it with me into the light."

Most people associate the term *shadow* or your *shadow side* with something evil, but your shadow is actually nothing to be afraid of. From a psychological perspective it merely refers to the unconscious or disowned side of our personality. In other words, it's any part of yourself you do not readily see, acknowledge or accept.

We all have one, and running from it is not the answer. This only allows it to grow bigger, which will eventually negatively affect you. Even though you may try to ignore it at times, life will always force you, in one way or another, to go back and deal with your shadow. It's part of what we all came here to do.

Your shadow actually helps you learn how to love because anything you judge in another is usually a part of your shadow. When you think of it that way, you can begin to ask, "How can I be kind to that part of me?" - just like you ask yourself how you can be kind to others who need your kindness when they are not behaving as their best selves.

Ultimately you must learn to love ALL of who you are - not just the good parts. In turn, this helps you love all of who others are. When you shine the light of your love on the dark parts of you, you realize why you should love them more. When standing fully in the light, you understand that your shadow helps you evolve.

Prayer: *"Source of Light, help me make friends with my shadow today rather than seeing it as my enemy. It is here to help me grow. Amen."*

Challenge Your Mind. Channel Your Power. Change Your Life.

February 26

REDEFINING MY SPIRITUAL PRACTICE

Inside Out

> ***Affirmation***
> *"Today I know and understand that inner transformation always precedes and supersedes outer transformation."*

I read a story about a woman once who was so unhappy with herself that she decided what she needed to do was radically change her body. In order to accomplish this she entered herself into a body-building competition that was sufficiently far enough in the future for her to get herself into shape. And... she did it.

By the time of the contest she felt she had attained the perfect body, or near enough to it at least. But, the surprise of her life was that nothing at all had changed about the way she felt about herself.

What she discovered was that it wasn't her body that needed changing, but her perspective. As a result of this experience, she began an entire campaign and filmed a documentary about body image positivity that has subsequently helped thousands of women.

Making changes to ourselves is indeed necessary in order to grow and evolve, but so much of the time, just like this woman did, we concentrate on changing the wrong things - those things that are external.

How many times have you heard someone say, "If I can just get out of this bad relationship / quit this dead end job / move to a better neighborhood / get my kids to behave - THEN I will be happy." Sometimes those things do need to change, but all of that is just rearranging outer circumstances. The real change must take place inside. As within, so without.

> **Prayer:** *"Transformative God, help me to change my inside before worrying about my outside, and to realize my search for happiness will never be solved by any source or circumstance outside myself. Amen."*

REDEFINING MY SPIRITUAL PRACTICE

February 27

Step Out of the Boat

Affirmation
"I will not get stuck in any practice that is no longer serving my spiritual needs."

Some spiritual practices are only meant to be a part of your life for a season. Once they have fulfilled the purpose they were meant to accomplish in your life you no longer need them.

We all move, learn and grow at a different pace. Some people are comfortable sticking with the same basic religion or spiritual philosophy for years, maybe even a lifetime, while others move through different seasons where a variety of practices are needed.

Let's think of our spiritual practice as a boat. Once you reach the shore, you step out of the boat because you no longer need it. And you walk on dry land for a while, but as you continue to live and grow, you inevitably come to another body of water, for which you again need a boat . . . maybe a very different kind of boat this time than last time.

People get stuck when they won't get out of a particular boat. Life is not static, just as bodies of water are not all the same. White water rapids are fast, wild and choppy. Lakes are calm and still. Rivers flow smoothly. Huge ships are useless in shallow water, whereas small motor boats have no business out in the deep sea. Different boats are needed for each type of water.

Whatever spiritual practice or religion you were born into may work for you most of the time, but it's not wrong to seek something more when that way no longer works for you.

Prayer: *"Progressive God, help me to seek out whatever spiritual practice best facilitates my connection with you during each season of my life. Amen."*

Challenge Your Mind. Channel Your Power. Change Your Life.

February 28

REDEFINING MY SPIRITUAL PRACTICE

Correcting Our Misperceptions

Affirmation
"Today I will perceive the Christ in me!"

Most of us are familiar with the phrase: perception is reality. Though that's not always true, our reality is indeed changed, shaped and affected by how we perceive things. That's why it's so important to correct any misperceptions we have, especially about God, Jesus and the nature of salvation.

Let's look at a physical example. Have you ever seen someone in the ocean flailing around, perhaps on their backs, kicking and splashing, coughing and sputtering, when suddenly someone tells them to put their feet down and they realize they can touch the bottom? They perceived they were in over their head, but that was not the reality. It's actually pretty comical when they realize this.

That's how I view Jesus and his role in our lives. When we're sure we're sinking and we cry out to him, he *hears our despairing cry*, as the old song says, but instead of lifting us out of the water, he calmly says to us, "Just put your feet down."

And if we still don't believe we can, he'll jump in beside us and put his feet down to show us how shallow the water is and say, "If I can do it, so can you!" (*The things I do, you will do and greater!*)

His purpose in our lives is to be our example; to show us the way. But we continue to splash around and insist that he pull us out because we believe we cannot be *saved* unless he does something for us that we perceive we cannot do for ourselves.

Prayer: *"God of Reality, help me today correct the misperception that Jesus must do for me something I am perfectly capable of doing for myself. Amen."*

FULLY AWAKE 365

REDEFINING MY SPIRITUAL PRACTICE

February 29

Swaying In Place

Affirmation
"When neither moving forward or backwards is a good option, swaying in place is the best choice - and perfectly ok."

Often we feel like the only two directions we can move in are either forward or backwards, and if we're not doing one, we're necessarily doing the other. But…there's a third option where we're still moving, but neither forward nor backward - we are swaying in place. This is achieved by keeping your feet planted in the same spot but moving your upper body from side to side.

What happens when you close your eyes while standing still? Your body automatically begins to sway on its own like this, helping you to naturally find and maintain your balance.

In metaphorical terms, when you close your eyes, you're going within. You're looking at yourself and evaluating which things need to go and which things need to stay in order to keep your emotional balance. During these times you are not making forward progress, but neither are you regressing or losing any ground. It's just a holding pattern for when you need a little breather.

Don't let others or your own mind force you to move forward before you're ready. There's nothing wrong with swaying in place for a while until you find your balance. Any forward motion will go much more smoothly from a balanced position. Taking the time to find your balance makes you more, not less, capable of taking positive action that will truly make a difference in your life.

> **Prayer:** *"God of Balance, help me stand still and take a breath emotionally before moving forward today if that's what is needed. Amen."*

Challenge Your Mind. Channel Your Power. Change Your Life.

March 1

THE POWER OF NOW

Your Appointed Time

> **Affirmation**
> *"My appointed time is not some moment in the future. And, I have not missed my appointed time somewhere in my past. My appointed time is NOW! This is the day the Lord has made. Today is the day of salvation. There is no thing, and no one, to wait on. This is my appointed time. I believe it. I perceive it. And now, I receive it."*

There is a generally accepted idea in many religious and denominational circles that God has specific seasons of favor, changes moods and says "yes" sometimes and "no" at other times. God does not have favorite people, favored times or even seasons of favor. Your appointed time and your season of favor is always now…whenever you awaken to your divine creativity and godlike capacity to think, speak and manifest the experience of life you desire by finding the vibration that yields that reality to you. The biggest threat, and greatest hindrance, to the kingdom of God coming among us is that it's somehow always on the way…not here now…waiting for appointed times and prophetic utterances to be fulfilled. Jesus taught that the kingdom of God is right now, not on the way or in the future:

> *"Now when He was asked by the Pharisees when the kingdom of God would come, He answered them and said, "The kingdom of God does not come with observation; nor will they say, 'See here!' or 'See there!' For indeed, the kingdom of God is within you."* (Luke 17:20-21)

Religious minds always get bogged down in the literal and miss the spiritual… unconsciously they give their creative power away to illusions of time and delusions of favor. There is nothing to wait on. God exists in eternity and doesn't submit to time. Be powerful by not giving your power away. Today is your appointed time. Now is where favor can be found.

> **Prayer:** *"Timeless God, I give thanks that this is my appointed time. Today is my season of favor. Now is my moment. Amen."*

March 2

Be Here Now

Affirmation
"Today I will live in the now and be present in each moment, giving it my full attention and my unconditional love."

Attachment is based in fear and dependency and has more to do with love of self than love of another. Love without attachment is the purest form of love because it isn't about what others can give you because you're empty, but what you can give to them because you're already full.

When you reach that level, you're up there with the ascended masters, willing to give everything - even your very life - with no expectation of getting anything in return. But that's a pretty high bar. So, what can we do in the meantime while we're walking in that direction? We can take some baby steps toward that deeper level of non-attachment (not the "I'm not going to care about anything or anybody so I won't get hurt" level) but the purest level of loving without being attached in an egotistical way.

In the Bhagavad Gita, Krishna says, "Let your concern be with action alone, and never with the fruits of action. Do not let the results of action be your motive." This doesn't mean we shouldn't be fully engaged with others and with the events of our lives, just that we should enjoy each moment or phase as it comes; concern ourselves only with what we're doing right now and surrender the final outcome. In other words, be present. Be. Here. Now.

Prayer: *"God of Our Present, teach us to do what is in front of us right now with all our hearts, letting go of what might come of it. Let us learn to love life as it is for its own sake. Amen."*

Challenge Your Mind. Channel Your Power. Change Your Life.

March 3

THE POWER OF NOW

Common Past. Uncommon Present.

> *Affirmation*
> *"Today, I will be aware that as I change and evolve I may not share common vibration with everyone from my past. I will not be a debtor to shared histories if they do not connect with my now. I give thanks for former friends and past experiences. And, I remain fully awake to this present moment."*

How many of us have stories of either great joy or tremendous pain from our past? All of us! And, each of those stories and experiences involve people. Some of those people shared great triumphs with us. And, some shared desperate moments of worry and stress. As life is a long journey, many times we vibrate or veer away from people with whom we shared significant life moments. This is the natural process of evolution and unfoldment.

Just because we share a common past with someone does not mean we are automatically connected in a common now. When an astronaut is mapping out the journey to the moon he or she must be cognizant of the reality that even the slightest turn can ultimately mean thousands of miles in shift. Imagine the vibrational, spiritual, emotional, psychological shifts we experience from our childhood to our senior years. A journey of shifting and sifting and even drifting. It is natural to lose connection with those from our past, even with those who played a significant role in our lives. Be at peace with it. Give thanks for it. And, live in the now moment.

> **Prayer:** *"Wind of the Spirit, thank You for each person and experience that has blown into my life and impacted me in any way. I give thanks for them all. Now, enable me to live in the present moment without obligation to my past. Amen."*

March 4

Happy For No Reason

Affirmation
"Today I know that happiness is my natural state and I need no specific reason to feel happy other than I want to."

When people ask you what you want, answer them, *"I want to be happy."* And when they ask, *"Well, what makes you happy?"* Answer, *"Being happy."* And when they then say, *"You're a nutcase."* Respond: *"Maybe so. But I'm the one who's happy and you're not."*

This somewhat comical fictional exchange given by spiritual teacher, Esther Hicks, makes a good point. Most people feel they need a *reason* to be happy. In fact, our culture tends to think that people who are happy too much of the time for no apparent reason are looking through rose colored glasses, not living in reality, and may even be a bit *crazy*.

That's because too many of us have allowed this world of duality and suffering to convince us that being miserable is not only unavoidable, but the norm, and that happiness is the exception. That's simply not true.

Happiness is our natural state, and we need no other reason to be happy than that we *want* to be. The true reality is that your brain can't tell the difference between *thinking* you feel happy and actually feeling or being happy. When you're not happy, what is it you want most? To be happy! As we know, thoughts become things. So think happy thoughts about happy things and it won't be long before happiness manifests in your reality.

Prayer: *"Spirit of Happiness, help me keep myself in the vibration of happiness and well-being today by taking my thoughts into captivity and directing them toward positive, happy things. Amen."*

March 5

THE POWER OF NOW

Temporary Containers

Affirmation
"I know that I am an eternal spirit having a temporary human experience. My body is not eternal and not who I am. My body is simply a container, or the temple, that houses my spirit... for now."

Water will always take the shape of its container. The container is not the water. The container is only the housing of the water. If you poured the same water into another container of a different shape, the water would, without hesitation, take the shape of the new container. No container could ever boast that it has trained the water or figured out the shape of water. Similarly, Spirit may be housed by many different containers. And, Spirit may even take the shape of a particular container. However, Spirit is not the container. Containers such as religions, holy books or religious buildings, are only containers. When Spirit is poured into them, it may take the shape of that specific religious container, but the container is not Spirit. It is just temporary housing for Spirit.

Water, or H2O, can actually take on 3 different forms...liquid (water), solid (ice) and gas (steam). Whatever form it takes, it is still the same substance. No matter its shape, texture or temperature, it is still water. Consider that the same Spirit that was working in the container we call Jesus was also present in Mahatma Gandhi, Martin Luther King, Jr. and is working around, in, through and as us. It was all the same Spirit, called by different names, just being housed in different containers.

Be conscious not to value the container more than the Spirit. Paul described our bodies as *"tents"* or temporary housing. Containers such as human bodies, churches, temples, synagogues, mosques are all just facilitation or temporary housing for eternal, shapeless, boundless Spirit. Build your hopes on things eternal, not on temporary things that will eventually pass away.

Prayer: *"Shapeless Spirit, give me the vision to recognize You regardless of the shape You take or the container You inhabit. Amen."*

You Have the Power

Affirmation
"I know the power of Christ is within me!"

In the fifth chapter of John, there is a story of a pool in a place called Bethesda where it was believed that the spirit of the Lord would come and *trouble the waters* once a day. Anyone who got into the pool at that time would be healed. It is unknown whether this had anything to do with the actual water, or was just a product of the strong belief in it the people had.

Jesus came to the pool one day and saw a man lying beside it who had been there for years. He asked the man one question, "Do you want to be made whole?" Instead of just answering, "yes," the man started explaining to Jesus why he hadn't been healed already - because no one would help him get into the water when it was troubled, and someone else always stepped in before he could get there.

This is a perfect example of how humans get conditioned by the scarcity mentality: *someone else took the healing power and that's all there was - there is no more left for me.* It's also an example of how we give our power away to others, always wanting someone else to do our spiritual work for us.

When you realize you want something, and the Christ Spirit is standing in front of you (more accurately, is residing within you) asking you if you want it - don't blame anyone else, explain why you don't already have it, or wait for someone else to give it to you - just say yes!

> **Prayer:** *"Christ Within, help me realize today that I already have all the power I need to get the things I need from life. Amen."*

Challenge Your Mind. Channel Your Power. Change Your Life.

March 7

THE POWER OF NOW

Nothing New Under The Sun

> **Affirmation**
> "Today, I affirm that God lives without timelines and above linear thinking. The Alpha and Omega, the First and the Last, the Beginning and the End, He who Was, and Is, and Is To Come exists continually, eternally, in eternity. Yet, allows me to awaken in time."

History repeats itself. For me. For you. For us. Whether it is sideburns and bell-bottoms, or one country (or religion) attempting genocide (in the name of God) against another, look deeply enough and you will see a discernable, definable, distinct historical pattern repeating itself. Thus, "Nothing New Under the Sun." And, this pattern repeats itself to give us a second chance at a first opportunity. King Solomon lays this wisdom out for us…

"That which is has already been, And what is to be has already been; And God requires an account of what is past" (Ecclesiastes 3:15). The Amplified Bible's translation of this verse says, *"God seeks what has passed by [so that history repeats itself]."*

Humanity's way of seeing history is usually limited to time and timelines. We think linearly. Yet, God is not linear. God is timeless. Cyclical. Said scientifically, energy is neither created nor destroyed. Said colloquially, what goes around comes around. What does this mean? God, in His, in Her, in "Its" timeless infinite cyclical existence, causes history to repeat itself so that we have several chances to learn lessons we could have, and possibly should have, learned the first time. Historical patterns of war, prejudice, discrimination, homophobia, xenophobia, religi-phobia, are all cyclically, painfully, predictably and even graciously repeating in the hopes that we will finally "get it." So, history is not only repeating. History is repeating for you! Give thanks. There is a historically repeating lesson for you to learn today.

> **Prayer:** *"Infinite Wisdom, thank You for causing history to repeat and for offering me another opportunity to 'get it.' I will! Amen."*

March 8

Sliding Door Moments

Affirmation
"Today I will take advantage of sliding door moments."

Contrary to what romantic movies may suggest, trust, in relationships, is not built by grand gestures, but rather in very small, sometimes seemingly insignificant, *sliding door* moments, which actually refers to another movie by that title that came out some years ago.

The plot was centered around a single event that took place in the life of a young woman and then forked into two distinct plot lines based on the sliding door of a subway train. She arrives on the platform just as the door is closing. In one scenario, she makes it onto the train just in time, and goes to work as usual. In the other scenario she misses the door by a fraction of a second, returns home to get her boyfriend to drive her to work instead, and finds him with someone else, ending their relationship and changing her life forever. The dual story lines then play out according to whether she made the train or missed it, and were vastly different.

The point is that huge shifts can occur as the result of a relatively small decision you make in a split-second - a sliding door moment. For instance, when someone you love really needs you, you have a choice to either drop what you're doing and connect with them, or pretend you don't notice they are struggling. Trust is built every time you make the choice to connect.

Just noticing when someone is a little off and asking, "How are you?" can ultimately mean more to them than any grand gesture you could offer, thus changing the entire trajectory of the relationship.

Prayer: *"Loving God, help me notice the small ways today in which I can earn others' trust. Amen."*

Challenge Your Mind. Channel Your Power. Change Your Life.

March 9

THE POWER OF NOW

Repent. Rethink. Renew.

> ### Affirmation
> *"Today, I will think, think about what I think, and think again. I will be aware of my awareness and thoughtful of my thinking."*

Jesus, and his cousin John the Baptist, had similar messages: *"Repent, for the kingdom of heaven is at hand."* (Matthew 3:1-2) The word *repent* is actually, originally two Greek words: *meta* and *noia*. Combined, metanoia. *Meta*, meaning mind, after and beyond. And *Noia*, meaning new, or modified. If we apply this understanding to Jesus and John's sermons, they were saying go beyond the known and welcome the new. Or, think, rethink, repeat. Think again, and then renew your mind to continue in this process.

Growing up in church I believed this message of repentance to be about showing regret, sorrow and guilt. As a child, many of my Sunday nights were spent in church, on the walk of shame, going to the altar to show regret for my sinful thoughts and ways. From a different look and deeper perspective, we can see this message is not really about sorrow, regret or guilt. It is about renewal. The renewing of the mind. In essence, Jesus and John were saying, "you have thought about the kingdom in a certain way. Repent! Think again. It is not physical. It is spiritual. It is not on the way. It is here. It is not out there. It is within." When Jesus said, "you have heard of old, but I say," He was saying go beyond what is known. When Jesus said, "you cannot put new wine into an old wineskin," He was saying renew your mind. When Jesus challenged old ways of thinking He was inviting religious minds to repent, rethink, renew.

> **Prayer:** *"Eternal Mind, grant me the strength to repent, the openness to rethink, and the flexibility to renew. Amen."*

March 10

Always Divine

Affirmation
"I know that I am divine and that my words hold power. I will use my words for healing and not for destruction."

In Mark 11 there is a story of Jesus cursing a fig tree because it was not bearing fruit. He and his disciples had been traveling from town to town and were tired and hungry. When they came upon the tree and Jesus saw there were no figs for them to eat, he got upset. So he commanded the tree to die. This was the human side of Jesus.

It could be argued that he could just as easily have commanded figs to appear on the tree's branches and they would have. This wouldn't have been at all out of the realm of possibility for a man who had just fed 5,000 people with two fish and five loaves of bread!

But he didn't. He chose to operate out of his lower nature and curse the tree instead. If he had been operating from his higher nature, he would have healed the tree.

Just like Jesus, we all have the choice to either curse or heal with our words; to operate from our higher or lower nature. This story shows us that even when Jesus spoke from his humanity, his words still had power, and so do ours. That's why it's so important for us to be mindful of what we speak - always - because even when we're speaking out of our human emotions, the divine within us is still divine.

Prayer: *"Source of Divinity, help me to understand and to honor the power of my own words today. Help me to use them to heal rather than curse, and let me always follow my higher nature. Amen."*

March 11

THE POWER OF NOW

The Eternal Me

> **Affirmation**
> "I am eternal. I was alive before I was born. I will live after my body dies. Today, I will reconnect with the Eternal Me as I resist being burdened by time or bound by any temporary label of race, gender or religion. I will upgrade my thoughts and focus on eternal ideas. I am skinless, sinless, endless, immortal, immutable, immeasurable and unmistakably an eternal spirit having a temporary human experience and expression."

When the young prophet Jeremiah was struggling with insecurity, instability and insignificance, God spoke to him: *"Before I formed you in the womb I knew you; Before you were born I sanctified you; I ordained you a prophet to the nations"* (Jeremiah 1:5).

In other words, God lets Jeremiah know that before his spirit took on physical form it was alive, known, sanctified and ordained. That's quite a bit of pre-incarnate activity before he showed up in his mother's womb. The First Law of Thermodynamics reminds us *"energy can neither be created nor destroyed."* The Hindu holy book The Bhagavad Gita enlightens us *"All that lives, lives forever. Only the shell, the perishable passes away. The spirit is without end. Eternal. Deathless."* The shell carrying Elijah's spirit was taken from the earth. But, that spirit showed back up in the shell called John the Baptist. Jesus said, *"For all the prophets and the law prophesied until John. And if you are willing to receive it, he is Elijah who is to come"* (Matthew 11:13-14). Your spirit is eternal. You were alive before you were born. You will live after your body dies (*"to be absent from the body is to be present with the Lord"* 2 Corinthians 5:6). So, don't align with or allow your eternal self to be limited by temporary labels of race or time-laden leashes of religion. This idea terrifies many church leaders because it diminishes the power of hell and defies its doctrines that want us to believe we only have one shot to get it right. You are externally fading, internally unfolding and eternally being. Rebuke time. Refuse temporary. Receive eternity.

Prayer: *"Timeless Truth, I am surrendered to the Eternal Me. Amen."*

March 12

THE POWER OF NOW

Get Happy, Stay Happy, Be Happy

Affirmation
"Today I will put consistent effort towards getting happy, staying happy and being happy."

Many people think happiness is hard to come by - that it's rare and random, reserved for only a few lucky people. But happiness is not something that comes ready made. It comes from our own actions, and it also comes through practice. Happiness is not something we find or happen upon. It's something we create and cultivate.

Recent advances in science show us that happiness is more than a simple feeling. It's a state of being that encompasses our mind, our heart, and even our cells. Because it's a state of being, we've first got to get there, and then stay there until we "be" there most of the time. But this takes some effort on our part.

Just like you can't exercise for six months and expect the benefits to remain for the rest of your life, you can't work on cultivating happiness for only a short period of time and expect it to make a permanent change. Both these things require consistent attention and need to become a part of your overall lifestyle.

One easy way to do this, among many others, is to start keeping a gratitude journal. It doesn't have to be elaborate. It can be as simple as writing down three things you're thankful for before you go to bed every night. This changes the ratio of what you're attending to or being aware of in your life and tips the scale to the positive side.

Small steps like this and others, practiced consistently, will do wonders to create happiness as your state of being.

Prayer: *"Source of Happiness, help me to know that happiness is something I can cultivate with consistent practice. Amen."*

Challenge Your Mind. Channel Your Power. Change Your Life.

March 13

THE POWER OF NOW

Iron Sharpens Iron

> *Affirmation*
> "Today, I will allow other people to both sharpen my dull places and smooth my rough edges. I embrace the truth that resistance makes me stronger, not weaker. I will not fill my life only with yes men or yes women. I will celebrate the contrast that creates wisdom."

Fish that live in a flowing stream, or exist in an environment that is full of strong currents or strong waters, are exponentially stronger than fish that sit and float in an undisturbed habitat. What do fish have to do with us? Specifically, how do fish relate to iron sharpening iron? Proverbs provides us with the wisdom that "iron sharpens iron." Obviously, this cannot be specific to iron, metal and other physical materials. The next piece of this passage says, "*so one person sharpens another.*" (Proverbs 27:17 NIV) Many times it is the dissenting voices, the opposing currents, not just the affirmations of friends and allies, that help to sharpen us. In preparing for a debate, the process involves cultivating an argument from the "other side" or from the opposing perspective of an issue as an exercise in being ready to answer and predict resistance. Do you have a family member, friend, neighbor or co-worker who shares a different opinion or perspective than you? Resist the temptation to float downstream. Refuse the temptation of the least resistance. And, allow the iron of their alternative view to sharpen you!

What does not kill us makes us stronger. And, those who do not agree with us only makes us sharper. The Apostle Peter encourages us to be "*ready to give a defense…for the hope that is in (us).*" (1 Peter 3:15) Set your intention to allow perceived enemies to sharpen and prepare you. We have a great hope. Our hope is that God is love and that all of creation came from God, exists in God, and will return to God. Anyone who does not agree with us can be a powerful catalyst inspiring us toward greater preparedness.

> **Prayer:** "God of All, give me the courage to swim upstream, the wisdom to avoid the path of least resistance and the confidence to avoid 'yes' people who only agree with me. Amen."

The Power of Silence

Affirmation
"My words are powerful and I will use them wisely. I will not allow the opinion of others to make me speak too quickly."

"People will remember not the words of their enemies but the silence of their friends." This famous quote by Dr. Martin Luther King, Jr. is often used as a reproach when people feel others should speak out about a situation or speak up for a certain cause or person and they don't.

However, there's a difference between silence that is an absence of presence because you don't care or you feel intimidated to speak and silence that is potent because its purpose is to listen deeply to your inner guidance and anchor down into the power that is produced from true righteousness *before* you speak. This type of silence is about gathering power before a battle just like a warrior.

If you don't go within and receive knowledge from your higher self before you speak, especially when the stakes are high and the situation is one in which your words could easily be misunderstood, you run the risk of your words and/or actions not being as effective as they could be.

Some issues do not require your immediate response. Don't let anyone rush you into speaking before you are sure about what it is you want to say.

Prayer: *"Patient God, help me today learn that pausing before I speak, especially on important matters, is wise. May I always use the most effective words available to me in every situation. Amen."*

Challenge Your Mind. Channel Your Power. Change Your Life.

March 15

Politicians and the Savior Complex

Affirmation
"I don't need a politician to save me."

We should be grateful to live in a democracy where everyone's voice is heard by way of the ballot box, but we must be careful not to put a savior complex on our politicians. When it comes to political leaders and our criticism of them, none of them are perfect because they are representations of us, and we are not perfect. Our leaders, especially the ones we elect, are reflections of us and our level of consciousness.

Instead of spending our energy either idolizing or demonizing them, we should try to work on and improve ourselves as a society. The more we do this, the more we are going to manifest leaders of a higher consciousness. It's that simple.

No one party or candidate is the answer to all our problems, and making elections a competition between light and darkness, where one is good and the other is evil, is very low vibrational energy.

All parties and all candidates contain both the light and the dark, because we as individuals and as a society have both within us. There is no such thing as a flawless politician because there is no such thing as a flawless person. If you think there is, you're falling into the deception of the savior complex, expecting one person or one political ideology to save us.

We must save ourselves. The more each of us can work on ourselves and stay in alignment with love and truth and live by our spiritual principles, the more we will see those same things reflected on the world stage by our political leaders.

Prayer: *"Source of Wisdom, I pray today for all political leaders as I work on raising my own consciousness. Amen."*

The WAY of Jesus

Affirmation
"I am aware that I cannot solve any problem by using the same consciousness that created it. Racial divides, religious wars and all segregations of the human family will only be solved as I create an environment of love and inclusion. Today, I will not only be a Christian...I will be a follower of THE WAY of Jesus. And, that WAY is LOVE!"

Jiddu Krishnamurti (philosopher and founder of the theosophical society) believed that a person practiced violence by labeling themselves as a Christian, Hindu, Muslim, etc. He believed that labeling encouraged separation, and separation eventually gave place to violence. Jesus left us several hints that He was more concerned with a person's thought process than their religion or label. He declared of the Centurion (a non-Jew and captain for the Roman oppression) that he had greater faith than anyone in Jerusalem. He told the disciples that He had *"sheep in other pastures"* that no one knew about. He told the woman at the well it didn't matter where she worshipped as long as she did it in Spirit. Jesus rebuked his disciples for condemning the Hellenists that didn't become His followers. He even scolded the Pharisees for making converts. Then He confuses the conversation by saying *"I am the Way the truth and the life. No one comes to God except through Me"* (John 14:6).

I wonder if Jesus meant no one comes to God unless they come through Him, His name and become a Christian? Or, unless they follow His Way... The Way of Jesus? The Way of love and higher thought. I believe promoting one religion over another is the cause of much of the strife in humanity. So, we cannot solve a problem (religious wars) using the same consciousness that created it (religious supremacy). Let us spend our time, money and energy, not converting people to Christianity, but convincing them of God's love...The Way of Jesus.

Prayer: *"Spirit of Unity, give me new a consciousness to create a world of peace and a beloved community of inclusion and coexistence. Amen."*

Challenge Your Mind. Channel Your Power. Change Your Life.

March 17

THE POWER OF NOW

St. Patrick's Day and a Break From Religion

> *Affirmation*
> "Today, and every day, I will honor MY spiritual practice by refusing to assimilate to someone else's idea of religious life. If I need a break from religion, I am practicing the wrong religion."

I look forward to green beer, green clothes and even green food! Green is one of my favorite colors. My Coexist and fitness training t-shirts are lime green! My Apple watchband is green. But, other than wearing, eating and drinking green, what is St. Patrick's Day all about?

March 17th, St. Patrick's Day, is a holiday originating in Ireland but observed all over the world. Traditionally, this holiday began as a day to take a break from the Christian Lent season and its sacrifices (February 22nd – April 6th). St. Patrick's day became a day to consume alcohol, to party with friends and to commemorate the birth of Christianity in Ireland.

Have you ever considered the insanity of having to take a break, or breaks, from a religion in order to celebrate it? If your spiritual practice needs constant time-outs and sabbaticals are you really being spiritual? Isn't one of the key differences between religion and spirituality balance? Every day of our lives we should seek TO DO something positive rather than strive to NOT DO something hurtful to ourselves or others. So today, drink green beer, be an active and empathetic listener to a hurting soul, laugh with friends and speak a word of encouragement to someone in need. Every day is a day for the spiritual practices of playing and giving.

> **Prayer:** "Every Day God, enlighten me to navigate and architect my spiritual practice with discipline, fun, helping others and caring for myself. Amen."

March 18

Telling Your Own Story

Affirmation
"I get to choose my story."

"I call heaven and earth as witnesses today against you, that I have set before you life and good, death and evil; blessing and cursing. Therefore, choose life, that both you and your descendants may live." (Deuteronomy 30:19)

This scripture reminds us that all options are always set before us. Ultimately, we get to decide what story our life will tell as well as which stories are true for us and which are not.

We get to question - constantly - the information we're receiving that's being filtered through our ego and the lens of our life experience. As we are brave enough to question our own truths, we gain more and more ability to change and shift what that truth and those beliefs are. And that's how we create our own reality. That's how we learn to tell our own story.

By taking responsibility for shaping our own stories in this way, we pass down better truths and perceptions about life to our children so that they can have better options to choose from as they form their own truths and tell their own stories.

What the divinity within you says about you is always your truth. Is that the story you will tell? Or will you continue to hold on to another, lesser story that says you are sick or not enough; that tells you you're a victim and can't change your circumstances.

For your own sake as well as those who come after you, make sure your story is aligned with what God says about who you are and what you're capable of. And don't accept anything less.

Prayer: *"Benevolent God, help me choose to tell a divine story with my life today. Amen."*

Challenge Your Mind. Channel Your Power. Change Your Life.

March 19

THE POWER OF NOW

Worshipping in Spirit and in Truth

> ### Affirmation
> *"I affirm that God is bigger than any religion, yet visits and can be occasionally discovered in most of them. I acknowledge that the fullness of God cannot be contained in any one holy book, confined to any one specific religion or defined by any one leader. God is not partial to location, sanctuary, temple or mosque, but is equally present in all of creation at all times. God is Spirit. And today, I will worship in Spirit and in Truth."*

Jesus is such an amazingly complex figure. At one point on His journey He told a Canaanite woman that He wouldn't help her or her daughter and informed her He wasn't even sent to help her or her people…who were dogs…yikes (Matthew 15:21-26). On another occasion, at Jacob's well, He engages a Samaritan woman in a conversation challenging her to see God as being bigger than any culture, impartial to any geographical location and unconcerned with religion (John 4:1-26). We can take comfort in knowing that as Jesus *"grew in grace and truth"* (Luke 2:40), so will we. And, as Jesus was *"perfected"* (Hebrews 5:9), we will be too. Like Jesus, we too will eventually ascend from the tribalism of cultural bias and overcome religious exclusivism. We will one day be able to worship Father God, Mother God, in Spirit and in Truth. And, pave the way for others to do the same.

A key point in this conversation is when Jesus tells the Samaritan woman that He is not coming to worship on her mountain and doesn't need to drag her back to His temple. After this declaration He explains why. He tells her that God is Spirit, and desires to be, or must be, worshipped in Spirit and in Truth. Jesus paints the picture that God is actively seeking worshippers who understand this spiritual truth. If God is Spirit, then God is neither male nor female. God is not a Christian or a Muslim. God is not an American or a Mexican. God is not a Democrat or a Republican. God is Spirit.

> **Prayer:** *"God As Spirit, I worship You without the boundary of culture or bondage of religion. I worship You in Spirit and in Truth. Amen."*

March 20

THE POWER OF NOW

Springing Into Rest

Affirmation
"Today, I will stop and smell the roses, be silent to hear the birds, pause long enough to feel the breeze and be still to enjoy the beauty around me."

March 20th is traditionally the first day of Spring (occasionally March 19th). Spring is a time for projects like planting flowers and Spring cleaning. For students, Spring is a time to cram for midterms, meet deadlines, complete projects and finish assignments. Accountants are swamped with filing taxes for stressed families. And, companies are anxious about their first quarter profit and loss margins. I engage in all of these necessary activities. However, I also try to be mindful that Spring is a time to break. Spring Break signals the end of stress and an opportunity to rest and rejuvenate.

Each Spring announces itself with new life and new growth. The flowers bud. The grass turns green. The leaves sprout on the naked trees. The baby ducks are born. Spring is a time to slow down, look around and take it all in.

This Spring, set your intention to finish your exams, complete your projects, meet your deadlines and file your taxes. Then, slow down and take it all in. Get outside and take a walk. Visit a botanical garden. After springing forward and then springing into action and activities, consider springing into rest, play, stillness and mindfulness. Rest just might be the action for which your soul is thirsty.

> **Prayer:** *"My Resting Place, grant me the strength to finish what I started and the wisdom to rest when it is complete. Amen."*

Challenge Your Mind. Channel Your Power. Change Your Life.

March 21

THE POWER OF NOW

Natural Mind vs. The Mind of Christ

> *Affirmation*
> "Today I consciously move from my natural mind to my Christ Mind."

Until you are able to accept that what is on the inside of you creates the world outside of and around you, you are never going to be able to connect with your Christ Consciousness (higher self) and observe from that vantage point.

If you believe that this earth consciousness, ruled by your natural mind, is all that exists, where everything is a reaction to outer circumstances and where you're always the victim, you're still living in a world of lack and scarcity. The only way to survive in this world is to be in constant competition with others for limited resources.

When you put on the Mind of Christ, you recognize yourself as a powerful creator and realize you have access to an infinite well of limitless resource that is always renewing itself.

Because the natural mind is born of this world of duality, it is subject to the swing of the pendulum which is constantly moving from good to bad, from happy to sad, from lack to abundance. The Christ Mind allows you to see that you are the one holding the pendulum.

In order to reach this level of mastery, however, you must do your own work. No spiritual teacher or pastor can do it for you. The most they can do is give you the tools and remind you how powerful you are.

> **Prayer:** "Christ Consciousness, help me to do the work necessary to take on the Mind of Christ that resides in me. Help me to recognize that I have the power to create my own reality because I am made in your divine image. Amen."

FULLY AWAKE 365

THE POWER OF NOW

March 22

The Ever-Present Christ Presence

Affirmation
"Today, I affirm that the Christ Presence has always been in the world, even before Jesus was born. And, I am open to waking up to the Christ Presence, Principle, Power, Purpose and Person within me."

Most Christians would agree that Jesus of Nazareth is the Christ Person. But, is it possible that the Christ Presence was in the world before the Christ Person showed up? And, does the Christ Presence still exist in the world now? After Jesus ascended? I believe we find the Presence of Christ all throughout the Bible before the account of the birth of Jesus. Genesis 1:2 *"and the Spirit of God was hovering over the waters."* The Christ Presence was in the lion's den with Daniel, shutting the mouths of the lions. The Christ Presence was in the fiery furnace with the three Hebrew children. King Nebuchadnezzar looked into the furnace and said, *"Look! I see four men loose, walking in the midst of the fire; and they are not hurt, and the form of the fourth is like the Son of God"* (Daniel 3:25). Paul refers to a High Priest named Melchizedek (who lived around 2,000 B.C.E.) who was called the, *"king of righteousness," "king of peace,"* and who was *"without father, without mother, without genealogy, having neither beginning of days nor end of life, but made like the Son of God, remains a priest continually"* (Hebrews 7:2-3). Sound familiar? And Jesus, happens to be a priest according to the order of Melchizedek. Consider this key verse: *"And it is yet far more evident if, in the likeness of Melchizedek, there arises another priest who has come, not according to the law of a fleshly commandment, but according to the power of an endless life"* (Hebrews 7:15-16). Jesus is the other priest who arises in the likeness of Melchizedek.

What's the point? Christ was in the world before Jesus. Christ was in the world as Jesus. And, Christ is now in the world as you. Christ in you, Christ through you and Christ as you, is the hope of glory.

Prayer: *"Ever-Present Christ Presence, I acknowledge Your Eternal Presence in the world and working in me. Amen."*

Challenge Your Mind. Channel Your Power. Change Your Life.

March 23

The Power of Our Words

Affirmation
"The power of life and death is in the tongue."

There are no such things as divine words and human words. Words are just words. They are tools. The underlying energy with which they are spoken determines their purpose.

Words are tools just like a hammer is a tool. You can use a hammer to drive the nails that build a house or to hang a beautiful picture on the wall. Or you can use a hammer to smash out someone's car window or hit someone over the head. The power to be "good" or "evil" is not in the hammer, but in how it is wielded. The person using the hammer decides the purpose for which it will be used.

The word "spelling" is exactly what it sounds like…it comes from the idea that words cast spells and that when we create words with letters, we are casting spells. To some in our modern culture that has an evil or scary connotation, so if it makes you feel more comfortable to hear it said this way - we are *calling things into existence* when we speak.

The reason people were healed when Jesus spoke is because he was backing up his words with belief. That's why what he said always came to pass. Our words coupled with our belief is the ultimate power. We can decide to kill with this power or to bring life.

> **Prayer:** *"Life Giving God, help me today understand the power of my words and let me use them to bring life rather than death to everything in my life. Amen."*

THE POWER OF NOW

March 24

Awake to my Time, Task, Treasure and Temple

Affirmation

"Today, I intend to be fully awake to my time, my task, my treasure and my temple. I am aware that when I am on time I am inviting money and people with money into my life. When I am on task and prepared I am declaring to the universe that I am available for opportunities and success. When I manage my treasure wisely I am opening a portal for more to arrive. And, when I am awake to my body temple I am laying a foundation for a long, healthy life."

In Luke chapter 19, Jesus teaches the importance of being a good steward over very little. The reward for this stewardship is to be trusted with more. I am not sure there is an exact science for finding success and welcoming money into our lives. But, being on time, showing up prepared for our task, making responsible decisions with our treasure and respecting our body temples are huge steps in the right direction. Obviously, these four areas all begin with the letter "T." There is one "T" word that is missing here that many people believe is the key to success. But, I have actually found that, although it may be helpful, it is not always necessary and sometimes can even be a hindrance to success. That "T" word is…Talent.

I have been around fabulously talented athletes, musicians, speakers, entrepreneurs and creative minds my entire life. Generally, the more talented a person is, the less they are on time, the less prepared they are when they show up late, the less they manage their money when they make it and the less they respect their body temple by feeding it, exercising it and resting it properly. Talent seems to be the most detrimental piece to managing time, task, treasure and temple. The great ones, who enjoy a long life full of money, opportunities, health and happiness are the ones who can mix in their God-given talent with their time, task, treasure and temple. Welcome a lifetime of success today by being faithful over little things. And watch, as God blesses you with more.

Prayer: *"Source of Blessings, as I am faithful over little I know You will trust me with more. Amen."*

Challenge Your Mind. Channel Your Power. Change Your Life.

March 25 — THE POWER OF NOW

The Same...Yesterday, Today and Forever

> **Affirmation**
> "God is not changing...WE ARE! God is not changing...I AM! I am not my beliefs. I am not my opinions. I am the Spirit who is aware that I have beliefs and opinions. I am bigger than my thoughts. I am the Spirit capable of having thoughts and changing beliefs. I am open and available for Spirit to guide me to Higher Ground!"

As God's messenger, Moses proposed ideas like: wearing blended fabrics was an abomination, a young woman was worth twice as much as an older woman and an eye for an eye and a tooth for a tooth was God's way of justice. Interestingly, as we progress through the pages and books of the Bible, God seems to be growing, expanding in thought, awakening to new dimensions of higher consciousness and managing His anger in a more civilized manner. Jesus provides us with a peculiar predicament as He began many of His teachings by saying, *"you have heard of old, but I say to you."* In other words, Jesus was saying, whatever God said to Moses years ago...He has changed His mind over time. At one time, God wanted us to seek justice and exact revenge on anyone who harmed us. But now, God wants us to forgive and turn the other cheek. What amazing growth and maturity has taken place in God over the years! Is God changing? Or are we?

God, Creator of the heavens and the earth, the original vibration who formed the universe with His words and breathed life into man, is not changing...not getting better with time. The Bible is not a record of God's gradually advancing mindset or an account of God's diversifying cultural opinions. The Bible is a beautiful, sometimes brutal, story of man's journey toward awakening, enlightenment and expanded thought. God, who never changes, desires to carry us from wisdom to wisdom, glory to glory, one level to another, line upon line and precept upon precept. Let's agree to go.

> **Prayer:** "Changeless God, give me the courage to change and challenge my beliefs and opinions. I desire to go higher. Take me there. Amen."

THE POWER OF NOW

March 26

The Problem With Making Assumptions

Affirmation
"Today I will consciously question my assumptions in order to make the best judgment possible."

Have you ever wondered why we tend to jump to negative conclusions more frequently than positive ones? It's quite literally the way our brains are wired. Hundreds of thousands of years ago, it was important to be able to size up another human who came into your space. Those who could make quick judgments - or assumptions - about others were the ones who survived. Assessing the negative - or threat level - was a crucial skill that is still with us.

Prehistoric man had to notice whether or not there was a club in someone's hand before they noticed anything else about them. Positive attributes had to take a back seat to anything that could negatively affect him. So, when we have limited information about a person or situation, our brain automatically starts trying to fill in the gaps with the negative first.

Everything our brains do is for the purpose of protecting us by avoiding uncertainty as much as possible. The irony of this is that uncertainty - or not knowing - is where we have to be in order to get the next piece of information. Being uncertain is the only thing that causes us to question, and questioning is the only way we ever learn anything new.

Being aware of this helps us learn how to make assumptions responsibly. We're always going to assume things. It's part of our nature. But in order to grow, we have to challenge and question our assumptions, and hold off making a final judgment until we have more information.

Prayer: *"All Knowing God, help me today to be more aware of how I make assumptions and let me use this ability responsibly. Amen."*

Challenge Your Mind. Channel Your Power. Change Your Life.

March 27

THE POWER OF NOW

The Mind Is Our Bridge

Affirmation
"I know that my mind is always subject to my spirit."

Each of us came here with a purpose and a mission. In order to accomplish it, the first thing we must do is re-connect with our higher self, or the divinity within that we all came here with. Over the course of our lives, this part of our nature gets buried underneath the layers of our story, or our history, which lives in our mind.

The mind, although limited in its power, is also the tool we use to call things into form. It is the bridge between our non-physical self, or what we refer to as our spirit, and our body, which is the vehicle we're working with here on earth.

What we must remember, however, is that although it performs a necessary function, we can never let the mind be in charge. The mind is not the leader and does not set the tone for our lives unless we let it. It's our job to get into our mind and explore it a little - see what's going on and re-train it by getting rid of all the subconscious programming we've been conditioned by.

The workings of the mind alone, without the intuition and guidance of the divine part of us, our spirit, are a waste of time and can even be destructive. But without the mind, we'd never be able to bring anything from our divine self (imagination) into form (manifestation) in this physical realm. When directed by our divine nature, the mind becomes the bridge between the two dimensions.

Prayer: *"Divine Creator, help me today understand the function of my mind as a tool, and to always allow my Christ-Consciousness to lead and guide it for my highest good. Amen."*

March 28

Being In The Room

Affirmation
"Today, I will be an active listener, thoughtful speaker, deep thinker and willing participant. I will focus my attention, with the intention, of being and staying in the room."

What does it mean to be "in the room?" Being in the room means to be completely available and fully present to the people and to the subjects being discussed. Being in the room involves considering an idea that may be foreign or even offensive. Being in the room suggests that the subject(s) being discussed can stand on their own merit and deserve our attention without rejecting, deflecting, or projecting.

We "leave the room" when:

1. We REJECT the necessity of working through an issue that may not be a concern to us.

2. We lose presence and DEFLECT away from an issue and attempt to change the subject.

3. We PROJECT our own bias into a conversation without giving space for alternative opinions, views and ideas.

Being in the room allows every voice to be heard.

Being in the room assures every journey will be considered.

Being in the room chooses to feel the pains and joys of others in the room.

Being in the room affirms every person in the room.

> **Prayer:** *"Attentive God, thank You for being in my room and feeling my pains and joys. Grant me the grace to be in the room for all who need connection. Amen."*

Challenge Your Mind. Channel Your Power. Change Your Life.

March 29

THE POWER OF NOW

I Can Only Create in the Present

> ***Affirmation***
> *"The power to create my reality is in the present moment. I will not blame anything or anyone in the past or wait on an outside force to intervene in the future. I can and will create my reality right here and right now."*

We talk a lot about our ability to create or to recreate our reality. There are two main clusters of reasons why some can't seem to grasp this concept.

- We've been taught that the devil is busy; that life is difficult and evil is everywhere; that adversity is normal; and you always have to watch your back because others are out to get you.
- We must wait on God to give us favor; to intervene on our behalf; or for our season to change.

The problem with these reasons is this. The only power you have to create anything exists in the present moment. You can't create from the past or recreate it. Neither can you create into the future.

When you blame the devil or anyone else for what's wrong in your reality, you're operating in the past - what he or she did to you.

When you're waiting on God to do something for you, you are operating in a non-existent future.

Neither the past nor the future hold any creative power. Both of these mindsets stop you from believing and knowing you have the power, in the present moment, to create or recreate anything about your reality you want.

> **Prayer:** *"God of the Now, help me realize the power I have to create my reality, and that the only time I can use it is in the present moment, right here, right now. Amen."*

March 30

It's Your Birthday

Affirmation
"Today, and every day, is my birthday. Each morning is new. Each day is a rebirth. And today, it is my birthday, as I set my intention to be reborn bigger, wiser, newer and more open than the day before."

One day out of every 365 days we take time to celebrate a birthday or the day we emerged from our mother's wombs. We probably should be celebrating our mothers on our birthdays, shouldn't we? Amen moms? This is why every day should be Mother's Day. But, why is it that we only celebrate ourselves once a year?

Many different cultures around the world recognize the importance of new birth and rebirth. In ancient Egyptian iconography we find the ouroboros, a depiction of a snake eating its own tail. Many times, this image is encountered as the snake being depicted either in the shape of an infinity symbol or a simple circle. These symbols speak of eternalness and the connection of life and death as a continuous, endless reality. This image also is one of constant renewal and rebirth. The reason the snake has earned this image is because snakes shed their skin. When the old skin is gone a new, bigger, more beautiful snake appears to have been reborn.

The apostle Paul describes this process as "dying daily" to be reborn anew. Jesus reminds us that new wine cannot be placed in old wineskins. Each and every day is a moment for rebirth, renewal, reimagining ourselves. As we remain open to the daily leading of Spirit in our lives we can rest in the peace that we are not old dogs, and there is always a new trick. Celebrate your birthday...today, and every day.

Prayer: *"Spirit of Rebirth, thank You for placing eternity in my heart. I am reborn every moment that I realize my journey is one of spiritual growth and eternal expansion. Amen."*

Challenge Your Mind. Channel Your Power. Change Your Life.

March 31

THE POWER OF NOW

The Power of Resonance

> ### Affirmation
> *"I recognize that I have a choice. I can resist the things I don't like, resign myself to things I don't prefer, or I can get into resonance with the way I want things to be.*
> *Today, I choose resonance!"*

Whenever we face a situation that we wish to be other than it is, or that we are in disagreement with, we've got several options as to how we will respond. The first option, which many of us choose, is to resist - to fight against what is. Another option is to just resign ourselves to the way things are; give up and give in to something we'd prefer to be different.

But a third option is to get into resonance with however it is we'd like for it to be. In this way, we're not resisting nor resigning, but rather, we're deciding to put all our energy and focus into lining ourselves up with a better, more desirable reality.

Resonance is more than a practice or something we do sometimes. It's a flow we get into and adopt as a lifestyle. Resonance means getting our words, thoughts and actions all flowing in the same direction. Energy flows where our focus goes. We must learn to spend more of our time building what we do want than fighting or giving in to what we don't want.

> **Prayer:** *"God of Resonance, whatsoever things are true; whatsoever things are pure; whatsoever things are of a good report - teach me to think, meditate and focus on these things! Amen."*

TRANSFORMATION

April 1

Loving Myself. Loving Others. Loving God.

Affirmation
"As I learn to love myself, I will be able to love others and then see the way to love God. I cannot give to others, or to God, what I do not possess myself. Today, I will love me, and then be able to give out to others from the love I have for myself."

In Sunday school I was taught to put God first, to put others second and to put myself last. I carried this idea for years. Then one day, I realized that it just didn't work. We cannot love others if we don't love ourselves. This foundational religious idea is actually in reverse order. We have to love ourselves first, then love others, then love God. Jesus asked a question, *"How can you love God who you have not seen? When you do not love your neighbor who you have seen?"* Jesus went on to remind us that the most important law was to *"Love God, and love your neighbor as yourself."* Every major world religion teaches some form of the Golden Rule: Do unto others what you would have them do unto you. The question we must wrestle with is this: if every religion teaches its followers to love their neighbor as they love themselves, why is it not working? Why are religions at war with each other? The answer is pretty simple. We cannot give what we do not have. Put plainly, we are loving others as we love ourselves. The problem is we don't love ourselves. Jesus realized this was an issue. He told us to love our neighbors as we love ourselves. Then, He discovered how little we love ourselves. So, He altered His original command and issued a new one, *"A new commandment I give to you, that you love one another; as I have loved you."* (John 13:34).

When you're taught your whole life that you're fallen, wretched, helpless, hopeless, sinful and shameful, it is difficult to love yourself. Tell yourself a different story about yourself today. You're made in the image and likeness of God and good. Believe it. And, watch as your love grows for others and for God.

> **Prayer:** *"Loving Creator, grant me the courage to love myself so that I may love others and love You with my whole heart. Amen."*

Challenge Your Mind. Channel Your Power. Change Your Life.

April 2

TRANSFORMATION

Agreeing With God

Affirmation
"Today, I will humble myself to agree with what God says about me, and I will agree with the God in me and as me."

When God told Moses he would be a messenger to Pharaoh and a deliverer for the Hebrews Moses began to inform God of all of his imperfections and shortcomings. Growing tired with Moses' false humility God says to him, "Humble yourself!" It would seem that Moses was already being humble. However, Moses was actually being prideful in his disagreement with what God said and thought about him. All of us struggle to believe we are made in the *image and likeness* of God and good. (Genesis 1:27) Even Jesus denied His own god-nature for a season. (Matthew 19:17)

Palm Sunday is more than just a chance to wave palm branches. Palm Sunday is celebrated as the Triumphal Entry of Jesus into Jerusalem. (Luke 19:28-40) What or who was Jesus triumphing over? The Pharisees? The Romans? Arguably. Yet, I would offer the perspective that Jesus was triumphing over Himself. Jesus was finally ready to accept His divinity. He was willing to humble Himself to agree with the God in and as Him. It may sound strange, but when we embrace our godlikeness we are walking in humility. Begin today!

Prayer: *"Inner Knowing, awaken the humility within me to agree with my own divine nature. Today, empower me to triumph over any spirit of pride that would stand in opposition to who I truly am. Amen."*

April 3

TRANSFORMATION

Say It. See It. Survey It. Shift It.

Affirmation

"My greatest gift is that I am created in the image and likeness of God (and good). This means, I am Created BY God…Creative LIKE God…and Creating AS a god. I am finally willing to stir up the gift of divine image and god-likeness within me. As I embrace my God-given divinity, I will awaken to my full power and potential. God SAID it. God SAW it. God SURVEYED it. Today, I will harness my full power as I SAY it, SEE it and SURVEY it!"

In the very first chapter of the Bible, we find a beautiful pattern of divine creativity. God said, *"let there be light."* Then God saw what He said. Then God surveyed what He saw (*"said that it was good"*). The divine pattern we discover is: First, Say it. Next, See it. Then, Survey it. This is a textbook example of responsible creativity. As divine creatures, created in the image and likeness of the Divine Creator, we must learn to create in the same way. We create by speaking. Then, we will eventually see what we have spoken. And hopefully, we will have the honesty and objectivity to survey what we have spoken and created.

What happens when we don't like what we survey? If (and that's a BIG IF) we have the courage to own what we have created, we have the ability to shift it…or re-create it. When God created man, we see the same pattern: God said it. God saw it. God surveyed it. But, this time, God saw that man was alone. God surveyed that this was not good. So, God created again (a companion) or shifted it. We have the same power! We can re-create our lives whenever we have the strength to own what we create and then create something new, something that brings peace, love and joy into our daily experience. This is the process of taking responsibility for our divine creativity. Or to make it plain, this is how we take responsibility for our lives and the experience of life we are creating.

Prayer: *"Creative Word, give me the wisdom to SAY IT, the courage to SEE IT, the honesty to SURVEY IT and the strength to SHIFT IT. Amen."*

Challenge Your Mind. Channel Your Power. Change Your Life.

April 4

TRANSFORMATION

Grace Abuse

> **Affirmation**
> *"Today, I am grateful for the grace of God in my life. And, I am deeply thankful for the price Jesus paid to offer me this free gift. However, I will not be guilty of grace abuse, or allow any idea of an unlimited supply of grace to lure me into an ongoing destructive pattern. I will not use grace as a crutch keeping me from becoming more like Christ or hindering me from learning to use my divine creativity to create the life I want to experience."*

I grew up under the teaching that our good works are like *"filthy rags"* and that salvation was *"not of works, lest anyone should boast."* I was taught that salvation was a "Finished Work" and I couldn't add anything to it. I don't believe this was intentionally meant to be harmful. It was just a way of promoting the strength of the cross or the power of the blood of Jesus. Although, it did become a bit of a bragging point and was common practice across the Evangelical world to actually diminish other religions (that taught personal growth) because they had to actually work on their character and become better people in order to reach Nirvana, or become enlightened, or find whatever their expression of heaven or eternal life might be.

There are some unintended problems with this expression of grace. Mainly, it requires no growth. All one must do is believe and confess Jesus as Savior. The result is people leaning solely on grace and never dealing with the condition of their heart. So, we have "followers" of Christ not following Christ. Hate, racism, homophobia, misogyny and discrimination of all sorts are tolerated, and sadly, promoted. As Christians, shouldn't we be on a path to becoming like Christ? There is also a strain of grace abuse dangerously allowing and promoting that people can do whatever they want because they can't lose the grace of God. Which is true. However, the devastation reaped with undisciplined living is a pain no one wants and a collateral damage no friend or loved one deserves.

> **Prayer:** *"God of Grace, I desire to be more than a Christian. I want to be more like Jesus. Give me the grace to get there. Amen."*

TRANSFORMATION

April 5

One Heart at a Time

Affirmation
"Today I am content to help heal the world one heart at a time."

Have you ever stood at your window and looked on as strong winds deposit leaves onto the yard it took you hours to clean in what seems like mere minutes? Nature has a way of keeping us humble, and also showing us the meaningless of our arbitrary divisions.

The wind doesn't recognize our invisible boundaries or give extra credit to the people who always keep their yards tidy. When it starts blowing, that dividing line between your yard and your neighbor's means nothing at all to it! In the face of this fact, we might be tempted to adopt the attitude of, "*What's the use?*" That attitude is easy to transfer over to other areas of our lives as well. Healing the world is a beautiful concept to talk and dream about, but sometimes seems too big, impossible and daunting to ever achieve in reality.

Of course we have compassion for everyone, but when these overwhelming thoughts of "*I can't help everyone, I'm just one person*" or "*it will just be more of the same tomorrow*" creep in, instead of putting it out of your mind totally, which is the easiest thing to do, or distracting yourself by thinking "happier" thoughts, or getting bogged down by spreading yourself too thin and trying to do too much – you can adopt this attitude: Today I will help those who God puts directly in my path to the best of my ability and not worry about the rest.

> **Prayer:** *"God of Compassion, help me to put my desire to help people to the best use possible by prioritizing my time and energy where it will do the most good. Amen."*

Challenge Your Mind. Channel Your Power. Change Your Life.

April 6

TRANSFORMATION

4 Levels of Thought Progression

> **Affirmation**
> *"I have the capacity to think on many different levels. When I was a child, I thought, spoke and processed information as a child. I existed on a lower level of conscious awareness. Today, I am willing to put away childish things and think on a higher plane."*

There are many different levels of thought. In my journey, I describe them 4 different ways: Absolute, Abstract, Mystic Receptivity and Spiritual Oneness. Absolute thought is concrete thinking, cut and dry, black and white, no complexities, no questions and no room for discussion. "Brush your teeth." "Don't get near the street." "Why? Because I said so." In Abstract thought, we begin to see that truth may not be found in the extremes, but rather, held in the tension between extremes where absolute thought encounters contradiction, crisis, surrenders and is then introduced to grey areas. In Mystic Receptivity, we begin to get comfortable with contradiction. We choose to celebrate truth as a journey, not a destination. Questions become as, or more, important than answers. Finally, we arrive at Spiritual Oneness where the truth we have been searching for is amazingly discovered within us. The kingdom we are waiting on is within us. The God we are praying to is within us. We begin to see ourselves as the offspring of God and an extension, example and earthly expression of divinity. In Spiritual Oneness we begin to *"behold in the mirror the glory of God."* Spiritual Oneness requires a strong connection to self-government as the laws that bound us, and the punishments that scared us, no longer exist in this higher level of thinking. In Spiritual Oneness we don't beg or even ask. We begin to manifest the life we desire through an awareness that we are created by God, creative like God and creating as gods.

We all change, but at our own pace and in our own space. Wherever you are in thought progression, keep walking, pressing, listening, asking, growing.

Prayer: *"Higher Mind, elevate me to higher thought…from one progression to another. I am ready. Amen."*

TRANSFORMATION

April 7

My Triumphal Entry

Affirmation
"Just as Jesus woke up to His divinity, I am waking up to mine. Today, I will behold the glory of God in the mirror. Today, I will unlock the mystery that the same Spirit that raised Christ from the dead is living in me. Today, I will remember I am created in the image and likeness of God and good. Today, is my Triumphal Entry."

For whatever reason, Jesus forgot that He was divine. He told a young lawyer that He was not good, and not God (Luke 18:19). We can only speculate that perhaps it was to fully identify with the human condition and to feel all we experience in our temporary amnesia to our own divinity? Or maybe He had to mentally be fully man for a season and then wake up to being fully God in order to show us that we carry the same potential of waking up? And still, maybe He actually knew He was divine but hid it for His own safety? No one can be certain. What we do know is that when He rode into Jerusalem, in the Triumphal Entry and what we call Palm Sunday, He was ready to declare His goodness and at was peace with His God-ness.

I love Palm Sunday. The music, the joy, the palms (especially the broken ones…I feel great joy watching the children try to trade their broken palm branches for their friend's unbroken ones). Yet, Palm Sunday is not about the palms, the praise or the people. Palm Sunday is the Triumphal Entry, the moment when Jesus accepted His own divinity personally, privately and publicly. What is your Triumphal Entry? Or better, when is it? It is a joyous day when we realize we are not fallen, hopeless, helpless or wretches saved by grace. When we *"turn"* from Moses (religious bondage) and *"to the Lord"* (Christ Mind) we experience a new *"liberty."* The liberty to *"behold in the mirror the glory of God"* (2 Corinthians 3:16-18). You are divine. Made by God. Made like God. It's personal, accept it privately and then declare it publicly. Let today be your Triumphal Entry.

Prayer: *"God of Awakening and Remembrance, help me to awaken from this sleep and triumph over this amnesia. I am ready. Amen."*

Challenge Your Mind. Channel Your Power. Change Your Life.

April 8

TRANSFORMATION

True Repentance

Affirmation
"Repentance does not mean being sorry for my sins.
It means: rethink!"

Accepting concepts because people tell you, "That's just the way it is" with no further supporting evidence is the height of unconscious living. It's about as far away from creating your own reality as you can get.

There's a much misinterpreted word in the bible called *repentance*. Most of us believe it means to be sorry for something you've done wrong followed by asking for forgiveness. The actual meaning of the word, however, is to *think* and then *think again* - or in other words, to *rethink*.

Repentance is a process of thinking and then rethinking in order to find out the *why* behind the *what*. So what's something in our current culture that needs rethinking? How about what we've been taught about how our physical bodies work and the degree of control we have over our own health and well-being?

We tend to think of our body as everything contained within our skin - a closed system - and everything outside of our skin as separate from us. Things from the outside affect or even attack our bodies, sometimes randomly in the form of illness.

Quantum physics tells a very different story about our bodies. Far from being a closed system, our energy field extends several feet beyond our body and is connected to the energy of everyone and everything else. Further, it is our beliefs, intentions and emotions that ultimately inform what goes on within our bodies. This is the basis of divine healing.

Someone somewhere had to *repent* in order for us to have this information today. Perhaps it's the concept of repentance that needs rethinking!

Prayer: *"Universal Intelligence, help me understand the true meaning of repentance and never be afraid to question things. Amen."*

TRANSFORMATION

April 9

The Same Spirit

Affirmation
"Today, I will get up, get out, and get something. I will celebrate Resurrection power. The same Spirit that resurrected Jesus also resides within me. I may fall, but I will get back up."*

Easter is celebrated all over the world. The Resurrection of Jesus of Nazareth is the most important holy day in the Christian faith. Easter church clichés range from the anti-secular "Easter is not about a bunny" to the more liturgical "Christ the Lord is risen today." But, what is the hidden mystery of Easter?

Easter is about the embodiment of Resurrection in our own lives. Proverbs reminds us that a *"righteous man may fall seven times and rise again."* (Proverbs 24:16) I am not suggesting that Jesus "fell" from grace. What I am suggesting is that there is no power in the world that can keep us from rising again after we experience difficulty.

Romans declares, *"He who raised Christ from the dead will also give life to your mortal bodies through His Spirit who dwells in you."* (Romans 8:11) So, the same Spirit that raised Christ from the dead is within us and working for us! This is how we apply Resurrection power to our journey. We can get back up from divorce, bankruptcy, bad choices, career failures and personal embarrassments. Jesus is no longer in the grave and we do not have to remain buried in the vicissitudes of life. Get back up again!

Prayer: *"Resurrection Power, awaken within me the same Spirit that raised Christ from the dead. I may fall. But, I know there is a power in me enabling me to get back up again. Amen."*

---

* Outkast, album: Southernplayalisticadillacfunkymusic, "Git Up, Git Out," 1994.

Challenge Your Mind. Channel Your Power. Change Your Life.

April 10

TRANSFORMATION

Muscle Memory Part I

Affirmation
"Today I will love myself enough to prioritize my emotional well-being."

Our muscles hold the memories of the actions we use them for repeatedly. Every morning our leg muscles remember how to walk. Our hands and fingers remember how to hold things, etc. The familiar phrase "just like riding a bike" originated from this idea - that once your muscles learn a specific action, they never forget it. Once you've learned to ride a bike, you always know how.

Although we don't always think of it in this way, our heart is also a muscle that needs to be exercised in order to make it stronger, just like our other muscles. One way we can do this is by regularly taking our emotional temperature.

Begin each day with a spiritual practice that balances your emotions. Then try stopping several times during the day to identify what you are feeling at that moment. Once you've identified the dominant emotion, rate its strength on a scale from 1-5. Taking note of what you are doing or what you are thinking about at the time may help you to see a pattern emerge.

Sometimes we feel tense all of the sudden and don't know where it has come from. Checking in with ourselves like this helps us to avoid the build up of unwanted and often unnoticed stress. Just like when you've lost an object, retracing your steps can help you find it again. When you lose your emotional balance, taking a moment to look back over your day to see exactly where you lost it can help you regain your equilibrium.

Prayer: *"Source of Balance, help me to know that it is always possible to regain my peace and restore my emotional equilibrium at any time. Amen."*

TRANSFORMATION

April 11

Muscle Memory Part II

Affirmation
"Today I understand that it is just as possible to exercise my emotional muscles as it is to exercise physically. I am determined to make my emotional muscles as strong as I can."

Target practice in military training involves aiming for the head or chest (center mass) of your target over and over until you do it without thinking about it. This is done because in the heat of battle, you don't have a lot of time to think or reason or weigh your options. In combat, a split second can determine whether you live or die.

Training for athletes and dancers is similar. They go over the same movements or steps repeatedly, which accomplishes two things. First, it strengthens the particular set of muscles needed, and secondly, it programs those movements so that when the big game, performance or competition comes and the pressure is on, no thought is required. The athlete or dancer just goes into automatic mode and their bodies carry out the movements that have been stored in their muscles.

In emotional terms, we need to practice over and over again facing and dealing with our difficult emotions no matter how strong they may feel in the moment. With regular practice, we can make our emotional muscles every bit as strong or stronger than our physical ones.

Prayer: *"Source of Determination, help me today to practice handling my emotions appropriately on a regular basis so that when a difficult situation occurs, my emotional muscles are strong and ready. Amen."*

Challenge Your Mind. Channel Your Power. Change Your Life.

April 12

TRANSFORMATION

The Gifts of Imperfection

> ***Affirmation***
> *"Today, I will bravely own my story. I will accept myself, my imperfections and my uniqueness. I will find the courage to be vulnerable, honest and open."*

What if all things actually, somehow work together for our good? Even our imperfections? We all experience a binary of reality. We are spiritual beings made in the image and likeness of divinity. And yet, we are in the material world, in human form, learning, at times struggling, even failing, to navigate our divinity in a way that creates the life we desire. Embracing our missteps and mistakes along the path of awakening is how we recover quickly, heal open wounds and evolve. Allowing ourselves to be mired in the swamp of shame and the sludge of guilt stunts our growth and hinders the realization of meaningful relationships.

When we own our stories, and tap into the courage to share our pain (pain we have both endured and created), we accept ourselves and also open a door to connect with others in a deep and purposeful way. Have you ever told an embarrassing story and had someone respond, "I thought I was the only one?" This type of connection is only made possible through vulnerability and authenticity. And, in a sense, the mistakes that lead to this openness operate as gifts of imperfection. When we live in shame, secrecy and sorrow we live a lie that disallows our true self, our organic vibration, to attract our tribe, our people, our family.

> ***Prayer:*** *"Authentic Spirit, grant me the courage to be vulnerable, the compassion to be empathetic, and the candor to connect. Amen."*

TRANSFORMATION

April 13

Created, Creative and Creating

Affirmation
"I am created BY God. I am creative LIKE God. And, I am creating AS a god. I am awake to the truth that life is not happening to me or around me. I am a created, creative and creating divine being and life is happening THROUGH ME and AS ME!"

In the first chapter of Genesis (1:27), we find possibly the most powerful truth in the entire Bible...we are created like God! This verse records, *"Let Us make man in Our image and according to Our likeness."* Then, we find out in the next chapter that mankind is commissioned to begin using this divine creativity. Adam begins the process of creating his reality by naming the animals, tending the ground, making choices...learning to use and navigate his God given power to create. It sounds strange to the religious ear, but we are walking divinities. If you will, we are little gods. Jesus attempted to explain this to the Pharisees when He quoted Psalm 98 reminding them, *"you are all gods."* Their response wasn't very accepting. They wanted to stone Him for this perceived blasphemy.

Why is it important to awaken to this revelation of being created like God? Sadly, until we get this truth we will remain powerless victims relying on power-stealing doctrines of chance and leaning on victimizing theologies of favor. When you know that you are created by God, creative like God and creating as a god, you begin to wake up to this truth...you can create the life you want to experience...today! No waiting on God, wishing for a blessing or wanting a new season. No devil can keep you from it and no pastor can prophesy you into it. You have a God given power to create. Use it!

Prayer: *"Creator of the Universe, Thank you for the blessing of divine creativity. I am grateful and amazed You imparted into me a piece of You. Open my eyes and let me see just how powerful I really am. Give me strength to manifest love and create peace. Enable me with courage to be daring enough to use the greatest gift You gave to me...You! Amen."*

Challenge Your Mind. Channel Your Power. Change Your Life.

April 14

TRANSFORMATION

Childlike vs. Childish

> ***Affirmation***
> *"Today I realize that being childlike and acting childish are two different things. I commit myself to growing in grace and to maintaining control of myself during each cycle of my life."*

What's ideally supposed to happen as we approach the golden years of our life is to reach an illuminated or enlightened state where we carry with us the wisdom from all the lessons we have learned along the way, but also return to a childlike state of being carefree.

But this only happens if we've done the work necessary to actually mature throughout our life. Some people get stuck at a certain stage emotionally that they can never seem to move past. The biggest way we get stuck in immaturity and all the behaviors and consequences that go along with it comes down to one simple concept, and that is self-governance.

The aim of growing up is to move from a place where boundaries have to be set for us (by parents, teachers, religion, and secular laws) into a place where we have mastered ourselves so completely that we no longer need these boundaries from others in order to behave maturely and appropriately.

The most important aspect of maturity is self-control. That's it. Period. You learn to do that and you're home free. If you learn how to control yourself, all your lessons will be learned appropriately and you will be able to move through all the cycles of your life right on time, enjoying each one to the fullest!

> ***Prayer:*** *"God of Wisdom, help me to age gracefully and mature into a person who knows how to self-govern. Amen."*

TRANSFORMATION

April 15

At Peace With The God IN ME

Affirmation
"Today, I am at peace with the God IN me. I am aware that God is not up there, over there, out there, on the way, held in the future or stuck in the past. God is around me, through me, IN me, for me, and as me."

Jesus rebuked a young lawyer for calling Him "Good rabbi" and insisted that He was neither good, nor God. (Luke 18:19) One chapter later Jesus tells the Pharisees that if people are not allowed to praise Him the "*rocks would cry out.*" (Luke 19:40) Impressive transition from not good enough to more than enough! I believe this shift alerts us to an awakening of His divine nature. Jesus had made peace with the good IN Him and with the God AS him. Can we make the same peace within ourselves?

When we hold God at arms distance, separate(d) from us and other than us, we fall into an existence of waiting on prayers to be answered, fasting for breakthroughs and repenting of sin that may be "blocking our blessing." When we make peace with the God IN us we cease from wondering if God is on the job and we escape from the vicious cycle of being disappointed every time we get passed over for a blessing or let the man of our dreams slip through our fingers.

Being at peace with the God IN us is not just about mustering the boldness to proclaim, "I am god." Uncovering our innate god-likeness is about waking up to our divine creativity. In a nutshell, we begin to understand that we are created BY God, creative LIKE God, and creating AS gods. And, when we arrive at this place of awareness, we don't have to take anything back from the devil. We simply choose to refuse to give our power away any longer.

Prayer: *"God IN me, I give thanks for Your presence, purpose, providence and power IN me. Give me the wisdom to look for You in the right place...IN me! Amen."*

Challenge Your Mind. Channel Your Power. Change Your Life.

April 16

TRANSFORMATION

Old Dogs and New Tricks

> **Affirmation**
> *"I am open and available for the Universe to send me whatever is necessary for the evolution of my soul. I boldly declare I am free from the lower mind and from literal thinking. I am not my beliefs and I am surrendered to the process of Spirit taking me from glory to glory."*

There is an old saying, "An old dog can't learn a new trick." Fortunately, you're not a dog, even if you consider yourself to be old. We are here to grow, evolve, unfold and surrender to being *"transformed into the image"* of God (2 Corinthians 3:18). So, along our transformational journey we will encounter situations, sometimes challenging ones, all designed to develop us into our higher selves. The disciple Peter is a prime example of this.

Peter is in desperate need of growth. Peter is a racist and a misogynist. Peter believes that only his Jewish brethren are worthy of being accepted into the family of God. So, God (the Universe) sends Peter what is necessary for the evolution of his consciousness. God gives Peter a vision of unclean animals and tells Peter to eat them. But, the vision is really a metaphor for Peter to understand that God is asking him to accept the Gentiles (or people from other countries and cultures) into the fold. When Peter awakens from the vision, God sends him to the house of Cornelius (a well-known Gentile). When Peter arrives at Cornelius' house he encounters Gentiles (people from other countries he doesn't accept or include) experiencing the presence of God. Peter finally gets the point of God provoking, poking, pushing and prodding him. Peter has the revelation that *"God is no respecter of persons."* God wouldn't leave Peter alone until he grew and evolved. And, there is good news for us all. God won't leave us alone until we surrender to this process of transformation.

> **Prayer:** *"Divine Change Agent, I surrender to the process of being transformed into my highest expression of divinity. Today, I ask You to send to me whatever is necessary for my unfoldment. Amen."*

TRANSFORMATION

April 17

Fixing vs. Healing

Affirmation
"Today I know that I am a powerful, divine being fully capable of addressing any area within me that needs healing."

If you've ever spent any time with pre-school children, especially age 4 and younger, you know that when something goes wrong or gets broken, their first instinct is to bring it to you and say, "fix it" rather than trying to figure it out for themselves, which comes a little later on in their development. How often do we approach our own issues like immature toddlers, wanting others to "fix" us rather than realize we are perfectly capable of healing ourselves?

The first thing we must understand is that there's a difference between *fixing* and *healing* with any illness, whether physical or emotional. To heal is much more than to just cure or alleviate the symptoms that appear on the surface. True healing gets to the root cause of the problem.

Healing should always be our goal, step one of which is not giving our power away. Medical doctors, counselors, spiritual healers as well as any form of treatment may be helpful and can certainly assist and guide us in our process, but healing is an inside job that no one else can do for us.

We are capable of so much more than we give ourselves credit for.

Prayer: *"God our Healer, help us to understand the power we have inside to heal ourselves and help us know how to access it today. Amen."*

Challenge Your Mind. Channel Your Power. Change Your Life.

April 18

TRANSFORMATION

Matrix, Mind, Mouth, Manifestation

> **Affirmation**
> *"Life and death are in the power of how I see and say. My matrix processes it. My mind presents it. My mouth proclaims it. My manifestation produces it. Today, I will be aware of the matrix, mind, mouth, manifestation connection."*

One of the most popular verses in the Bible is *"Death and life are in the power of the tongue"* (Proverbs 18:21). This verse assures us that the power is not in life or in death. The power is in the tongue. But, when we think this through, the power is actually not in the tongue either. The power is in the mind that controls and tells the tongue what to say. *"Who can tame the tongue?"* (James 3:8). A masterful mind tames the tongue!

So, life and death are in the power of the mind. Yet, if we look a little more deeply, the mind is actually a servant of the matrix, the filters, the theological framework and sociological grid-work that all discriminate, decide and deliver what gets to the mind and how. Matrixes like education, experience and exposure. Filters like culture, country and class. All of this unseen force-field decides how and what information gets to the mind. Finally, we arrive at the matrix, the origin... *"Death and life are in the power of the matrix, that filters information to the mind, that controls the mouth."* Our mission, as awakened spirits, is two-fold. First, we must be aware of this matrix, mind, mouth, manifestation connection. And, that our lives, or manifestations, are directly connected to how we process information and then choose to declare it. Second, we must ask the Holy Spirit to remove the filters, take away the biases, delete the prejudices, extract the religious leanings and cultural learnings so we can perceive neutrally, purely, clearly and cleanly whatever the Holy Spirit sends to us. This way, we are not merely manifesting with our mouths, minds and matrixes, more separation and segregation into the global human family.

> **Prayer:** *"Master, I surrender my matrix, mind, mouth and manifestation to You. Amen."*

TRANSFORMATION

April 19

Press Into It

Affirmation
"Today, I will press into the new and press away from the old. I will surrender my old, lower thinking to new, higher concepts."

The kingdom *"suffers violence, and the violent take it by force."* (Luke 16:16-17) That sounds aggressive! Almost like some type of encouragement to form a militia or the propaganda for a military coup d'état. And yet, this is not what Jesus was saying at all. If you continue to follow Jesus' line of thinking in context, He is talking about a violent separation from an old way of thinking. Thus, the next verse says, "the prophets and law were until John, since that time the kingdom has been preached, and all people are pressing into it." Whew! We can put down our ax handles and gas masks. No government overthrow in the name of Jesus. However, the spiritual task that lies ahead of us, as followers of the Christ Mind, may be more daunting than any physical battle.

Jesus is asking us to violently press away from old mindsets and press into new ones. Have you been in the mindset that you were born in sin and shaped in iniquity? Violently separate from that lower mind and press into the new mindset of being fearfully and wonderfully made, created in the image and likeness of God and good. Have you been in an old mindset of unworthiness? Violently detach from this diseased way of thinking and press into the new mind that can behold the glory of God in the mirror. Old habits, and thoughts, die hard. So, they must be violently forced out!

> **Prayer:** *"New Mind, grant me a violent spirit to overthrow any thought that keeps me from my highest good and best self. Amen."*

Challenge Your Mind. Channel Your Power. Change Your Life.

April 20

TRANSFORMATION

Be Ye Transformed

> *Affirmation*
> "Today I will keep my heart open in the face of ugliness and hatred. I will not return evil for evil, but will endeavor to love even those who act and speak in abusive ways."

Over the past few decades participation in organized religion has dropped dramatically, especially by young people. Ever wonder why? Perhaps it has a little to do with them hearing pastors behind pulpits or teachers in Children's Church say to them, "God is love and we're all supposed to love each other…even our enemies" and then walking outside into the "real world" and witnessing us all treat each other terribly.

They know this is wrong. They know this is hypocritical. And when they, themselves, are treated less than lovingly, they instinctively know that as a human being they deserve better. We all do. They know hate speech when they hear it, no matter how cleverly disguised. Yet when they express their feelings about this state of affairs they're often called names like "snowflake" and told not to be so sensitive. They don't buy it. And they shouldn't.

Yes, at times the world does seem cruel and heartless, but toughening up in order to be able to withstand the cruelty is not the solution. Continuing to open your heart and behave lovingly, even when it is not reciprocated, is the only way forward.

> **Prayer:** "God of Transformation, help me to be daily transformed by the renewing of my mind rather than conforming to my surroundings when they are less than loving. Help me to remember that the love and light inside me is greater than any darkness, and that being sensitive is not a fault or disadvantage, but a gift. Amen."

TRANSFORMATION

April 21

Caring for the Earth

Affirmation
"Today, I acknowledge my interconnectedness to all people, to all living things, and to the earth. I am not separate from any living thing. I inter-BE with all that exists."

Dr. Martin Luther King, Jr. and Vietnamese Buddhist monk Thich Nhat Hanh worked together, both in the Civil Rights movement in America and in the campaign to end the war in Vietnam. Both of these men understood their connectedness to each other and gave voice to the ideas that we are all trapped in a *"network of mutuality, tied to each other in an inescapable, single garment of destiny"* (Dr. Martin Luther King, Jr.) and to the reality that all things *"inter-BE"* (Thich Nhat Hanh) with all other things. Yes, all people are connected in some direct or indirect way. But, what about the earth? Are we interconnected to the earth? Do we really inter-BE with nature?

Climate Change is ubiquitous, and a global pandemic that affects us all and sometimes can seem to be an insurmountable problem to solve. You may ask, "What will my small contribution do?" We cannot give in to hopelessness or accept any semblance of powerlessness. We can all play a part and effect change in our own way. Eating less red meat reduces the methane that causes climate change. Driving a fuel efficient or electric car helps to reduce fossil fuel emissions and reduces our carbon footprint. Recycling plastic, glass, aluminum and buying products that are either recyclable or made to biodegrade assists in caring for the earth. The earth is the Lord's! And, we have been given the responsibility to care for it. Let us all set our intention to play our part.

Prayer: *"Mother Nature, thank you for life, water, air and for the overwhelming beauty of creation. Amen."*

Challenge Your Mind. Channel Your Power. Change Your Life.

April 22

TRANSFORMATION

Earth Day

> *Affirmation*
> *"Today, I am aware that the earth is the Lord's, yet placed into my care. I set my intention to respect the earth and to care for the creatures inhabiting the earth."*

Despite appearances, science and religion are not enemies. And, God seekers should not be science deniers. The earth is getting hotter. Ocean water levels and temperatures are rising as glaciers are melting. Prayer, denial, and politicizing this existential threat is not working. What can we do? Be practical! Power plants, transportation, deforestation, farming and garbage are at the top of the list of what is effecting climate change.* What is obvious? We can become less oil dependent and utilize green energy (solar and battery). We can cut down less trees, breed and eat fewer cows (reduce methane), reduce, reuse, recycle and produce less garbage. Sounds pretty cut and dry. Right? Yet, we are missing the common denominator that fuels all of the top threats to the environment: PEOPLE!

Biblical literalists take the Genesis command to be *"fruitful and multiply"* seriously. (Genesis 1:28) I have visited third world countries where starving families regularly boast fifteen, twenty or more children. Often times, the churches in these areas are more concerned with saving souls than with feeding families and educating people regarding birth control. Fewer power plants and less electricity is more easily solved if there are LESS PEOPLE on the earth. Smog, demand for wood, fast food restaurants, steakhouses and landfills are all just symptomatic consequences of people producing too many people. Trust me. We have been fruitful and multiplied enough (refer to Atlanta traffic)! It is time to shift our paradigm about how many children we need in our houses and how many people we need on the earth.

> *Prayer:* *"Mother Earth, thank You for surrounding me with breathtaking beauty. Enable me to preserve it by giving me the wisdom to have fewer children. Amen."*

---

* Joe Kelly, The Top 10 Causes of Global Warming, sciencing.com, 2019.

TRANSFORMATION

April 23

Send Me What I Need

Affirmation
"The Universe will send to me whatever I need for the evolution of my consciousness. I am open and available for this growth and unfoldment...however it finds its way to me."

Hidden things unexpectedly find their way to the surface every day and in various ways. Occasionally, situations arise in our lives that seem to be unfair and even strange. Yet, we can be at peace knowing that even the most bizarre and challenging seasons carry with them a lesson and a wisdom that possess the potential to emancipate us from mental stagnation, force us to rethink and elevate us into our higher and highest selves. The Apostle Paul spoke of a *"thorn in his flesh"* that was used by God to enable him to receive and relay deep revelations and unrevealed mysteries. Jesus was *"driven into the wilderness by the Spirit to be tempted by the devil"* and afterward returned with great power and a new authority. Peter was stuck in religious bondage and mired in prejudicial perceptions of other cultures. So, God put him into a deep sleep and sent him a vision regarding his need to be more open and inclusive.

Every day, I experience something new that is designed for the evolution of my consciousness. I also observe this process happening in those around me. The racially prejudiced father has a daughter who marries someone of another race. A homophobic mother must come to grips with the reality of having a gay son. A male chauvinist must learn to work for a powerful female boss. A religious zealot finds a new friendship with someone who believes differently. All of these scenarios are the Universe's way of letting us know that we are loved, supported and cared for in an interconnected and interactive way that demands us to expand, unfold and evolve.

Prayer: *"Universe, send me whatever I need for the evolution of my soul. I don't want to be stuck, stale or stagnant. I relinquish my resistance and surrender to the lessons and wisdom You send my way. Amen."*

Challenge Your Mind. Channel Your Power. Change Your Life.

April 24

TRANSFORMATION

Water Magic

> **Affirmation**
> "Today I will recognize and honor the magical connection between my emotions, my speech, and my body."

Water is so ubiquitous in our world and essential to our lives that we often take it for granted and fail to recognize its almost magical nature. Scientists have discovered that every one of water's properties is unique and does not easily fit into the generally accepted laws of physics.

For instance, it is the only substance on the planet that can exist in three states - liquid, solid and gas. Also, its density expands when it freezes rather than contracting like every other known substance.

Dr. Masuru Emoto of Japan has done extensive studies on water and found that it actually has memory. It receives and then makes an imprint (or record) of any outside influence, remembering, as it were, everything that occurs in the space that surrounds it, much like magnetic tape.

In one experiment, a group of people were asked to project (verbally and mentally) onto jars of water placed in front of them positive emotions such as love, tenderness and concern, while another group was to do the opposite and project onto their jars fear, aggression and hatred. Measurements were then taken showing changes in the actual molecules of the water that were clearly formed in one direction or the other.

It was concluded that love increases water's energy levels and stabilizes it, while negative emotions reduce the energy and make radical changes in the water's structure.

Our bodies are 70 - 90% water. Knowing this information serves to emphasize the importance of how we speak to ourselves and others because the water inside is always listening.

> **Prayer:** "Creator of Nature, help me remember today the absolute importance of speaking kindly as often as possible. Amen."

TRANSFORMATION

April 25

Poison or Promise?

Affirmation
"Today, I choose promise, freedom, liberty and peace. And, my study of the Bible and other holy books will not lead me toward poison, enslavement or restriction."

Frederick Douglass and Henry Garnet were both public figures and Civil Rights leaders during the struggle for abolition. In 1849, a very fiery debate drew these two men to opposite sides. Garnet lobbied to send Bibles to Southern slaves while Douglass regarded the Bible as a "Book of Poison." Is the Bible a book or promise or poison? Does the Bible foster peace or build a prison? Is the glass half empty or half full? Interesting thoughts! The Bible teaches equality and promotes slavery. The Bible envisions an egalitarian society while it simultaneously speaks degradingly toward women. Wow! How complex and contradictory. So, how do we decide? Throw it out? Or study it? Abolish the Bible? Or promote it? When the choices are so extreme it is difficult to find balance.

There is a middle path that allows us to keep the Bible while not allowing it to become a poisonous weapon. This path involves *"rightly dividing the Word of truth."* (II Timothy 2:15) The difficult reality is that the Bible is full of both promise and poison. The same Bible that delivers us is also capable of imprisoning. So, we must leave the debates of biblical accuracy knowing that we can prove just about any philosophy from the Bible. If reading the Bible is not about accuracy, perhaps it is about presenting us with a mirror or revealing personal consciousness. So, the questions are no longer simply who is right or wrong, but rather why are you attracted to specific teachings. From this perspective the Bible can be seen as a revealer of consciousness, showing us who we are. Let us choose the higher vibration!

Prayer: *"Higher Mind, strengthen me to choose promise rather than poison! Amen."*

Challenge Your Mind. Channel Your Power. Change Your Life.

April 26

TRANSFORMATION

Break On Through

Affirmation
"I know today that the willing sacrifice of Jesus makes it possible for me to approach God for myself at any time."

According to the biblical account, the veil in the Jewish Temple separating the outer court from the Holy of Holies was torn in two at the moment of Jesus' crucifixion.

Symbolically, we have come to believe that event represents Jesus, in his willingness to sacrifice himself (not meet a requirement for blood initiated by God, the Father), showing us that the system of religion we were following was man-made and founded on an idea of separation that was not based on the truth. Jesus' finished work on the cross put an end to that idea of separation and gave every person equal access to God.

The destruction of the veil presumably happened of its own accord as the result of his willing sacrifice. Yet, over 2,000 years later, we act as if he physically still stands in the Temple waiting for us to "check in" with him in order to get to God. But he's not there. In fact, he never was. All we have done is replace the idea of a veil separating us from God with Jesus separating us from God.

When we believe this way, we make his sacrifice meaningless. He opened the door so that we could all walk in freely, but many of us still wait in the outer court for him to pick us up and carry us to God. He's done his part. It's time for us to do ours and break on through to the other side!

Prayer: *"Christ Consciousness, help me to understand that there is no separation between me and God. Amen."*

TRANSFORMATION

April 27

Creating Good

Affirmation
"I am created in the image and likeness of God. That means I am creative like God. I have the power to create good. And, I have the power to create evil. I am learning to use this power the way God intended. I am a mature spiritual creature. This means, I don't need the threat of hell in order to do what is good and right. I do good because I came from Divine Good, and because I am good! I love God without the promise of heaven or the threat of hell. I love God because God is God!"

Creative power is neutral. It is neither good nor bad. Similar to all forms of power, creative power is completely at the mercy of the mind wielding it. The good or evil produced totally depends on the way it is used. This creative power is sometimes referred to as "free will" in religious and theological circles. This is exactly what it is…freedom to use our divine creative power any way we want. This wonderful freedom is potentially very dangerous. To be plain, our freedom can enslave us. We are free to create peace and prosperity. Conversely, we are also free to create sorrow and suffering. The freedom isn't to be blamed. The Creator who endowed us with this freedom isn't to be blamed. Learning to navigate this freedom, for good purposes, is the reason we incarnate and come to earth. In essence, we are learning, on a smaller scale, how to handle being like God. How do we control this power?

One of the ways religion has attempted to control this creative power is by incentives, or the promise of rewards (and the fear of consequences). If you create good, you go to heaven. If you create evil, you go to hell. On the surface, this doesn't seem so harmful, until a majority of people begin doing good to get to heaven instead of doing good for the sake of doing good. Ulterior motives, lower vibrations and base levels of consciousness are the results of these fear driven strategies and we wind up serving God out of fear or some hidden manipulation. Let's do good…because we are good!

> **Prayer:** *"God of Freedom. Today, I know there is an open door set before me. I can choose life or death. I choose life! Amen."*

Challenge Your Mind. Channel Your Power. Change Your Life.

April 28

TRANSFORMATION

Spiritual Maturity

> *Affirmation*
> *"Today I understand that living by the law of love puts me in a much higher vibration than living by any set of religious rules."*

Living your life in a certain way being motivated only by the fear that "God's gonna get you" if you don't is a very low vibrational level to live on. But many people who are grown adults - at least physically - still do.

That's the level the Hebrew children were on when they had to be given the Ten Commandments. They still had to be told: Don't take things that don't belong to you. Don't kill people. Be good to your parents. Go to church on the Sabbath, etc. because their love relationship with God, themselves and each other was not strong enough to ensure those things would, or in some cases would not happen without some threat of punishment or promise of reward.

People operating on this level are spiritually immature and still need the container of a religion with a strict set of rules.

When Jesus came, he gave only two commandments: *Love the Lord your God with all your heart, soul and mind. And love your neighbor as yourself.* He even went a little further and added, *on these two hang all the law and the prophets* - meaning basically, if you just follow these two laws, you don't really need any of the others because when love is the highest law, smaller, more specific laws become obsolete.

> **Prayer:** *"God of Perfect Love, help me today to live in the higher law of love and not have to be told what to do and what not to do like a child. Help me be the most mature spiritual person I can be. Amen."*

TRANSFORMATION

April 29

Does God Need Praise?

Affirmation
"Today, I am aware that God does not need my praise, nor does God depend on my praise. I am also aware that praise raises my vibration and connects me with a divine atmosphere."

There are so many church clichés regarding praising God and God's apparent need for constant adulation and affirmation: "Let's give Jesus a great big hand clap…When the praises go up, the blessings come down… If I only had two praisers…Enter His courts with praise, and His gates with thanksgiving." We get chided from worship leaders that our praise is not good enough for God. Does God really need praise? Is God somehow incomplete without our praise? Does God come running when we praise? If God is omnipresent and expressing evenly throughout the universe, how do we get God, who is always ever-present, to "show up?"

God is not an egomaniac. Spirit is not self-absorbed. God is Spirit. God is Vibration. So, how do we explain the genuine, experiential presence of God in church services? What about the tears and joy and love…and the miracles that take place? When we raise our conscious awareness, we create an atmosphere where love, joy, peace, gratitude can do miraculous things. In essence, when we raise our vibration, God "inhabits our praise" as God already exists in that higher vibration. Or, we inhabit the vibration of God when we praise with gratitude, thanksgiving, joy. So, God does not show up as much as we go up! Hey! Blessings actually do come down. But, really more than blessings coming down, blessings come through us when we raise our vibration.

Prayer: *"High Vibration, today I will ascend to Your vibration of love, peace, joy and gratitude, as I enter into praise. Amen."*

Challenge Your Mind. Channel Your Power. Change Your Life.

April 30

TRANSFORMATION

Heart Alchemy

Affirmation
"Today I will use love and forgiveness to transmute negative experiences into positive lessons."

Alchemy is the process of transmuting one substance into another, particularly attempting to convert base metals into gold. Metaphorically it is a form of philosophy that gives more value to things that would otherwise be less valuable.

As we know, the anti-venom used to stop the effects of a snake bite is made from the venom itself. Many vaccines contain a little part of the virus or disease they are trying to prevent. There are a number of substances that contain both healing properties and poison; and medicine given in the wrong dosage or handled improperly can make you very ill or even kill you.

In order to get to the part that is medicinal, you've got to take the poison itself and then somehow separate out or strip away the harmful part. That's very similar to the process of alchemy, which involves distilling the substance down to its essence and extracting the part that is useful.

When, for whatever reason, we have taken in something that could have a poisonous effect on us emotionally, we must spiritually alchemize it so that it can no longer harm us. We do this by distilling it down to its essence, or more accurately, neutralizing it with our pure essence, which is love. Love is the only thing that can transmute something that was meant for evil into good.

Prayer: *"God of Transformation, help me understand today that I have the power to alchemize any harmful emotion that comes up in me through the power of love. Amen."*

May 1

I'M NOT IN TROUBLE. I'M IN TRANSITION.

Generational Curses or Blessings?

Affirmation
"Generational curses have no power over me or my family. I will not be a victim of any former generation's choices. I am the BREAKER of bad choices, harmful cultures or negative cycles. Today, I choose life and blessing! Today, I create righteousness, joy and peace to be passed down to the next generation."

There is actually no such thing as a generational curse. On the surface, it may look like a curse that has been passed down for generations. However, as we dig deeper we discover that it isn't a curse at all. Generational cycles exist from generational cultures and customs that are the result of generational choices.

Contrary to popular belief and faddish preaching, God does not play favorites. God doesn't favor Jacob over Esau. God doesn't bless Isaac and curse Ishmael. The "curse of Ham" has not been passed down to people of color throughout generations. We are not helpless victims.
We are powerful victors!

There may be a cycle in your family that has been accepted as a way of life for generations. Yet, you can change this cycle and choose a different experience of life by simply making different choices. You are the creation of a creative Creator and you carry the same divine DNA. What does this mean? Your Creator gave you the power to create! So, wake up to who you are and stop giving your power away to any idea of being the victim of an unbreakable family curse. Create the life you want to experience by making good choices that become powerful customs that create healthy cycles that yield positive cultures. You can do it!

Prayer: *"Heavenly Father, thank you for gifting me with the power to choose, change and create. I give thanks that I am blessed, not cursed. Today, I pass down blessings to generations who come after me. Amen."*

Challenge Your Mind. Channel Your Power. Change Your Life.

May 2

I'M NOT IN TROUBLE. I'M IN TRANSITION.

Just Say No!

Affirmation
"I know today that an appropriate no is just the starting point for the many 'yeses' that will open the door for me to live my life more fully and abundantly."

Saying *no* can be positive sometimes. For instance, when you know your own self-worth and you find yourself in a situation where it's not being recognized by others.

This is the *no* Rosa Parks felt on the bus that day.

It's the *no* black men felt as they carried signs saying, "I am a man."

It's the *no* the prodigal son felt when he, the son of a prominent and influential man, looked around and realized he was living and eating with pigs.

It's the *no* every addict feels when they realize an addiction has taken over their life, changed everything about them and they finally say *no more*!

It's the *no* you feel when you're tired of living every day with the disempowering thought patterns of fear and negativity and you make a decision right then and there to make a change.

This kind of *no* begins an emotional chain reaction and sets into motion an energetic shift within you that ripples out through every part of your life.

Learning to say no appropriately is just as important as learning to say yes.

> **Prayer:** *"Source of Divine Guidance, help me today to have the courage to say no to the things in my life that are holding me back and hindering my growth. Amen."*

FULLY AWAKE 365

I'M NOT IN TROUBLE. I'M IN TRANSITION.

May 3

Ending With the Beginning in Mind

Affirmation

"Today, I will position myself for success by ending this season the way I wish to begin the next. I will not waste time or energy predicting my future. Instead, I will create my future by agreeing to the process of transformation. I may not be exactly where I want to be. But, thank God I know I'm not where I used to be. There is a deposit of divinity anxiously waiting to be expressed through me. God desires to be God in, through and as me. And today, I will let God, be God, as me."

We have all heard motivational speeches for sports, education, fitness regimens, investing, that include the phrase, "Begin with the end in mind." In other words, begin a season the same way you want to end it. Today, we are looking at this idea, but in reverse, "End with the Beginning in Mind." In other words, end one season of your life as if the way you ended it determined the beginning of your next season. Let's go a little further. What if, in reality, there is no beginning or ending? What if it is all connected and continuous? Seasons, jobs, relationships…all of it, connected.

Life is not segmented into disparate, disconnected sections. All life is connected. If a butterfly in California can flap its wings and affect the weather patterns in Hawaii…you know the rest. This life philosophy is about more than just protecting our professional reputations so that former employers will give us good references when we want a new job. This is about setting up the conditions of our minds to emit an endless vibration that continually declares to the Universe that peace, possibility and prosperity are the order of the day. On a deeper level, if God is eternal, Alpha and Omega, First and Last, Beginning and Ending, then as we awaken to the idea that one season is connected to another season, that all of life is interconnected cyclically, not linearly, we begin to surrender to the truth that we are like God, divine, without beginning or ending. And, we open up a portal that empowers us to continually experience happiness and fulfillment.

Prayer: *"Beginning and Ending, I get it now. Thank You. Amen."*

Challenge Your Mind. Channel Your Power. Change Your Life.

May 4

I'M NOT IN TROUBLE. I'M IN TRANSITION.

Take Only What You Need

> **Affirmation**
> "I make it my intention today to let go of any pain which is no longer serving me. I will learn the difference between the positive and temporary pain of learning a lesson and the unnecessary pain of suffering."

We're all familiar with the old adage our moms and dads told us as kids in an effort to teach us how to be polite, "Take only what you need." It's a wonderful concept to promote conservation, avoid waste, and is also a good lesson in how to share.

We usually think of this in physical terms - not taking more food, dessert, toys, than we can reasonably consume or enjoy - the idea being: *leave some for others.* Or, in terms of another form of resource management - *let everyone have a turn, don't have another go until everyone has had a chance, etc.* Children who do not learn these behaviors are considered greedy and ill-mannered.

Oddly, we never seem to think of holding on to our pain as being greedy, but in a sense, it is. If you keep holding on to your pain *beyond* learning the lesson it comes to teach you, allowing it to turn into suffering, you are taking more of it than you need. After the lesson is learned, there is no more need for the pain. Learn to let go when the time is right. In this way, pain benefits rather than harms you.

> **Prayer:** "God of Wisdom, help me to discern between pain that is necessary and helpful and pain that has turned into suffering because I have held onto it for too long, and taken more of it than I need, failing to let it go once its lesson has been learned. Amen."

FULLY AWAKE 365

I'M NOT IN TROUBLE. I'M IN TRANSITION.

May 5

Cinco de Mayo

Affirmation
"Today, I will be open to seeing the importance of someone else's holidays and holy days. I will celebrate my culture while remaining curious about all of the cultural expressions around me."

Cinco de Mayo, or the fifth of May, is a holiday that celebrates the date of the Mexican army's May 5, 1862 victory over France at the Battle of Puebla during the Franco-Mexican War. The day is also known as Battle of Puebla Day. While it is a relatively minor holiday in Mexico, in the United States, Cinco de Mayo has evolved into a commemoration of Mexican culture and heritage, particularly in areas with large Mexican-American populations.[*]

There are many different holidays, and even diverse holy days, in various nations, cultures and religions. There may be times when you celebrate a holiday that is not necessarily significant to a friend of yours. Many Americans celebrate the 4th of July as an Independence Day or America's freedom from the tyranny of Britain. Yet, African American abolitionist and social reformer, Frederick Douglass, begged the question of how America could hypocritically celebrate being freed from the bondage of Britain while simultaneously placing Africans in bondage.

Keep your mind open to seeing new perspectives, and your heart open to feeling the passion, and protest, others may experience around significant days. Every holiday, culture and religion can enrich our understanding of the global human family.

Prayer: *"Divine Parent with many children, today I set my intention to learn from all of Your children. Amen."*

---

[*] History.com

Challenge Your Mind. Channel Your Power. Change Your Life.

May 6 — I'M NOT IN TROUBLE. I'M IN TRANSITION.

The Truth of Self-Acceptance

Affirmation
*"Complete self-acceptance does not mean I can never change.
It only means I must love all of myself."*

Many people view what has come to be known as "radical" (which is just another way to say *complete*) self-love or self-acceptance as a cop-out because they think what people are saying when they suggest this is to accept all of your negative behaviors without trying to change them. They think the statement "just be who you are" means only who you are at your worst.

But that's not what it means. Self-acceptance is seeing very clearly who you are - the characteristics, attributes and behaviors you judge as good or positive as well as those you judge as negative, unappealing or even destructive - and then being able to still love yourself completely.

Because your eternal spirit, the core essence of who you are, is your Christ Nature, that part of you is indeed perfect and contains no flaws. It's the human part that has been damaged, influenced and shaped by other people and by the circumstances of your life that has created any flaws or negative aspects of your personality.

You can change those things about yourself if you will:
1. See them.
2. Accept they are there. Don't live in denial.
3. If you can determine where they came from, forgive the person or situation that caused them, and more importantly, forgive yourself.
4. Love yourself in spite of them.

When you are able to do these four things, the change will happen of its own accord.

Prayer: *"God of Truth, help me today see all of who I am, not just the positive and not just the negative, and help me to change the things about myself that I can through radically loving and accepting myself. Amen."*

FULLY AWAKE 365

May 7

I'M NOT IN TROUBLE. I'M IN TRANSITION.

Get the Devil Out of Your Mind and Out of Your Mouth

> ***Affirmation***
> *"I no longer need the devil because I am done with blaming others for my life experience. I choose to eat from the Tree of Life and refuse the fruit of the knowledge of good and evil. Today I affirm there is only One Power in the universe. And, that Power is working in, through, as and for me."*

"The devil made me do it." No phrase has lulled and kept more people asleep to their power in the history of mankind. Having the devil to blame is a luxury feature that keeps us completely comfortable and incapable of seeing that we are the only devil to blame. Blame is a power thief. And, blaming the devil for what we do takes more of our power than we know. I have had the unfortunate experience of being around intoxicated individuals who behave poorly. Then, later on, in a sober state, blame their inappropriate actions on the alcohol. The alcohol is not to be blamed. The alcohol just provides an excuse to do what you want to do sober, but don't have the nerve or an excuse. Many Christians are drunk on the devil, blaming him for all of their poor choices and bad behavior.

I am not sure I just stopped believing in the devil one day. I feel like I just realized I didn't need the devil anymore and the devil just kind of faded away. I like to say, "Get the devil out of your mind and out of your mouth, and the devil will get out of your life." Or, from the words of Jesus, *"make no place for the devil and he will flee."* There doesn't have to be an official exorcism or even a rebuking of the devil. Just simply make no place for the devil by not needing him or anything else to blame. You will never truly have power until you realize there is only One Power in the universe. And, that Power is not separate from you. When we praise God for the good and blame the devil for the bad, we subtly and subconsciously continue to eat from the Tree of the Knowledge of Good and Evil. It's all God. Humanity's misuse of its divine creativity can at times certainly seem like the devil. Yet, it's only a lack of navigating our divine creativity. Keep your power. Hone your power. Own your power. And, watch the devil flee.

Prayer: *"Strong Deliverer, today I will make no place for the devil. Amen."*

Challenge Your Mind. Channel Your Power. Change Your Life.

May 8

I'M NOT IN TROUBLE. I'M IN TRANSITION.

Generational Curses

Affirmation
"Today I will make positive, healthy choices in order to create my own life."

The relatively new field of study called Epigenetics tells us that our genes are like light switches. Each gene you have has the potential to either be switched on or off, and which position it's in determines how it expresses in your body. So, genes are really just potential. You can control their behavior by what you choose to do or not do. We have the power to either activate or suppress particular genes.

Previously, it was thought that changes in gene expression happened at the level of our DNA and was a lengthy process, but now we know that the change actually occurs in the *processes that surround* the DNA, not in the DNA itself. Therefore, it's dynamic rather than static.

That's a lot of scientific talk to simply convey that we've now learned we can affect and alter things in our body through lifestyle changes that we used to think we just had to live with because they were passed down to us from our parents.

Therefore, things we view as, or have been told are generational curses, whether physical or behavioral, are no longer beyond our control. Even the genetic make-up we were born with is just a starting point. If we live unconsciously, those programs will just keep running on auto-pilot. But if we decide to live our lives on purpose by making good, healthy choices, we can, in a very real sense, create our own reality.

Prayer: *"God of Destiny, help me understand today that the power to create my own reality is within me. I am not the victim of any generational curse or genetic illness. My destiny is in my own hands. Amen."*

May 9

I'M NOT IN TROUBLE. I'M IN TRANSITION.

Set 'Em Up and Knock 'Em Down

Affirmation
"Today, I am aware that I am not what people say about me... good or bad. I am neither the flattery nor the criticism of others. I am what I say about me. I am the thoughts I have about myself."

Is it of interest to you that the same "crowd" that celebrated Jesus with *"Hosanna, blessed is he who comes in the name of the Lord"* just a few short days later demanded his blood... *"crucify him!"* (Matthew 21:19, 27:22 NIV) Can we avoid the pinnacle of flattery and pitfall of criticism?

Scripture reminds us that flattery *"deceives the minds of the naïve."* (Romans 16:18 NIV) We all desire to be told wonderful things about ourselves. However, there are times when flattery is used manipulatively to achieve a hidden agenda. "Yes" people find a way to offer affirmation to those who cannot affirm themselves. Conversely, criticism can be utilized as a tool to promote the critic to some sense of an advisory position. In essence, as one becomes critical there is an assumed promotion to being the solution.

Flatterers focus only on the good. Critics are never satisfied. We may never be rid of either. Yet, we can rid ourselves of our need for them. When you know who you are flattery and criticism become non-issues. Receive the flattery with a grain of salt. Consider the criticism if there is any application that is helpful. Assume best intention from flatterers while remaining vigilant to manipulation. Assimilate the negative from critics without becoming beaten down by mean-spirited people. And remember this: never let any of it touch your spirit!

Prayer: *"One Voice, awaken in me the wisdom to wear flattery and criticism like a loose garment – that is always near me, but never truly touching or restricting me. Amen."*

Challenge Your Mind. Channel Your Power. Change Your Life.

May 10 — I'M NOT IN TROUBLE. I'M IN TRANSITION.

Spiritual Restoration

> ***Affirmation***
> *"Today, I set my intention to be spiritual, not religious. Therefore, I will walk in a spirit of love with the desire to restore others."*

There is a modern trend that has birthed a popular cliché:

"I am not religious. I am spiritual."

I would venture to guess we have all heard someone, or even heard ourselves, say something similar to this. So, if there is a current societal demand for spirituality, how do we approach achieving spiritual status? The Apostle Paul exhorts the Galatian church: *"Brethren, if a man is overtaken in any trespass, you who are spiritual restore such a one in a spirit of gentleness, considering yourself lest you also be tempted."* (Galatians 6:1) Wow! There is so much here to unpack. I do not offer that spirituality is limited to this scriptural definition. Yet, it might be a good place to start.

Let's grab the two basic exhortations offered to us here. 1) Instead of tearing down or attempting to disqualify, restore others who have veered from the path of purpose. And, 2) Restore in gentleness, not with an insensitive, damaging strength or with a self-righteous attitude, remembering that you could also fall from your intended destiny.

Yes, we meditate. We read enlightening books. We dialogue with those of other religious traditions. We watch Oprah's Super Soul Sunday. All spiritual! But, maybe the journey of a thousand miles begins with lovingly restoring others with a spirit of kindness.

> **Prayer:** *"Restorative God, awaken true spirituality within me. Give me the compassion to restore others with gentleness and from the awareness that I might need the restoration that I give. Amen."*

I'M NOT IN TROUBLE. I'M IN TRANSITION.

May 11

From Chaos to Balance

Affirmation
"Today I will seek the middle way in all things knowing this is the path of oneness."

When you find yourself in a chaotic situation, your first instinct might be to feel that what is needed is its opposite - order. However, if all we ever do is go from chaos to order (which can be rigid and restrictive at times, not allowing for much creativity) then we'll only be participating in a never ending swing of the pendulum.

We will find ourselves going back and forth between the two extremes forever; from chaos to order, then back to chaos (because no change can occur without chaos, and as we know, the only constant in this world is change), and then back to order again - that is the nature of extremes.

So what we should be seeking, when we find ourselves in the midst of chaos, is not order, but balance. As always, the middle way is best because it is only there that we can stop the pendulum from swinging and achieve stillness.

Chaos to order is duality. Chaos to balance is oneness.

Prayer: *"God of Perfect Balance, help me today stop the never ending pendulum swing from chaos to order. Help me to find the perfect balance that the middle way provides and come into stillness. Amen."*

Challenge Your Mind. Channel Your Power. Change Your Life.

May 12

I'M NOT IN TROUBLE. I'M IN TRANSITION.

Get Back Up... Again

> **Affirmation**
> "Today, the Resurrection is alive and well as it is happening in me! The love, the light and the life of Jesus are waking up on the inside of me. As I show kindness, as I express care, as I extend help to the hurting, as I spread hope, the Resurrection is happening through me. Jesus is alive today. And, the Spirit of Jesus is alive within me."

Easter is a big day for churches. And, Easter is a lot of pressure for most pastors. There is an unspoken expectation from the faithful members that one sermon, specifically the Easter sermon, is going to transform all of the first timers and members, who only attend once a year on Easter, into somehow miraculously becoming weekly attenders. And, by the way, this magical sermon is to be short enough not to interfere with families' pre-planned events. After about 20 years of killing myself to deliver a "best of the best" sermon every Easter, I realized that Easter, for people who don't have a weekly spiritual practice, is really just a social event, a pseudo high school reunion or a fashion show. So, what is Easter?

Easter is the powerful hope that as Jesus rose from the grave, so can we. But, in most Christian circles we believe our resurrection is a future event, when Christ calls all of the sleeping faithful saints out of their graves to meet Him in the sky. Easter is not only a future event. Easter is now, today, when we wake up to it. Because He lives, I can face tomorrow…not next year. The same Spirit that raised Christ from the dead is in us, the Kingdom is within us, Christ in us is the hope of glory. This means we can get back up now…from poor choices, financial ruin, divorce, sickness or from the heavy burden of guilt. We all fall down. But, we get up. And, because *"a righteous man may fall seven times,"* we may be getting back up…again. Easter is about resurrection, redemption and restoration. Today!

> **Prayer:** *"Resurrection Power, awaken the power of Easter within me today. By Your Spirit, I will get back up…and get back up again. Amen."*

May 13

I'M NOT IN TROUBLE. I'M IN TRANSITION.

Everybody's A Hero

Affirmation
"I embody the Christ-Consciousness."

Especially in times of crisis, people start looking around for a hero; for someone to save them, or us, collectively. It's funny how infrequently we think to look for a hero in the one place that it's actually easiest to find - inside ourselves.

We, as a culture, have been conditioned to be very externally oriented when we think of this character type. There's an old Bonnie Tyler song from the 1980's that accurately describes our vision of a hero:

> He's gotta be strong and he's gotta be fast; and he's gotta be fresh from the fight. I need a hero. I'm holding out for a hero 'til the morning light. He's gotta be sure and it's gotta be soon; and he's gotta be larger than life.

That says a lot about our expectations, and also about our level of self-confidence. Most of us don't think we could ever live up to that description. We don't think it's possible for us to show up for ourselves or for others in this way - so - we look outside ourselves for someone else to swoop in and save the day.

For much of humanity, Jesus is that hero. But right now, the world needs people who know how to do more than just *call on* the historical Jesus. It needs people who know how to embody Jesus.

It's time for each of us to realize that through the Christ Spirit that lives in us, we can all be the hero of our own story; we can show others how to do the same; and we can collectively create an entirely new future for ourselves.

> **Prayer:** *"God of Clear Vision, help me see myself as you see me today, as the hero of my own story. Amen."*

Challenge Your Mind. Channel Your Power. Change Your Life.

May 14

Love Has No Date

I'M NOT IN TROUBLE. I'M IN TRANSITION.

> ***Affirmation***
> *"Today, I will celebrate those I love and those who are near and dear to my heart. I will honor special dates of the year while also choosing to never limit my love to any specific date."*

Does it seem strange to you that children are born, raised, fed, clothed, nurtured, educated, and loved in a home for twenty plus years, then one day follow a spouse or career across the country and only spend Mother's Day, Father's Day, Thanksgiving and Christmas with the parents who raised them? If you are perceptive you might have picked up on the fact that I am about to be an empty nester.

Prior to the Industrial Revolution, families were generally agrarian, working on, and living off of the land, together, in close proximity. With the advent of trains, cars, and airplanes, families have never been farther apart from each other. Whether we move thousands of miles away or merely down the street, each day provides us with an opportunity to celebrate the ones we love.

Every day of the year should be honored as a wedding anniversary, a birthday, Mother's Day! Saving gifts, meaningful words, and valuable time for a few days of the year subtly projects our love into the realm of obligation and ritual. Begin today! And, always remember, every day is Mother's Day!

> **Prayer:** *"Abiding Love, awaken my heart today, that I might live each day to love with all of me. Like You...I am love. Today, help me surrender to my true nature. Amen."*

I'M NOT IN TROUBLE. I'M IN TRANSITION.

May 15

Shaken. Not Stirred.

Affirmation
"Today, I will be aware that the rain falls on the just and the unjust. When a shaking comes my way, I will not be shattered. Rather, I will be shaken into an awakening that moves me toward positive action and healthy growth."

James Bond certainly had style. How many Bond movies have we seen James Bond in a sharp tuxedo, hair slicked back, and casually introducing himself as "Bond, James Bond?" He also had a specific way of ordering his dry martini… "shaken, not stirred." All of us experience events and circumstances that shake our faith. Do these shakings stir up anything positive? I believe these difficult moments are not designed to shatter us, but to shake us. How can we allow shaky moments to stir us? Teach us?

One safeguard against being shattered is cultivating a spiritual flexibility. Don't grow too attached to people, places, things, preachers, doctrines, beliefs or ideas. Flexibility allows us to move and sway and flow as Spirit leads us. We also avoid being shattered when we can decipher the hand of God from an attack of an enemy. The wind blows and causes roots of a tree to go deeper. Seasons of shaking can stir up gifts within us that have been lying dormant. Sometimes you don't know what you can do until you're forced to try. Today, as shakings come our way, allow these moments to strengthen, stir and teach us.

Prayer: *"Unchanging Spirit, grant me grace to be shaken, and stirred, but not shattered. I give thanks for the strength, resilience and flexibility that each shaking produces in my journey. Amen."*

Challenge Your Mind. Channel Your Power. Change Your Life.

May 16

I'M NOT IN TROUBLE. I'M IN TRANSITION.

Performance. Proving. Prerequisites.

Affirmation
"Today, I am aware that my self-worth, and my worthiness, are not dependent on my performance, proving myself or satisfying any prerequisite. I am worthy right now…just as I am."

How do we operate in loving relationships if we do not feel as if we deserve to be loved? Sadly, no matter how passionately someone endeavors to love us, we can only receive love in direct proportion to how much we love ourselves.

Perhaps we were raised with the skewed definition that love is about performance, proving and prerequisites. Whether we perform beautifully, prove ourselves or meet particular prerequisites is absolutely beside the point of love. Love is about worthiness and self-worth. Unfortunately, many religious adherents are burdened with generations of "unworthiness" teaching. And, the unlearning of unworthiness can take a lifetime.

First, we are worthy of love because we come from a loving Creator and from a loving space. Our behavior, successes, failures, strengths, weaknesses are a part of our human development. Yet, they do not factor into our worthiness of love. Second, our self-worth either invites or blocks love from finding its way into our lived experiences. When we love ourselves, not only do we attract the love of others, we tap into our capacity to love others. We cannot give what we do not have to give.

Prayer: *"Unconditional Love, today I set my heart to love me, to be loved, and to love others. Help me to accept my worthiness. Amen."*

I'M NOT IN TROUBLE. I'M IN TRANSITION.

May 17

Jesus and John Wayne[*]

Affirmation
"Today, I choose to take back what Christianity stole from me…Jesus."

Who hijacked Christianity? And, who has been sneaking test boosters into Jesus' matzo ball soup? Modern evangelicalism is abundant with beefy heroes, legendary warriors and "real men." Politicians, actors and reality television stars assert their masculine prowess in support of their ideal Christian "…Mmmerica." Consciously, or unconsciously, these so-called Jesus followers take their cues from John Wayne, an iconic figure, lost in time, who exists as a reminder of manhood: unafraid of being politically incorrect, willing to tell the truth (or a subjective version of it), and anxious to brandish a gun at a moment's notice. Many of us are shocked when a majority of Christian Americans back candidates who are the polar opposites of Jesus of Nazareth, yet successfully campaign under the Christian flag. Where does this disparity come from? And, why are we so shocked?

I would offer that these painful discoveries are not mere betrayals of a faith founded on love, compassion, sensitivity and inclusivity. I argue that these reality checks are simply revealing that the majority of American Christians resonate with these public figures because they are desperate for the second coming of John Wayne, the reassertion of patriarchy, and the enforcement of aggressive foreign policy that turns it nose up at diplomacy anxiously waiting to kick some …! Jesus turned the other cheek, ordained the first woman minister, washed His friends' feet, engaged foreigners with love and absolutely never showed any symptoms of homophobia. Who has hijacked our Christianity, our Jesus, and crafted a new faith founded on guns, testosterone and authoritative rigidity? Are we worshipping Jesus? Or John Wayne?

Prayer: *"Sensitive Savior, awaken me to the testosterone-free, genderless expression of who You are. Amen."*

---

[*] Du Mez, Dr. Kristin Kobes, Jesus and John Wayne: How White Evangelicals Corrupted a Faith and Fractured a Nation. Liveright Publishing Co, NY. 2020.

Challenge Your Mind. Channel Your Power. Change Your Life.

May 18

I'M NOT IN TROUBLE. I'M IN TRANSITION.

The Sacred Yes

> **Affirmation**
> *"Today I will remember that while control is often out of my reach, surrendering to the present moment will always increase my peace."*

In her book entitled *The Sacred Yes*, Rev. Deborah Johnson says this, "When your prayers appear to be answered, it is not because God has come to your understanding, but because you have come to his. It is you who have changed your mind, not God." That's why the commonly uttered phrase *prayer changes things* is deceptive, for it is not the "things" that are changed, but the individual. A more accurate expression would be *prayer changes me to accept things as they are*.

This involves surrender. The teachings of Jesus are full of paradoxes, and this is one of them - that the ultimate way to be in control is to give up all control. The greatest example of this is what Jesus did on the cross. He had done nothing to deserve the situation he found himself in, yet he decided to accept the experience for what it was, just as it was. And because he chose to be powerless, he was given all power and authority forever.

There are always going to be circumstances beyond your control. The only thing that is totally in your control at all times is your attitude and how you decide to perceive things.

> **Prayer:** *"God of the Sacred Yes, help me to understand that all things are working for my good at all times even when there is little evidence of that. And help me to know that surrender will ultimately lead me to the place I want to be. Amen."*

I'M NOT IN TROUBLE. I'M IN TRANSITION.

May 19

Like Water Off of a Duck's Back

Affirmation
"Today, I will be conscious that negative interactions, mean looks, and rude tones are not necessarily personal. I will encounter angry, unhappy people. Their energy is not about me. I will allow insults, overreactions, harsh words, and abrupt conversations to roll off of me like water off of a duck's back."

Unfortunately, we do not have the privilege of knowing exactly what someone else is going through. Unless we are close to people and have intimate knowledge of their situation, we do not know what others are facing. When we encounter someone who is rude, defensive, harsh, impatient, demanding, ungrateful, angry – there are two responses that will help us maintain a high vibration and allow the other person to experience a different reality from whatever it is they are used to:

1. **Fly above the turbulence.** Maintain your joy and peace. Don't add fuel to the fire by lowering your vibration.

2. **LET IT ROLL OFF!** Don't take it personally. Let the lower energies roll off of you like water off of a duck's back. It is not personal. Not about you. When you take it personally you make it about you.

So many people we encounter have a long history of past hurt and even present pain. Unawakened, unenlightened, self-absorbed souls will attempt to project all of their pain onto you. When we react defensively or aggressively, we allow the projection of lower energy to take up residence within us. Don't be drawn into this trap. Simply let it roll off. And, give thanks for your state of awareness and awakedness. It is only from this mindset of maintaining our peace that we can offer help and hope to others.

Prayer: "All knowing God, only You know the heart, and the hurt, of every person. While I do not have this knowledge, I can rest in the knowing that difficult interactions are not always about me. Amen."

Challenge Your Mind. Channel Your Power. Change Your Life.

May 20

I'M NOT IN TROUBLE. I'M IN TRANSITION.

Joy and Sorrow

Affirmation
"Today I recognize that no sorrow lasts forever and that joy is always on the horizon."

"Some of you say, *Joy is greater than sorrow,* and others say, *No, sorrow is the greater.* But I say to you, they are inseparable. Together they come, and when one sits alone with you at your table, remember that the other is just asleep upon your bed." ~ Kahlil Gibran

I love the idea in this quote that sorrow clears out space for joy. It's like a forest fire. We tend to always think of those as tragedies, and they can indeed be destructive. But the ash and detritus that they leave behind is some of the most fertile soil there is.

Forests sometimes get too crowded and dense. The bigger, older trees block too much of the sun and drink up too much of the water supply so that the newer, smaller plants can't get enough nutrients to their roots to grow properly. But Mother Nature always knows how to right this imbalance. That's why some forest fires start spontaneously, and are actually healthy for the forests from time to time.

Mother Nature helps us out as well. Even though we may not like it and it may be uncomfortable, sometimes we just need a good cry to release stuck emotions. So next time you are feeling sorrow, try to shift your perspective and look at it as if it's just clearing out space; making room for new joy!

__Prayer:__ "God of our silent tears, help us to understand the value of both sorrow and joy. Both are necessary parts of life. One is simply making space for the other. Amen."

May 21

I'M NOT IN TROUBLE. I'M IN TRANSITION.

Joy and Happiness

Affirmation
"Today I will learn the difference between happiness and joy. One comes and goes, and the other is eternal. I can choose joy in any situation, even the situation of temporary unhappiness."

Even though people use these words synonymously, joy is deeper than, or at least different from happiness. Joy is rooted in our relationship with God, or Source. Since this is the case, it is more serene and more stable than mere happiness which is based in emotion.

You can be sad or unhappy because your particular life situation is temporarily not the best, yet still be joyful in general about other things going on around you in your greater world. Because it is an emotion, happiness is necessarily dependent upon your current circumstances. Current circumstances, however, have nothing to do, really, with your joy, which is not an emotion that comes and goes, but rather a fruit of the Spirit and a result of your identification with God and your eternal divine nature.

The actions or words of another may make us unhappy; and as we know, the actions of others are beyond our control. But because joy is a fruit of the Spirit that we always have access to, we always have the ability to choose it in any circumstance, at any time.

> **Prayer:** *"God of Joy, help us to understand that joy is truly always available to us whether we are currently happy or unhappy with our life situation. True joy is in the knowledge that all things are working together for our good and that 'trouble don't last always'. Amen."*

Challenge Your Mind. Channel Your Power. Change Your Life.

May 22

I'M NOT IN TROUBLE. I'M IN TRANSITION.

Count It All Joy

> **Affirmation**
> *"Today, I will count it all joy having confidence that faith-testing trials will teach me patience, and patience will bring a completeness and perfection in my life. I am grateful for the wisdom I have gleaned and remain open to receive more. I am persuaded that God wants to share wisdom with me. I live in gratitude for a benevolent universe that responds to my openness and sends the Teacher when I, the student, am ready for Him to appear!"*

Count it joy when we face hardships? Joy in tests? Joy in trials? We may find it difficult to feel joy (or even want to) while we are in the middle of stressful seasons. Look closely at the order of how James describes goodness unfolding throughout challenging times:

> *"My brethren, count it all joy when you fall into various trials, knowing that the testing of your faith produces patience. But let patience have its perfect work, that you may be perfect and complete, lacking nothing. If any of you lacks wisdom, let him ask of God, who gives to all liberally and without reproach, and it will be given to him"*
> *(James 1:2-5).*

Trials bring Testing…the Testing develops Patience… Patience yields Completeness/Perfection…the end result is that there is no lack of anything. And, as an added bonus, if we still don't have wisdom after this process is over, we can simply ask God and it will be given to us. The Bible describes Jesus approaching His most difficult moment (the cross) with a *"joy set before Him."* If we could see the end result of these growth pangs, we would be able to set a joy before us. Or, as we said in church growing up, not "wait 'til the battle is over…Shout Now!" It's all good and all God. And, we can count it all joy knowing it's not happening to us…it's happening for us!

> **Prayer:** *"God of Joy, today I give thanks for the process of You developing me into my highest and greatest good. Amen."*

I'M NOT IN TROUBLE. I'M IN TRANSITION.

May 23

Finding Stillness in the Chaos

Affirmation
"Today I will not give my attention to any chaos that presents itself in my life, but I will learn to shift my focus to the stillness I can always find within myself instead."

"Chaos never needs your attention . . . it's an indication that stillness needs your attention." ~ Dr. Kim D'Eramo

Far too often when we find ourselves in the midst of confusion or disorder we think we must shift all of our focus and energy onto the chaos because we've got to put that fire out before we can do anything else. We feel that in order to restore calm and stillness, we must take some action to resolve the chaos.

But actually, the exact opposite is true. When you come across a chaotic situation and you're the person looking at it from the outside, what is the first thing you say to the people involved? *"Calm down."*

Instinctively you know that putting more focus on the hysteria at that point only gives it more fuel and creates more chaos. You try to get the person to shift their focus away from whatever the disorder is and toward stillness.

Although it's much easier to tell someone else to do this than to do it yourself, it is a skill worth cultivating. Shifting your focus away from the chaos is the way you come back to your stillness.

Prayer: *"Source of Calm, help me to remember that when I find myself in turbulent circumstances I can always come back to stillness by focusing on the Christ within who leads me beside still waters. Amen."*

Challenge Your Mind. Channel Your Power. Change Your Life.

May 24

I'M NOT IN TROUBLE. I'M IN TRANSITION.

Victim of Chance? Or Agent of Change?

> **Affirmation**
> "I am not a human victim of chance. I am a divine agent of change. I am not the things that happened to me. I am what I do with the things that happened to me. I am not the names people have called me. I am only what I answer to. And today, my name is not victim. My name is victory."

In a counseling session years ago, I sat with a middle-aged individual who was heavily burdened with painful memories from their childhood and the neglect from their father. They explained how the lack of fatherly love was now affecting their ability to be affectionate with their spouse and their own children. Tears, tantrums and a lot of tissue later, I finally suggested that this person needed closure and should go to their father and express how the neglect had affected their life. The individual then paused from the emotional outburst and said, "I can't do that. My father has been dead for twenty-five years." I was stunned that this level of emotional pain was still present all these years later. I said to this person, "A man who has been in the grave twenty-five years is still running and ruining your life?" This seemed to strike a chord and bring about an awakening that enough was enough. The individual said to me, "Why should I allow a person who is dead to destroy the life and good years I have left?"

All of us carry painful memories and images from our childhood. Some people believe we chose to come here and even chose our parents and families. Whether we choose our parents or it is all a game of chance, we can create purposeful change that provides us with a life full of love and joy. Pain unreleased and unresolved can be passed down for generations. Don't allow chance to run and ruin your life. Be a change agent. If your parents were neglectful, be the change in your kid's lives. If you grew up without love, be the change and give love. You will find that when you give out of the place of your pain you will experience a powerful sense of healing knowing that what may have happened to you by chance is now the fuel empowering you to create change.

> **Prayer:** "Divine Change Agent, help me be the change today. Amen."

I'M NOT IN TROUBLE. I'M IN TRANSITION.

May 25

Standing Up to Systems

Affirmation
"People are not inherently evil. Therefore, I will not focus any anger, even if it is righteous and justified, toward any individual. I will love all people, and seek to liberate those caught up in the conditioning of destructive systems."

Standing up for what you believe in and against things you don't is important. However, we need to learn how to stand for a message, a teaching, a principle - something we believe to be right and true - without blaming others or pointing fingers at individuals.

When we fight each other as individuals, we're fighting the wrong thing. We're wasting our energy. What needs to be "fought" - if you even want to use that terminology - are the dynamics of concepts like inequality, patriarchy, racism, classism, injustice in its many forms, and all incarnations of oppression.

The Bible tells us in Ephesians 6:12 that *we wrestle not against flesh and blood, but against powers and principalities*. It's systems that need to be destroyed, not people. The people caught up in these systems are the victims of the conditioned beliefs of these systems and need our love.

A major way we can change the world is by *not* going to war with others, but by doing what we can to dismantle the systems behind their behaviors that make us angry and cause something inside us to want to stand up. There's nothing wrong with standing up; we just have to make sure we're standing up to the right thing.

Prayer: *"God of Justice, teach me to look beyond the anger I feel at people and see the system that created their behavior. Help me to love the people caught up in the destructive dynamics and work to dismantle the systems that have conditioned them. Amen."*

Challenge Your Mind. Channel Your Power. Change Your Life.

May 26

I'M NOT IN TROUBLE. I'M IN TRANSITION.

From the Pit to the Pinnacle

Affirmation
"Whether others throw me into a pit, or whether I wind up there of my own volition, I will not stay there. I may be in a pit today. Yet, there is a pinnacle in my future."

When studying the biblical account of Joseph, we can find ourselves on a roller coaster of highs and lows. Joseph is this favored son, then he is thrown into a pit, then he winds up as second in command in Egypt. What a ride! The question that I would like for us to consider is this: isn't Joseph the same person in the pit of slavery that he is in the pinnacle of Pharaoh's palace? The answer is…yes! Joseph may be in very different circumstances. Yet, he is essentially the same person through it all. Furthermore, the same God that guided him to the palace of power was with him in the pit of pitifulness.

We may not always understand exactly what the meaning of our highs are lows may be. I posit that some of the pits I have graced were those of my own making. While some of the difficulties in my life were a direct result of others' actions and choices. There have also been moments of great achievement and success that I worked hard to experience. And yet, there have been instances when I did nothing to deserve good fortune and it just came my way. What remains the same is this – you are the same person in triumph and in tragedy. I have been the same person on a national stage as I am in the quiet moments of despair. Joseph helps us see panoramically the goodness of God when he tells his brothers "what you meant for evil, God meant for good!" Through it all, God is working things together for your good.

Prayer: *"God of the Pit and Pinnacle, Your abiding presence has comforted me every step of the way. Help me rest in the knowledge that it is all good and all God. Amen."*

I'M NOT IN TROUBLE. I'M IN TRANSITION.

May 27

Inspiration or Desperation

Affirmation
"It's always my choice."

The desire to experience change can show up as either inspiration or desperation. The lower frequency manifestation of this shows up as frustration, hopelessness or anger. The higher shows up as: "I'm not where I want to be, but I can get there. I can do this!"

Whether you are feeling the pull of inspiration toward a new way of living and being or the desperation of getting away from somewhere you don't want to be, change is your destination. How you get there is up to you.

Have you ever realized there's not a whole lot of difference, physically, in the way you feel when you're nervous and when you're excited? It's that same *butterflies in your stomach* feeling. How you choose to interpret it determines the outcome.

Right before giving a presentation or going into a job interview, if you decide the feeling is nerves you might mess up, get tongue-tied and forget your points. But if you decide it's excitement and look at it as an opportunity to share some beneficial information with a group of people who have come to listen to you, or to tell someone why you would be perfect for the job, then the outcome will most likely be much better.

Feelings are subject to the meaning we give them. If you think of it as reaching into a grab bag, you're using the same amount of effort to reach in no matter what. It's not the amount of effort that is the determining factor, but what you choose to focus on and pull out. You can pull out inspiration or desperation. Your choice.

> **Prayer:** *"Source of Inspiration, help me to choose the highest frequency available for my emotions today. Amen."*

Challenge Your Mind. Channel Your Power. Change Your Life.

May 28

I'M NOT IN TROUBLE. I'M IN TRANSITION.

Right Livelihood

> ***Affirmation***
> *"Today, no matter where I work, I will bring joy to others. I will have a good word for my brothers and a gracious heart toward my sisters. Everyone needs an encouraging word. And, I will be that word."*

How many days have we all spent working? Too many to count. During these working days we encounter coworkers, bosses, vendors, delivery workers, customers, strangers. Do these people leave our presence with joy, knowing that they are worthy of love? No matter what our job might be, there are little opportunities each day to bring a little light into someone's world.

In his first sermon after being enlightened, the Buddha laid out an Eightfold Path leading to peace. The fifth "fold" on this path was Right Livelihood. In a nutshell, Right Livelihood suggests the way we support ourselves financially should not bring harm to others. Said another way: *"The way you support yourself can be an expression of your deepest self."* (Thich Nhat Hanh) Whether I am teaching, coaching, driving, delivering, stocking, cleaning, fixing or cooking…I can find a way for my true essence to be a blessing to all that come my way.

From the Bible we find a similar strain of thought: *"Whatever you do, work at it with all your heart, as working for the Lord."* (Colossians 3:23-24 NIV) What does it mean to work as unto the Lord? It means, the task ahead of us is not merely to complete a project so that we can be paid. Whatever we set our hands to can be a tool for sharing love with God's creation in some big or small way.

> ***Prayer:*** *"Jehovah Jireh, thank you for providing for and through me. I give thanks for the money that comes through me and for the opportunities to spread love while I am making money. Let Your light shine through me today. Amen."*

I'M NOT IN TROUBLE. I'M IN TRANSITION.

May 29

Weathering the Storm

Affirmation
"My faith is in the Christ in me."

The reason we have faith, or believe that we need it, is to get us through the difficult times in life; to get us through the storms. Let's face it, when everything's going well we don't really need faith. Coming to church, believing in a higher power, or practicing other aspects of our faith might be enjoyable and are certainly beneficial to us all the time, but when we really need to rely on our faith is when we're facing a storm.

Sometimes, the wisest thing to do in the middle of a storm is not to fight it, but to let go of control and just ride it out. The most brittle trees are those that break in the storm, whereas the ones that bend usually survive.

One of the greatest examples of letting go of control is what Jesus did on the cross. He had lived a sinless life and had done everything that had been asked of him. He was an innocent man, suffering for no justifiable reason. He could have tried to fight, but he decided to accept the experience as it was and do what he knew he had agreed to come here and do.

True freedom and ultimate control (of yourself) is living as if you had completely chosen whatever you are feeling and experiencing in every moment. That's when you know your faith is strong - when you decide that no matter what, you know your own Christ nature's got you and that you're always safe - even in the face of death.

That's when your faith can weather any storm.

> **Prayer:** *"Faithful God, help me to have a faith strong enough to withstand any storm I face today and always. Amen."*

Challenge Your Mind. Channel Your Power. Change Your Life.

May 30

I'M NOT IN TROUBLE. I'M IN TRANSITION.

When Two Halves Do Not Make a Whole

Affirmation
"Today I will work on becoming whole and complete on my own."

Ultimately, you're responsible for keeping your own emotional cup full. Think about it this way - whatever frequency or vibration you send out, that's the vibration you will attract back to yourself.

If you're sending out the vibrations of needing someone to complete you because you feel incomplete on your own, or if you're sending out the frequency of wanting someone to come into your life and fix you because you feel broken and unable to fix yourself, then what are you inviting in? Someone else who is also vibrating on the frequency of being needy, incomplete and broken.

Sometimes we like to think in terms of two halves making a whole, but that's not the way it works in relationships. That's just two broken people coming together - which usually results in a broken relationship.

A better solution is to work on making yourself whole and complete. Fill your own cup first and *then* connect with another person who is whole and complete in themselves.

Prayer: *"Source of Wholeness, help me to understand that I do not need anyone else to make me feel whole and complete. I am whole and complete within myself, and when that's the vibration I send out, that's the kind of person I will attract to myself. Amen."*

I'M NOT IN TROUBLE. I'M IN TRANSITION.

May 31

Recognizing Destructive Patterns Quickly

Affirmation
"Today I choose to make the most of this lifetime by recognizing destructive patterns quickly. I am aware that destructive thoughts lead to destructive choices; destructive choices become destructive behaviors; and destructive behaviors invite, enable and create destruction in my life. As I begin to think new thoughts, I am also cultivating new choices, establishing new behaviors and walking down new paths."

One of my mentors shared a piece of wisdom with me while I was in high school that still haunts me today. He said, "Some people can learn by hearing or observing. Other people learn through experience. But, there are some people who only learn by way of tragedy." People who refuse to learn any other way than by tragedy have an inability and an unwillingness to recognize destructive patterns quickly. We have all headed down paths that were either dangerous, or at the very least, unproductive. Realizing this quickly is the way we avoid a lifetime of pain and resist detours that put our destinies on layaway. Our lives are all on a long trajectory. When we get off track, the quicker we shift our trajectory the less severe the course correction will be down the line. Getting off course without recognizing it, or refusing to yield to a course correction, can result in finding ourselves in another galaxy far, far away.

Jesus offered a course correction to the woman at the well, to the woman caught in adultery, to the rich young ruler, to Zacchaeus the tax collector, to the Pharisees and to many others. Some received it, made quick adjustments and found their way back to purposeful living. Others rejected His wisdom and continued down the path toward tragedy. Today, set your intention to be a quick learner and visualize yourself heading directly toward the realization of your full potential.

Prayer: *"Course Corrector, with Your help, I will recognize destructive patterns quickly, adjust and enjoy a happy and fulfilled life. Amen."*

Challenge Your Mind. Channel Your Power. Change Your Life.

June 1

RESPECTING THE JOURNEY OF OTHERS

Get Off My Ship

> **Affirmation**
> "Today, I will be conscious of who is on my ship, how they influence my direction and ultimately determine my destination. I will trust that the same Spirit guiding me toward my destiny is also ordering the steps of others. I will release those not destined to ride with me and rest in the knowledge that the same God who is perfecting those things concerning me is actively making a way for all of His children."

In the story of Jonah, he is commanded by God to go to Nineveh (Mosul, Iraq). Instead, he chooses to disobey and boards a ship headed for Tarshish (Lebanon). So, Jonah is going the wrong way. And, the ship heading toward their appointed arrival is carrying a passenger, Jonah, who will eventually detour their direction and distract from their destiny. Not long after their departure, the ship encounters an epic storm. Jonah informs the other passengers that he is the reason for the storm and insists they should throw him off of the ship. They refuse to throw Jonah overboard and instead being to throw everything else imaginable into the sea in the hopes that they will satisfy the anger of the storm. Finally, as a last resort, they put Jonah off of the ship. Immediately, the storm subsides, the ship makes it safely to Tarshish and then God provides Jonah transportation to Nineveh via the help of a large fish.

It may seem cruel, throwing Jonah off of the ship and into the turbulent stormy waters. Yet, Jonah got to his designed destination. Further, the ship survived the storm and arrived at its intended port. However, had they stayed connected to each other neither would have survived. Are you on the wrong ship? Are you carrying the wrong person on your ship? Trust that God desires everyone involved to fulfill their purpose and disconnect, give it to God and watch as things fall into place.

> **Prayer:** "Captain of the Sea, give me the wisdom to board the right ship and the courage to carry the right passengers. Amen."

RESPECTING THE JOURNEY OF OTHERS

June 2

Are We There Yet?

Affirmation
"Today, and each day, I agree to the endless me. I choose to embrace truth as a journey, not as a destination. My endless nature is not awakened by ending, or by concluding. I set my intention to be endless, and to follow this intention with the action of not ending. Therefore, my endless, infinite, eternal self is at peace practicing endlessness."

Today, June 2nd, is my dad's birthday. Happy birthday dad. I can remember as a child being impatient on family road trips. The drive seemed to never end. I, along with every child in the world, badgered my parents with this question: "Are we there yet?" The desire to arrive at a physical destination after a long drive is normal. Yet, on the spiritual journey, asking "are we there yet?" is symptomatic of lingering religious indoctrinations.

If God is endless, eternal, and we accept that we are also endless creations of an endless God, then arriving, concluding, ending are practices that should be left in the temporal, religious, material expressions and experiences.

Truth has no arrival, no destination. Truth is a way. Truth is a journey. Truth is a process of unfoldment. Questions, curiosities, searches all lead us to temporary answers. We can honor those answers and continue to make room for more questions that bring new answers and higher levels of expanded consciousness.

Prayer: *"Endless Mind, awaken the endless mind and eternal capacity lying dormant within me. I surrender to the journey of unfoldment and ever-expanding truth. Amen."*

Challenge Your Mind. Channel Your Power. Change Your Life.

June 3

RESPECTING THE JOURNEY OF OTHERS

Let Others Be

> **Affirmation**
> *"Today I understand that just as others cannot do my work for me, I cannot do theirs for them."*

Part of maturing and evolving is realizing that no one was put here to do our work for us. But just as importantly, we must also realize that we were not put here to do anyone else's work for them; not even our children's and definitely not our partner's.

When someone is ill, physically or metaphorically, you can lift their head so they can drink, but you can't take the drink for them. You drinking water will do nothing for *their* body. Similarly, trying to bear someone else's emotional burden for them only slows their progress and stunts their growth.

We all know the difficult journey we have often had to undertake in order to experience growth in our own lives. And each person's journey is individual to them. If we take that away from them, we take away their growth as well.

For their sake, as well as our own, we must learn how and where to draw the line. We do others a disservice by not letting them grow and evolve on their own.

> **Prayer:** *"God of Balance, help me to see that no matter how much I love and care for others, I am only hurting them when I try to do their spiritual or emotional work for them. The only person I can ever change is myself, but in doing so, I help them as well. Amen"*

RESPECTING THE JOURNEY OF OTHERS

June 4

Don't Choose Sides. Choose Love.

Affirmation
"Today, I choose NOT to choose sides. Instead, I choose peace and I choose the highest good for ALL who seek my help."

Early on in my ministry I learned a difficult lesson. During a marital counseling session, I encountered a spousal partner who had a long list of grievances against their partner. As I listened, I lost objectivity and neutrality. I chose sides. I was upset and wanted to follow up with the villainized partner. As we talked, I learned about the other side of the story. I heard details that equally upset me with spouse who had initially come to me with accusations and complaints. As I stepped back and took a breath, I realized who I was really upset with…myself!

I had allowed myself to choose sides. In my initial reactions, I lost sight of my purpose. I was there to create peace, to initiate change, to build a bridge, to instigate redemption. I apologized to the couple for my subjectivity and thanked them for a lesson that would journey with me for a lifetime.

God has called us to repair the breaches between people, to fill the chasms dividing loved ones, to be a balm of healing. If we choose sides we forfeit this purpose. When we remember our purpose, function will follow.

> **Prayer:** *"Highest Good, empower me to be a bridge over troubled waters, a voice of peace, a presence of redemption and a spirit of restoration. Amen."*

Challenge Your Mind. Channel Your Power. Change Your Life.

June 5

RESPECTING THE JOURNEY OF OTHERS

Saving Souls or Revolutionizing Systems?

> ***Affirmation***
> *"Today, I will be concerned with the salvation of an individual as well as the systems that affect individuals."*

One of the critiques of the Evangelical American church is that it has been overly focused on saving the souls of individual persons and disinterested in reforming the systems that tend to oppress those same individuals. While I do not consider myself an Evangelical, I am familiar with the American Christian Evangelical Church world. To attend to this accusation, I have only a short journey to make.

My paternal grandfather was a fiery, Evangelical, Pentecostal preacher. He preached heaven, hell, the sanctifying power and fire of the Holy Spirit, and warned of sinner's destiny in the lake of fire. He was an Evangelical. However, during the Great Depression, he began a soup kitchen and bread line. He saw this action as a natural step to follow the example of Jesus who came to redeem souls of humanity while also refusing to neglect empty stomachs that needed fish and bread. He was criticized as being a socialist and a communist. During this season of American Christianity there arose a chasm between the Gospel of salvation and the Social Gospel. Protestants and Catholics alike were asked to pick a side: either save souls or feed the hungry. I am persuaded that there is a Middle Way! We can attend to the spiritual well-being, and the physical needs, of humanity.

Souls or systems? Let us not make a choice. Let us set our intention to attend to humanity as a whole. The individual may need salvation. Yet, the systems that make up an individual's environment and quality of living may need saving as well.

> **Prayer:** *"God of Humanity, give us the wisdom to attend to the spiritual and physical needs of Your creation. Amen."*

RESPECTING THE JOURNEY OF OTHERS

June 6

Two Trees

Affirmation
"Today I understand that no one has to lose in order for me to win."

In this dualistic world we are presently living in, an outcome that is *good* for one person or one group of people can be *bad* for another. This is always the way it is when competition is involved - someone must win and someone must lose.

The Tree of the Knowledge of Good and Evil introduced duality into this realm. But there is no duality in the Tree of Life. Everyone who eats of the Tree of Life wins. The fact that at some point mankind chose to eat from the Tree of Knowledge is what makes it difficult for us to achieve oneness in our present reality and why "win/win" situations can be rare.

There are so many people in this world who are still living on the level of winning and losing, and who will step on whoever they must, break whatever rules they can get away with, in order to win.

But ideally, in a perfect world, or as we might describe it - the Kingdom of God - everyone would get all of what they want with no conflict. That will happen only when mankind makes a different choice - The Tree of Life, which brings into our world the knowledge that because we are all one, whatever hurts you hurts me, and whatever is good for you is also good for me.

Prayer: *"God of Oneness, help me to choose to eat from the Tree of Life rather than from the Tree of the Knowledge of Good and Evil as often as I possibly can. And help me to always remember that my brothers and sisters and I are one. Amen."*

Challenge Your Mind. Channel Your Power. Change Your Life.

June 7

RESPECTING THE JOURNEY OF OTHERS

Living Above the Political Divide

> ***Affirmation***
> *"Whether I call myself a Democrat, Republican, Liberal or Conservative, I can find biblical backing to support my particular political platform. My political views are not necessarily the politics of Jesus nor are they the official platform for political Christianity. My political views are mine and they are evolving. I am not my political views or my religious beliefs. I am an eternal Spirit capable of having and changing temporary opinions. As a peacemaker, this week I will endeavor to find a way to bring people together, not cause further division."*

Jesus taught that a rich man could not enter the Kingdom. He also instructed that if we don't receive interest on our investments, we will be cast into outer darkness (parable of the talents). Jesus told the rich young ruler to sell everything and give the money to the poor. He also rebuked Judas (wanting to sell an expensive fragrance and give the proceeds to the poor) by saying *"the poor you have with you always."* Jesus scourged Peter for using a sword and then later told the disciples to sell everything and buy some swords. It would be inaccurate to make Jesus a Democrat or a Republican. He seemed to vacillate between the two political platforms. Similarly, Paul taught the early church to *"hold all things (possessions) in common."* Paul also instructed that if *"a person doesn't work they don't eat."* Who knew Paul was both a Socialist and a Conservative?

What is the purpose of this? To encourage all followers of Christ to cease from using the Bible, or Jesus, as political weapons to support their particular political platform. The Bible and its teachings are complex, and at times contradictory. Instead of focusing on a few verses to promote a candidate or cause, why not focus on verses that foster unity and help to fill the chasm created by Christians misusing scripture for political gain.

> ***Prayer:*** *"Father, make us one. Help us focus on our commonalities. Use me as an advocate for peace, not a pawn for politics. Amen."*

RESPECTING THE JOURNEY OF OTHERS

June 8

All Things To All People

Affirmation
"Regardless of race, gender, culture, religion, language, sexual orientation, economic status, politics, geography or country of origin, I have something in common with every other human being on this planet that I come in contact with. I am open to seeing our commonalities and I will endeavor to find ways of connecting with all of the global human family."

The Apostle Paul famously wrote *"I become all things to all people…"* (1 Corinthians 9:22). This verse has been much maligned by many fear-based Christians with comments like: "If you're all things to everyone you're nothing to no one," and "If you don't stand for something you'll for anything." Finding common ground with people doesn't mean you immediately become brainwashed by them or give up all that is sacred to you. When you are confident in who you are, you have no need to approach every new connection with fear and suspicion.

Paul's desire to connect with people from different cultures and various expressions of religion was both beautiful and uncommon for people of his religious background. Yet, his passion to reach across boundaries was not totally selfless and sincere as he had an ulterior motive… *"to save some"* or to convert them to be followers of Christ. So, Paul's connecting point can be seen as a set up or a call to repentance and salvation. Our motive and motivation to connect with a diverse group of people should be that we are all people. We all breathe the same air, drink the same water. We are all warmed by the same sun and gaze into the same sky. We are all eternal spiritual beings having a temporary human experience and expression. We do not connect with other humans to sell anything, not even Jesus. We connect to bring comfort and encouragement. And in this way, we allow each person we touch to sense Christ in us.

Prayer: *"God of All, enable me to become all things to all people in order to share Your love and light without an agenda. Amen."*

Challenge Your Mind. Channel Your Power. Change Your Life.

June 9 — RESPECTING THE JOURNEY OF OTHERS

Looking Through the Lens of Our Filters

> ***Affirmation***
> *"Today I understand that just as I look through the lens of my own filters, so do others. I will not be offended or take things personally, but will understand that it's just projection. I will keep the actions of others in perspective and be gracious and forgiving."*

Sometimes when things aren't exactly as we want them to be in our inner world, instead of dealing with it, we choose to project our feelings outside ourselves, frequently on those around us. Something that complicates this is the fact that you can never really have any perspective or perception other than your own.

Unless you consciously decide to put yourself in someone else's shoes, the only eyes you ever truly look through are your own. And even when you manage to put yourself in someone else's place, listen to and try to understand their story, the experience is only temporary and you eventually return to your default setting - seeing through your own eyes and the unique filters you have acquired over time. No matter how much we practice listening to others and seeing through their eyes, the strongest influence on us will always be our own personal experience.

And this is the reason we can't and shouldn't take anything personally. We have to realize that everything that comes toward us from others is not actually directed at us but is a projection of their experience and a reflection of their journey and unique filters. They are seeing through their eyes first and foremost just as we are.

> **Prayer:** *"God of Perspective, let me understand that everyone projects their issues onto others at times. Give me patience, grace and most of all perspective when I am feeling the projections of others. Amen."*

RESPECTING THE JOURNEY OF OTHERS

June 10

Christ Is All, and In All

Affirmation
"Today, I will be open to seeing Christ in all of creation. I will even allow myself to recognize Christ outside of the boundaries of Christianity. I am willing to see the Christ in me and in others. I will be awake today to the truth that Christ is all, and in all."

If all of creation came from God (or the Word of God), then all of creation carries the DNA of God. We find out in the first chapter of Genesis that we are made *"in the image and likeness of God."* So, *"Christ in us…the hope of glory"* is not something to be acquired. Christ is already in us…in all of creation. Christ in us is something to be uncovered and discovered within us. The Apostle Paul was speaking to the Colossian church about this idea of Christ being present in all of creation and said it this way:

"…put on the new man who is renewed in knowledge according to the image of Him who created him, where there is neither Greek nor Jew, circumcised nor uncircumcised, barbarian, Scythian, slave nor free, but Christ is all and in all" (Colossians 3:10-11).

When you understand the depth of this verse it opens our minds to what Paul was really saying. The new man is renewed in knowledge. What knowledge? The knowledge of the image of Him who created us! Wow! The barbarians and Scythians did not even have a definable alphabet. In other words, Paul was declaring that those who had never heard or read about Christ, had the Christ Spirit within them. So in essence, Paul was not preaching Christ to the Colossians, Barbarians and Scythians…he was preaching to the Christ already present in these people in an effort to wake it up. Once we wake up to the Christ in us, we begin to grant ourselves permission to recognize the Christ in other people and places.

Prayer: *"Christ In All, give me confidence to see You in me, courage to see You in others and openness to see You everywhere. Amen."*

Challenge Your Mind. Channel Your Power. Change Your Life.

June 11

RESPECTING THE JOURNEY OF OTHERS

How We See Each Other

> ***Affirmation***
> *"What I see in others directly affects how they see themselves. I will reflect the positive in people back to them today rather than focus on any negative I see."*

Because we are all connected, how we see each other has the ability to affect big change in the collective consciousness. It's a little like putting grains of sugar in a glass of water. If you put one grain in, it will just dissolve. If you put another in, it dissolves too.

But if you keep putting in enough individual grains of sugar, you will eventually reach the point of saturation, and once that happens, the very next grain of sugar you add will result in crystalized sugar inside the glass. Any one of us could be that final grain of sugar that crystalizes the awakening of our entire species.

So if we practice seeing each other in our wholeness rather than focusing on each other's negative aspects, we actually create a positive feedback loop that, grain by grain as it were, builds a bridge for others to step across more fully into their wholeness.

When we choose to tear others down, we are only hurting ourselves. Conversely, when we help others and lift them up - when we see the best in them - we are actually doing it for ourselves. We are helping to saturate the universe with wholeness and goodness, crystalizing our collective enlightenment.

> ***Prayer:*** *"Spirit of Connectedness, help me know today that when I see and encourage the good and wholeness in others, I am making it easier for them to see the same in themselves as well as promoting the well being of all mankind. Amen."*

June 12

RESPECTING THE JOURNEY OF OTHERS

Christ Outside of Christianity

Affirmation

"Today, I am awake to the truth that God is omnipresent everywhere and evenly present in all of creation. I am willing to see Christ in all of creation, even outside of Christianity. I am aware that Christ cannot be defined by, nor confined to, any religion. I embrace my interconnectedness with all people and I am surrendered to the idea that in Christ, there is no separation!"

I often ask people, "What was the difference between Mahatma Gandhi's Civil Rights work in India and South Africa and in Martin Luther King, Jr.'s Civil Rights Movement in America?" Usually, people agree that both men, and both movements, were very similar. And, even have an awareness that Martin Luther King, Jr. met with and then patterned the American Civil Rights Movement after Gandhi's non-violent resistance philosophies and strategies. Then I ask, "What spirit was working in Martin Luther King, Jr. guiding him to create change?" The answer is always the same…the Spirit of Christ. Then I ask, "What spirit was guiding Gandhi in his work?" Then comes the predictable, expected and confused pauses. And, then the answers, "I don't know?" "Maybe an evil spirit?" "some false Hindu god?" It is very difficult for people to recognize that the same spirit was working in both men, and that they just called it something different.

Interestingly enough, Gandhi was a Jesus fan. Gandhi actually said on one occasion, "I love your Christ…and will encourage all Hindus to follow His teachings on the kingdom of God…I just don't like your Christians. They are not like your Christ." Very telling. In this same vein, Jesus said to His disciples, *"I have sheep of other pastures that you don't know about"* (John 10:16). All of these sheep don't say the sinner's prayer and confess Jesus as their savior. However, the Spirit of Christ is undeniably, recognizably, obviously resident within them. Be willing to see Christ in others, in all of creation and outside of Christianity and religion altogether.

Prayer: *"Omnipresent Spirit, I give thanks that You are evenly present in all of creation. I am open to seeing You everywhere. Amen."*

Challenge Your Mind. Channel Your Power. Change Your Life.

June 13

RESPECTING THE JOURNEY OF OTHERS

Rock 'n' Roll Jesus

> **Affirmation**
> *"Jesus is Love. And, love is undeniable and magnetic. People of all ages, colors, countries and cultures are attracted by love. Love also crosses the boundaries of sacred and secular. No matter where you go, Jesus is Just Alright with most people."*

You might not think Jesus and Rock 'n' Roll are synonymous. However, you can't listen to rock music for very long without running into lyrics and admiration for Jesus. Lenny Kravitz, singing about Jesus asked *"Are You Gonna Go My Way?"* U2 dedicated the music and lyrics of *"Pride"* to the love of Jesus. The Commodores made it plain that *"Jesus is Love."* Evanescence asked if they could go too far to be saved by Christ in *"Tourniquet."* The Doobie Brothers weren't ashamed to tell the world that *"Jesus Is Just Alright."* Carrie Underwood surrendered and let *"Jesus Take The Wheel."* Kanye West admitted he could only make it because *"Jesus Walks"* with him. Andrew Lloyd Webber wrote an entire musical, *"Jesus Christ Superstar,"* spotlighting Jesus and His teachings. John Legend recently played the role of Jesus in Webber's timeless rock opera on live television Easter Sunday night. I could reference hundreds of secular rock, pop, country, rhythm and blues and hip-hop songs speaking about the love of Jesus and artist's attraction to, and admiration of, Jesus.

Jesus spoke a mystery one day regarding music and the secular marketplace. He said, *"But to what shall I liken this generation? It is like children sitting in the marketplaces and calling to their companions, and saying: 'We played the flute for you, And you did not dance; We mourned to you, but you would not lament.'"* (Matthew 11:16-17). Jesus described His generation as children playing music in the marketplaces and crying out without much sympathy or response from the religious order. Not much has changed. Rock 'n' Roll holds a special place for Jesus. Always has.

> **Prayer:** *"Rock of Ages, I wanna go Your way, take the wheel, walk with me, You will always be just alright with me. Amen."*

RESPECTING THE JOURNEY OF OTHERS

June 14

High Vibes

Affirmation
"Today I will remember the words of Dr. Martin Luther King, Jr. when he said, 'Let no man pull you so low as to hate him.'"

Sometimes we like to refer to people as *toxic*, but none of us is either completely one thing or another. We are all a complicated mixture of good and bad, light and shadow, higher and lower nature. Of course, as in everything, there are exceptions. And there are certainly people who have allowed the toxicity in their lives to stay at a higher level than others. But there are very few people, if any, who are completely evil.

Unfortunately, however, we all encounter *toxic situations* from time to time, and our first instinct might be to confront the person who is creating the situation. While there's a place for that, it's not the only option.

An alternative is to just continue vibrating on as high a level as you can until those people fall back and fade out of your life because their low vibration approach to you is no longer providing them the emotional payoff they desire.

Even in a physical battle, the person who is standing on the higher ground usually has the advantage. When someone approaches you from a low vibration, their intention is to bring you down to their level so they can take a swing at you. When you react and confront them, you give them that opportunity. But if you continue holding the high ground with no response, or better yet, a loving response, they find themselves swinging at nothing but air.

It takes two to fight. If you refuse to engage, they will eventually leave.

> **Prayer:** *"Source of Peace, help me today refrain from lowering my vibration to respond to a toxic situation."*

Challenge Your Mind. Channel Your Power. Change Your Life.

June 15

RESPECTING THE JOURNEY OF OTHERS

Father, Forgive Them...They Know Not

> **Affirmation**
> *"I absolve you of any guilt or wrongdoing. I know you were doing the best you could with the information you had. This is not to say you had the right information or to say that what you did to me was justifiable in any way. However, peace is ordained in my life and the order of the day. And today, you and I are at peace. I release you into your next season free from any guilt or obligation. And, I pray for your happiness and well-being."*

How would our lives be radically changed if we could say these words to those who have hurt us? Even if the words aren't uttered audibly, saying these words within our own hearts and minds could spark a mental restoration and begin an emotional healing that would welcome a sense of peace and closure that we have longed for. Notice, we are not saying what happened was right. We are not even saying we understand or sympathize. We are acknowledging that people who know better, do better. And, people who do not know better, do not do better.

In this framework, consider the words of Jesus as He was dying on the cross, *"Father, forgive them. They don't know what they are doing."* Like Jesus, we can forgive ignorance, and the hurt it inflicts upon us, without agreeing that the ignorance is accurate. It is entirely possible to forgive family ignorance, to protect our children from it, and to live in a higher realm of conscious awareness, without ever promoting it or passing it on to future generations. The hurt was and is real. Bad things do happen to us at the hands of ignorant people. Yet, give thanks! What didn't kill us only made us stronger. We have learned the power of forgiveness. And, we have realized that we do not share the same ignorance of those who hurt us because of theirs. We know better. We can now do better. Choose forgiveness. Cherish peace. Channel freedom.

> **Prayer:** *"Merciful Father, today I give thanks that You have helped me survive ignorance, forgive it, heal from it and learn from it. Amen."*

RESPECTING THE JOURNEY OF OTHERS

June 16

Every Voice Matters

Affirmation
"Today, I will be open and available to wisdom…no matter from where, or from whom, it may come. Every voice matters. And, my ears are ready to hear them all."

Proverbs 11 and 24 remind us that there is *"safety in a multitude of counselors."* (Proverbs 11:14, 24:6) In other words, every voice matters in our lives. Voices of agreement and affirmation, as well as voices of dissent and disagreement…they all matter. The white mind needs a black voice. The straight ear needs a gay voice, and vice versa. To accept a reality that is replete with only one type of voice or one singular way of thinking is to miss the beauty, and safety, of diversity.

King Arthur and his famous "round table" offer us an image that breeds safety. Each voice sees and provides a different perspective. Each friend in our lives allows us to see life from a new angle. Hear it all. See it all. And then, get quiet and by yourself, and ask the Spirit of Wisdom to help you assimilate and apply whatever is helpful. If some of the counsel is not for you, simply let it pass on by. But, be conscious that although a specific idea might not be for you in one season does not mean that it is necessarily wrong. It might just be in the wrong season of your unfolding and expansion. Give thanks for every voice in your life and for the Holy Spirit that helps you apply whatever it is you need, whenever you need it!

Prayer: *"God of Diverse Thought, I give thanks for the many voices speaking into my life and for the safety and wisdom they all provide. I also give thanks for spiritual discernment helping me to decipher when, how and if a particular voice is to be adhered to. Amen."*

Challenge Your Mind. Channel Your Power. Change Your Life.

June 17

RESPECTING THE JOURNEY OF OTHERS

Holding Space

Affirmation
"I am a willing space holder."

There will be times when someone you love will need space held for them because they are going through a time of crisis and they don't have their normal capacity for dealing with whatever the situation is.

To hold space for someone is to *learn the song in their heart and sing it to them when they have forgotten it.* This doesn't mean singing it *for* them - everyone's song is unique to them. But you can sing it *to* them until they, again, remember the words.

The place of oneness that we all share in our divine Christ Consciousness is like the middle of a great wheel. That's the source, where we're all one with our higher selves and with each other. When we incarnate into a physical body, each of us becomes a smaller expression of this and the image looks like many spokes coming from the center of the wheel.

Our physical existence occurs on the edge of the wheel at the end of our particular spoke. This far away from the center, it seems as if we are all separate from each other. It is also on the edge where we encounter situations that challenge us, but that also help us grow.

When we hold space for someone who is going through a challenge, the song we sing to them is telling them to remember who they are and where they came from. It's easy to feel alone out on the edge, but if they can follow their spoke back to the center of the wheel, they will find the oneness again. Oneness with God and with their own divine nature.

Prayer: *"Center of Being, help me be a space holder today for someone in need. Amen."*

RESPECTING THE JOURNEY OF OTHERS

June 18

Casting Pearls Before Swine

Affirmation
"Today, I will not cast my pearl(s) before swine. I will only share my truth with those who can receive it, and with those who will appreciate its beauty and worth."

When Jesus said, *"do not cast your pearls before swine, lest they trample them under their feet,"* (Matthew 7:6) he was obviously not talking about jewelry. Pearls, in the Jesus way of teaching, are considered metaphorical for treasures of truth. Jesus goes on to teach that the kingdom of God is *"like a pearl of great price."* (Matthew 13:45-46) Pearls, to Jesus, were precious ideas. Perhaps even ideas that only a select few might be willing to grasp. Swine, in this passage, are not literally pigs. Swine are people who will never understand your thoughts and truths. Further, swine are those who will trample on your truths and who mean you harm for having a way of thinking that is disparate from their way.

So, let us glean some wisdom from this passage. 1) Value your pearls. Be grateful when Spirit entrusts you with treasures of truth…precious, priceless pearls. Jesus paints a picture that precious ideas are worth selling everything to attain. 2) Be careful with whom you share, or show, your pearls. Everyone will not celebrate your truth. If you perceive resistance, don't force it. 3) Let it be! Our job is not to change anyone…even family and friends. Neither attempt to convince nor covert others to your way. This will only bring frustration and foster estrangement. Live your truth. And, allow your vibe to attract your tribe. Swine, or those who despise your truth, are God's creation as well. Allow them to change at their own pace and in their own space.

Prayer: *"Priceless Truth, I treasure the truths You have revealed to and in me. Enable me to share them with wisdom and to allow people space on their own journeys. Amen."*

Challenge Your Mind. Channel Your Power. Change Your Life.

June 19

RESPECTING THE JOURNEY OF OTHERS

Freedom From The Past

Affirmation
"Today, I will celebrate my freedom, honor my past, and respect my ancestors by living in the Now."

Juneteenth has been celebrated in the U. S. as Jubilee Day, Emancipation Day, Freedom Day or as Black Independence Day since 1865. This federal holiday commemorates the proclamation of freedom for enslaved people in Texas, which was the last state of the Confederacy plagued by institutional slavery. Slavery is a stain on the soul of America that will likely never be washed away. The images, stories and pain can be overwhelming and suffocating. Being raised in Georgia, I grew familiar with the lingering racial tensions and cultural chasms created by the memory of America's original sin.

After speaking at a church in Toronto years ago, the pastor took me downtown to grab some food and to see the city. While walking the busy streets of Toronto, I noticed a different atmosphere than what I was accustomed to in the Southeastern U. S. I saw Africans, Jamaicans, Canadians, Frenchmen all coexisting peacefully and seemingly happily and harmoniously. I asked the pastor why I did not sense the usual racial tension that had become my norm. He told me the reason I did not sense the racial animosity was because Canada did not have as painful of a past as the U. S. I flew home wondering if I should move to Toronto.

Of course, I am not suggesting we merely forget the past or even worse simply get over it. I am offering a different perspective that shines a light on the power of being present and the joy available from living in the Now. The past, and its pain, cannot be changed or erased, no matter how hard some have tried. The past can serve as a powerful teacher, enabling us not to repeat it. There are lessons in the past that serve us well. However, the greatest lesson is always in the Now, this moment. And, in this moment I choose to be at peace, to live, love and laugh in honor of those who have gone before me.

Prayer: *"Now Moment, I invite You to teach me from the pain of the past and to overwhelm me with joy in the present. Amen."*

RESPECTING THE JOURNEY OF OTHERS

June 20

The Sin of Jonah

Affirmation
"I have been included. I will include. I have been forgiven. I will forgive. I have been accepted by God. I will accept others."

Most of us know that Jonah was swallowed by a great fish. We may even know that Jonah was disobedient in fleeing to Tarshish while God told him to go to Nineveh. But, do we know why Jonah refused to go to Nineveh? Growing up in church I somehow adopted the interpretation that Jonah was afraid of dying at the hands of the Ninevites. As you read through the story of Jonah you discover this was not the case. Jonah refused to go to Nineveh because he did not want God to include a foreign group of people.

As we read the end of the story, Jonah is vomited onto the shores of Nineveh. God indeed includes the Ninevites. Now, Jonah wants to die. In this harsh climate, God causes a plant to provide Jonah with shade. The plant then dies. Jonah mourns the loss of the plant. And, God asks Jonah why he cares more for a plant than he cares for four hundred thousand people. Jonah answers God and bemoans the loving, inclusive character of God. In essence, Jonah refused to go to Nineveh because he knew God wanted to include the Ninevites. Wow! Is this spirit of exclusionary thinking alive in the church today? If it is, it does not have to find space within us. Jonah finally repents of his own limited vision and remembers the way God's love reclaimed him from a lowly existence.

Prayer: *"Spirit of Inclusion, help me to learn from the sin of Jonah. I have been included. Strengthen me to include. Amen."*

Challenge Your Mind. Channel Your Power. Change Your Life.

June 21

RESPECTING THE JOURNEY OF OTHERS

Learning to Share

> *Affirmation*
> "Today, I will share of my time, of my talent, and of my treasure.
> I will allow money to flow to me and through me."

By my fifteenth birthday I had saved several thousand dollars working Summers as a lifeguard, landscaping yards and also working a host of odd jobs. While in a worship service one Sunday, I felt a strong impression to give all that I had saved as a seed faith offering. So, I did. I had saved this money with the intention of buying a car on my sixteenth birthday. At this time, there was a member of our church who owned an auto dealership. He found out about my gift. It moved him to action. He approached me and said, "I heard about what you did. When you turn sixteen come to my dealership and pick a car that you want. It is my gift to you." Look at God! After this experience, the gentleman who gave me the car was promoted to manage a much larger dealership. And, since that moment in my life, I have given away seven cars to those in need and have never been without solid and reliable transportation.

This is how the universal law of giving works. Actually, this is how the universe works. Giving and receiving. Sowing and reaping. Inhale and exhale. Karma. For every action there is an equal and opposite reaction. As we raise our vibration from lack to more than enough, we become a conduit, a channel for blessings to flow to and then through.

> **Prayer:** "Giving Spirit, awaken me to love, live and give from a place of more than enough. I am open and available for good things to flow TO ME for my prosperity, and THROUGH ME for the prosperity of others. Amen."

RESPECTING THE JOURNEY OF OTHERS

June 22

Out of Many, One

Affirmation
"Today, I am stronger because of the many voices I have heard, places I have gone, and people I have encountered. This wealth of diversity will guide me, inform me, and keep me safe."

In 1776, American Founding Fathers John Adams, Benjamin Franklin and Thomas Jefferson proposed the first great seal of the United States: *E Pluribus Unum*, meaning "One From Many" or as it has been commonly used, "Out of Many, One." The idea is that people from different continents, customs and cultures, come together to form one people. And yet, the creation of one people does not assume one idea, suggest one religion, or allow for only one opinion. Reaching a collective consensus is literally the result of many different, diverse voices finding a common wisdom.

Solomon reminds us there is *"safety in multitude of counselors."* (Proverbs 11:14 KJV) This safety is not found in listening to one voice, following one way or agreeing with one counselor. Although safety may indeed be the end game, it is only realized by hearing from diverse perspectives, and then applying the appropriate wisdom by filtering down to what is helpful for a given situation. Desires for purity, mandates for uniformity and pushes for singularity derive out of fear and insecurity. If we all thought exactly alike what would be the need for so many of us? Learn from every voice. Glean from every friend. Gather wisdom from every experience. Then, ask the Holy Spirit to help you assimilate Many, into One.

Prayer: *"Voice like the Sound of Many Waters, I give thanks for every voice that speaks into my life and spiritual journey. I welcome the Holy Spirit to help me decipher exactly what to apply from each voice. Amen."*

Challenge Your Mind. Channel Your Power. Change Your Life.

June 23

RESPECTING THE JOURNEY OF OTHERS

Healthy Mutts

> *Affirmation*
> *"Today, I am grateful for mix ups and impurity. I am not a pure bred. I am a mutt. And, mutts are healthy!"*

Strange way to start a devotion? I would agree. Mutts?

As a dog lover, I have raised Rottweilers, Mastiffs, Giant Schnauzers, Labrador Retrievers, Shih-Tzus and other pure-bred dogs. Although pure-bred dogs bring a higher sales price, they usually have innate genetic defects with their hips, sight, hearing, and health in general. Amazingly, the dogs I loved growing up were mostly mutts…sweet dogs that wandered into our yard with nowhere else to go. These dogs were a mixture of all types of breeds. I don't remember these mutts having hip dysplasia or cataracts. They were amazingly resilient and healthy, genetically strong dogs.

What does this have to do with spirituality?

Remember, everything is spiritual…even dogs! As a mutt is healthier than a pure-bred, a person exposed to diverse cultures, and religions, has a stronger, more exhaustive and flexible spiritual foundation than a purist, or fundamentalist, seeking to be monolithic or separate. There is an old saying that *"Travel is fatal to prejudice, bigotry and narrow-mindedness."* (Mark Twain) A well-traveled person, exposed to the beauty of the world's diversity, would have to work very hard to hang onto prejudice. Furthermore, aren't we all mutts in some way? The purity of any race is really a myth. We are all "part" something. Embrace your mutt-ness. There is a strength hidden in your mixture.

> **Prayer:** *"Creator of Diversity, I am grateful for the diverse people, places and experiences You bring my way. They make me stronger. Amen."*

June 24

RESPECTING THE JOURNEY OF OTHERS

Agree Quickly With Adversaries

Affirmation

"Today, I will attract openness and refuse stalemates. I will agree with those of different vibration quickly and move on to those of my tribe. I will not expend energy trying to convince people of my perspective or convert them to my approach. Today, I let it be!"

In the fifth chapter of Matthew, Jesus drops a nugget of wisdom that seems odd: *"Agree quickly with your adversary…"* (Matthew 5:25) Why would I agree with an adversary? Further, why should I do it quickly? Jesus goes on to say if you refuse to settle disagreements quickly they can magnify into larger conflicts. Have you ever heard the saying "no one wins in court except lawyers?" Of course, we need legal advice. And, I am grateful for trained professionals and their expertise. However, elongated court battles and unending disputes keep us from peace and invite anxiety.

How can we apply this wisdom in our personal and private lives? Here it is: Agree quickly with people of lower vibration! Family, co-workers, neighbors, anyone who has set up camp in a negative mindset…don't spend time trying to convince them of your social, political or theological stances. Agree quickly and save your energy, maybe even your sanity. Our job is not to change anyone. Our purpose is to create the life we desire to experience and to help others as the doors of opportunity open. When there is curiosity present, that means a door is open. When dogmatism is the vibration, agree quickly and sashay away!

Prayer: "Higher Mind, give me the wisdom to agree quickly with those of different mindsets. And, grant me open doors to invest my energy with those of curiosity. Amen."

Challenge Your Mind. Channel Your Power. Change Your Life.

June 25

RESPECTING THE JOURNEY OF OTHERS

Look Before You Leap

> **Affirmation**
> *"Today I understand that thinking only of how an action will affect me can lead to unintended consequences."*

The phrase "I am living my truth" has gotten a bad rap in some ways because people have misused and abused it. They have used the concept of "their truth" to justify behaving in any manner they want. But it's not a free pass to say and do whatever you want, when what you want shows no regard for the feelings of others.

For example, it is indeed a good thing to set personal boundaries, but so many people use this as an excuse to just not cooperate with others or to get out of something that is actually their responsibility because they don't feel like doing it.

When people misuse the concept in this way there are always what is known as unintended consequences - negative circumstances that your behavior caused even though you didn't intend for them to. If you find that "living your truth" is creating a lot of these, maybe it's time to take a look and make some adjustments.

The first thing to do is to follow the old axiom "Look before you leap." Traditionally, the purpose of this was so that you wouldn't land on anything that would harm YOU. But a deeper, more mature and evolved meaning is to make sure you don't land on anyone else and hurt THEM in the process of living your truth.

Unintended consequences will happen less frequently when you live your life consciously and become more aware of the decisions you make.

> **Prayer:** *"Considerate God, help me to strike an appropriate balance between setting personal boundaries and caring for others so that no unintended consequences occur as a result of my behavior. Amen."*

RESPECTING THE JOURNEY OF OTHERS

June 26

Don't Fix It

Affirmation
"Today, I acknowledge that it is not my job to fix anyone. I will listen. I will be present. I will provide a safe space. I will reserve my judgment."

When we see a person, or even an animal, in pain, most of us desire to help alleviate this pain. If it is a cut or scrape, we basically know how to bandage a wound. But, what happens when we see someone suffering from emotional baggage or from a long history of bad decisions or poor friend choices? How do we fix someone's mind? Usually we cannot. And, our attempts to fix someone become more or less a projection of our own opinions onto others.

In counseling settings, I have found that most people already know the answers they are searching for, they just need affirmation or permission to apply their own truth to their process of creating their lives. With this realization, I have tweaked my methodological approach. Where I once would have offered answers or advice, now I just listen. I listen intently for clues to uncovering the answers that lie within the person asking for counsel. Instead of attempting to fix someone, I simply listen actively and compassionately, even inquisitively. My job is not to teach or instruct. My role is to help uncover the truth that a person already knows deep within their being.

Here are some Do's and Don'ts when we share sacred space with those in need of answers:

1. Don't Fix It.
2. Don't Judge It.
3. Don't React To It or Defend It.
4. Do be Present.
5. Do Provide a Safe Space.
6. Do Listen for the Answer Already Present Within Others and Help to Uncover it.

Prayer: *"Restorative Spirit, stir up the gift of wisdom within me to avoid fixing others and awaken in me the gift of listening to help uncover the answers that already lie deep within others. Amen."*

Challenge Your Mind. Channel Your Power. Change Your Life.

June 27 — RESPECTING THE JOURNEY OF OTHERS

Love is a Listening Ear

Affirmation
"Today I will be an open, listening ear to everyone's story - even those who have hurt me because I know behind their hurtful behavior, there is unhealed pain of their own."

Here in the West, we're not very good at listening because we don't really value it. We place much more value on speaking. In fact, when we say the word *communication*, we usually are only thinking of the speaking part, but those words are not synonymous.

We must all learn to be good listeners, because if we don't start listening to each other, we'll never have any hope of understanding each other. And if we don't start understanding each other a little better, we're going to be in trouble!

Love must be practiced in three directions: toward ourselves, toward others (who we get along with) and also toward those we view as our opponents - especially those who have hurt us, because their stories too are worthy of our listening.

It's easy to listen to the stories of those we love. It's easy to tune out or not be interested in the stories of those who hurt us. It's hard to listen to their stories so that we can understand why they do what they do. But if we want to make any progress, if we're going to grow spiritually, we must.

No one is born wanting to hurt others. There's always a reason. It's usually because they have allowed their own hurt to harden into hate. But we can help them begin to break the cycle by being an open and listening ear to them.

Prayer: *"God of Grace, help me listen as willingly to the stories of those who I consider my enemies as I do to those I love. Amen."*

RESPECTING THE JOURNEY OF OTHERS

June 28

One Blood

Affirmation
"We are all the offspring of One Source…One Creator. And, we all share One Blood. Every country, culture and child must learn to coexist, cooperate and then celebrate our contradictions, complexities and commonalities. And today, I am willing to be a light of love and interconnectedness shining into the darkness of fear and separation. Whether we are Caribbean or Canadian, African or Anglo, we can live, move and have our being and becoming in the Christ Mind where there are no cultural boundaries separating God's creation. Today, I declare I am One Blood with all of humanity."

In 1980, the Jacksons released the song "Can You Feel It." The words are so powerful we actually sing this secular song at our church:

"All the children of the world should be, Loving each other wholeheartedly. Yes, it's all right, Take my message to your brother and tell him twice. Take the news to the marching men, Who are killing their brothers, when death won't do. Cause we're all the same, Yes, the blood inside me is inside of you."

Can you feel it? Not just the beat (which is really good). Can you feel the message in these lyrics? We all share the same blood. The blood flowing in your veins is the same as mine. People of different races can actually donate blood to each other. The blood being shed on battle fields is all the same blood, no matter which side we are on or which country or government we fight for. All the children of the world, the global human family, come from One Blood.

The Jacksons didn't create this idea, they borrowed it from the book of Acts:

"And He has made from One Blood every nation of men to dwell on all the face of the earth." (Acts 17:26).

Prayer: *"One Source, today I am aware that I share the same blood with all of Your creation. Let me be a symbol of harmony. Amen."*

Challenge Your Mind. Channel Your Power. Change Your Life.

June 29

RESPECTING THE JOURNEY OF OTHERS

Labels Are Lazy

> **Affirmation**
> *"Today I will focus on knowing rather than labeling people."*

If we know that labels separate us and are a distraction from our ultimate goal of oneness, then why do they continue to be so prevalent in our society? We begin this habit of labeling very early.

When a woman gets pregnant, the first thing people want to know is if it's a boy or a girl. The answer to that question sets that child up for a whole lifetime full of things we've decided are appropriate or inappropriate for their gender. That label can affect what kinds of toys they are given, what sports they play, and eventually what kind of career they choose.

One reason labels exist is because we don't want to take the time to get to know who people are on the inside as individuals. Labels exist because we aren't brave enough to relate to people spirit to spirit.

Labels are a shortcut. They are the easy way out. Labels are lazy.

You know who didn't use labels? Jesus. In the musical *Godspell* there is a song that shows Jesus relating to his disciples. During the course of the song, he approaches each of them with a special greeting or gesture that is unique to them and them alone. It's something the two of them share together that no one else does.

Why? Because he truly loved them. When you truly love someone, it's no chore to get to know them without any labels, without having to put them in a box, without having to define them.

> **Prayer:** *"Unique God, help me to drop the habit of labeling and learn to see and get to know people as individuals, loving them for who, not what they are. Amen."*

RESPECTING THE JOURNEY OF OTHERS

June 30

Walk A Mile In My Shoes

Affirmation

"Today, I will endeavor to see life through someone else's eyes. I will dig beneath the surface of inappropriate behaviors and be open see down into root causes. I will resist the urge to become critical or judgmental. And, I will ask the Holy Spirit for wisdom in how to seek out non-threatening ways to lighten someone's heavy burdens."

In the 1970's Joe South wrote a song entitled, *"Walk A Mile In My Shoes."* Consider just a few of the words: *"If I could be you, if you could be me, for just one hour. If we could find a way, to get inside each other's mind. If you could see you through my eyes, instead of your own ego. I believe you'd be surprised to see, that you've been blind. Walk a mile in my shoes. Before you abuse, criticize and accuse. Walk a mile in my shoes."*

Is this even possible? To really understand what another person is going through? Perhaps the best we can do is want to understand and maybe relate it to something similar in our own lives…even if it's not an exact parallel. I consider myself to be a compassionate person. One thing that really angers me is animal cruelty. Mistreating or neglecting a harmless animal is beyond me. But, in my journey I have come to grips with the truth that hurting people hurt people, and sometimes animals. The question came to me one day, "What has a human endured to lower them to animalistic, abusive, cruel behavior?" I donate to the ASPCA and Humane Society. And, I treat my dogs like human beings (they sleep in my bed). What causes me to treat an animal like a human? What causes a human to abuse an animal? And, what causes a human to treat another human like an animal? With broader vision, what have people with inappropriate behavior endured on their journeys? Jesus presented the Pharisees with a difficult challenge, *"If you are without sin, cast the first stone."* In other words, before you abuse, criticize and accuse…walk a mile in their shoes.

Prayer: *"God of Compassion, help me see past behavior and into hurt, past the surface and to the root, to walk a mile in another's shoes. Amen."*

Challenge Your Mind. Channel Your Power. Change Your Life.

July 1

THE INNER KINGDOM

The True Meaning of Living by Grace

> **Affirmation**
> *"Today I know that living by grace is not about the forgiveness of so-called sin, but about graduating into the higher law of living in relationship with Spirit."*

Go, eat your food with gladness, and drink your wine with a joyful heart, for God has already approved what you do (Ecclesiastes 9:7).

The question is not whether or not God approves of what you do, but do *you* approve of what you do? And, is it working for you? That's really what matters most because it is you who must look at yourself in the mirror every day. And it is you who must live with the results of the choices you make.

Galatians 5 is all about the difference between living under the law and living by the Spirit, and the freedom we now have because of the finished work of the cross.

Believing Jesus' sacrifice "saved" mankind once and for all is not the equivalent of saying "Ok, now that no one is going to hell for all eternity, you can behave however you want with no consequences."

Jesus' death didn't destroy the law, but fulfilled it - by surpassing it! He kept all the law and then rose above it to the higher level of living by the Spirit. So when we live by the law only, expecting that to save us, we actually fall away from grace.

The true meaning of living by grace, then, is graduating into the higher law of relationship where the fruit of our life is the limitless fruit of the Spirit.

> **Prayer:** *"God of Grace, please remind me that the higher law of living in relationship with you is what will bear the most fruit in my life. Amen."*

THE INNER KINGDOM

July 2

To Me. Around Me. Through Me. As Me. For Me.

Affirmation
"Today, I will be aware that life is not happening to me or around me. I am awake to the truth that life is happening through me, as me and ultimately for me. I am not a helpless victim without options or power. I am not an innocent bystander watching as life is created around me. I am a change agent and conscious participant in the creation of my life."

The *"same Spirit that raised Christ from the dead"* is living in us. We are positioned to do greater things or *"greater works"* than Christ. We are *"more than conquerors."* We *"can do all things through Christ." "Christ in us is the hope of glory."* We are *"made in the image and likeness of God"* and can *"behold in the mirror the glory of God."* Wow! So, we are not wretches saved by grace, lowly worms born in sin and shaped in iniquity or Adam's fallen helpless race. We are *"the righteousness of God in Christ," "predestined for good works"* and ordained before we showed up in our mother's wombs.

What does all of this good news mean? It means we are more powerful than we ever imagined. Life is not happening TO US (victim mentality). Life is not happening AROUND US (bystander mentality). Life is happening THROUGH US (participant mentality). Life is happening AS US (divinely awake mentality). And, life is happening FOR US (goodness of God mentality). These are five different lenses that we use to perceive life. Two of these lenses are power-thieves (To me, Around me). Seeing life as happening to us or around us places us in a never-ending cycle of blameful bitterness and eventually becomes an endless existence of powerlessness, poverty and paralysis. Conversely, three of these lenses are power-boosters (Through me, As me, For me). Our thoughts, words and choices show up as our lives. When we see life this way, we reclaim our creative power and realize that it is all working through us, as us and for us.

Prayer: *"God of Power, strengthen me to create my life consciously from a position of power and purpose. Amen."*

Challenge Your Mind. Channel Your Power. Change Your Life.

July 3

THE INNER KINGDOM

As Above, So Below

> **Affirmation**
> *"Today, I will be aware that my outer world is only a reflection, and a manifestation, of my inner world. My thoughts are seeds. My life is the fruit. And today, I will reap a healthy harvest from positive, powerful thoughts."*

Universal truth is never limited to one religion or region, one teacher or testament, one person or philosophy, one area or era. If it is timeless truth, it will survive and flourish as it finds its way into the hearts and minds of eager learners and hungry spirits throughout history everywhere. It may be said a little differently, but the message is the same:

> *"As a man thinks in his heart, so is he."* -Proverbs 23:7
> *"As above, so below. As within, so without."* -Hermes
> *"All we are is the result of what we have thought."* -Buddha
> *"Let Your kingdom come…on earth as it is in heaven."* -Jesus

This timeless truth, taught by diverse sages in different ages, is leading all of its adherents to the same place…within! Jesus said it beautifully, *"Let Your kingdom come, let Your will be done, on earth (in manifestation) as it is in heaven (in imagination)."* Heaven, or the kingdom of God, is not a place, but a space…a space in thought. The earth represents the material world. Or better, the earth becomes the outer experience of our inner expression. The earth is an outer harvest of our inner planting. Our thoughts are seeds. And, we can either grow flowers or weeds. We create our lives from our thoughts. Our thoughts become vibrations that both attract things to us and repel other things away from us. Spiritual teacher Esther Hicks always reminds us that *"We are vibrational beings in a vibrational universe."* Set your intention today to purposefully plant thought-seeds that will yield a harvest of peace, power and prosperity.

Prayer: *"First Thought, let Your kingdom come in my manifestation as it is in my imagination. Amen."*

July 4

Love Is the Road to Freedom

Affirmation
"Nobody is superior, nobody is inferior, but nobody is equal either. People are simply unique; incomparable." ~ Osho

Love isn't lazy. Love doesn't need labels, and labeling people is a lazy shortcut. Only our ego needs labels, but they are only a distraction from love. If we've decided to filter everything in our lives through love and to build our lives on the foundation of love, then we're going to have to drop the labels.

The world is full of labels because defining what someone or something is or is not helps the human brain to sort them into categories. But this only differentiates and separates. The ego completely depends on *us vs. them* scenarios, and to set those up, you must label.

Only love leads to true freedom, and true freedom means to be free from all conditioning, all attachments, and all identifications. The ego always needs a label to identify with and a label to identify others with. It cannot survive just being, doing and living without labels and defined roles.

No labels are necessary when we begin to trust what resonates with us, whether it be a person, an idea or a feeling. We don't necessarily need to know what to call it as long as our inner guidance is telling us it is true for us and beneficial to us.

Anything that creates a feeling of separation is coming from the ego. Only the authentic self, grounded in love, can create wholeness.

Prayer: *"Source of Oneness, help me to drop all the labels my ego wants to put on others, myself or ideologies and trust my inner knowing to guide me to what resonates with my authentic, loving self. Amen."*

Challenge Your Mind. Channel Your Power. Change Your Life.

July 5

THE INNER KINGDOM

No Secret Thoughts

> *Affirmation*
> *"I am aware that I create my life with my thoughts. My private, secret thoughts show up in my life and as my life. Nothing remains hidden. And in essence, my life becomes a looking glass for everyone to see what I have been thinking."*

As we begin to understand the creative power of our thoughts, we also notice that they do indeed show up as our reality and our experience of life. It may seem like a negative, a warning or maybe even a threat, the idea that our secret thoughts show up as our lives. On the contrary, our thoughts are not displayed publicly with the intention of embarrassing or humiliating us. Our secrets surface to engage us fully in the process of self-awareness, "knowing thyself" and fully awakening to our divine potential and god-like power to create, and hopefully, re-create our lives.

What Job "feared the most" came upon him and surfaced as his life. Peter, secretly struggling in his commitment and loyalty to Jesus, denied Him just as Jesus predicted. Paul, privately burdened with his bias toward women, manifests a doctrine that women should remain silent in church and even encourages some of his male disciples to reconsider the necessity of marriage. David, privately desiring Uriah's wife, Bathsheba, manifests his lustful thoughts, destroys another man's life and almost his own. All of these are difficult and hurtful moments…embarrassing. Yet, none of these and other scenarios of public revelations are intended for our or anyone's humiliation or devastation. Our thoughts come to the surface and manifest because the Universe desires for us to be transformed, to be self-actualized and to become fully awake. And, the Universe will faithfully and frequently send to us whatever is necessary for the evolution of our consciousness and for the maturation of the goodness and god-ness within us.

> **Prayer:** *"Universal Mind, thank you for the opportunity to see myself and for the chance to fully own the creative power of my thoughts. Amen."*

THE INNER KINGDOM

July 6

Christ In Us

Affirmation
"Today I will affirm the knowing that Christ in me is the hope of glory. I know that I am divine just as Jesus is divine."

I love Jesus. It is never my intention to take Jesus away from anybody or to diminish the value of His story, but we need to talk about the fact that the reason we often feel powerless is because of how we have erroneously viewed Jesus.

We are taught, in traditional Christianity, from birth, that we are sinful creatures and the world we live in is angry and inhospitable. Therefore, we are in need of someone or something to come along and save us because we are not worthy enough to possess the power it would take to do so ourselves.

Enter Jesus. But the context we are given is of the historical figure, Jesus of Nazareth. We are taught that belief in him (the human man) is the only hope we have of salvation. This places the emphasis on an external source, rather than on looking within ourselves.

However, the Bible clearly states that the Kingdom of God is within us, and Jesus refers to Himself as *"the firstborn among MANY brethren"* as well as referring to us as *"joint heirs"* along with Him.

Jesus of Nazareth was and is a container of the Christ Consciousness. The part traditional Christianity leaves out is that so are we, or can be if we choose. At birth we inherited the very same divinity Jesus did. He came only to wake us up to that truth.

Prayer: *"Christ Consciousness, help me to wake up to my own divinity and realize I have all the power I need within myself to create and maintain a spiritual life. Amen."*

Challenge Your Mind. Channel Your Power. Change Your Life.

July 7

THE INNER KINGDOM

Happy In My OWN Clothes Part I

> ***Affirmation***
> *"Today, I will celebrate my uniqueness. I am an individual and God created me, and works through me, in His/Her own way. I can respect how others connect to God and create their lives while honoring my own."*

All of us have borrowed a friend's clothes. Most of us have also been the recipient of a "hand-me-down" item from an older sibling or cousin. If we are lucky, these clothes fit us. If we are truly blessed, the clothes are still in fashion. However, there is a greater joy when the clothes you wear are your own clothes, picked by you and specifically for you. How do clothes apply to our daily lives?

In the Old Testament, we find the story of David preparing to fight Goliath. Part of David's preparation was to receive some of Saul's (at that time the current king of Israel) armor and weaponry. David tried on all sorts of protective armor and tried out Saul's weaponry. (1 Samuel 17:32-40) None of it was the right size and none of it suited David's style. David was accustomed to using his slingshot. When he told Saul that he would not wear his clothes, Saul questioned him about this decision. To paraphrase David's answer, he replied, God does not work with me like this…I cannot wear your clothes.

Are you wearing someone else's clothes? Approaching life through another's methodology? Borrowing a friend's definition of success and happiness? Allow me to encourage you to return all borrowed clothes! Be you. God made you unique and uses you in your own beautiful skin.

> ***Prayer:*** *"Unique God, there is none like You… and none like me. Give me the courage to wear my own clothes, connect to You in my own way, and to be authentically me. Amen."*

THE INNER KINGDOM

July 8

Happy In My OWN Clothes Part II

Affirmation
"Today, I am fully me. Faithfully me. Originally me. Organically me. Authentically me. Unalterably me. Unapologetically me. This me, is who I was created to be."

The Triumphal Entry, or what most Christians celebrate as Palm Sunday, was a big deal in the life and ministry of Jesus. This was the moment when He was going to openly declare His kingship, the nature of His divine mission and the essence of His own divinity. For his entry into Jerusalem, He tells the disciples to go and gather a young colt, that had never been ridden, as His transportation. (Luke 19:28-40) On their way back with this colt, they put their clothes on the colt. I find this antithetical to Jesus' purpose of choosing a colt, unridden, untrained, unconditioned. And yet, the metaphor here is beautiful. Jesus desires to establish his kingship through the means of openness that is a result of youthful ignorance, and not through rigidity that many times is the result of both older age and more experience.

How do we apply this to our lives? Have you been under pressure to conform to someone else's method or approach? Are you suffocating under the heaviness of parental fantasy? Has someone put their clothes on you? Have you borrowed someone's clothes? If the answer of these questions is yes, take them off, return them, say thank you, and come back to yourself and to your senses!

Prayer: *"Formless God, grant me courage to be myself in all circumstances of life. Give me confidence to wear my own clothes. And, awaken in me the grace to offer this same freedom to those I encounter. Amen."*

Challenge Your Mind. Channel Your Power. Change Your Life.

July 9

THE INNER KINGDOM

Happy In My OWN Clothes Part III

> *Affirmation*
> "Today, I celebrate the beauty of God creating me as a unique individual. Therefore, I will wear my own clothes. I will be authentically myself because I am happy with myself."

Allow me to share 4 principles that might assist us in applying this idea of wearing your own clothes:

1. **Wearing your own clothes is being happy with yourself.**
   Whoever you are. Whatever your expression. Happiness comes when you embrace you. Role playing, false identities and living to please others or get their approval will only produce regret, breed resentment and assure inauthenticity.

2. **Wearing your own clothes brings authenticity.**
   Know who you are. Be who you are. Remember that your vibe attracts your tribe. When you wear someone else's clothes you will never find your own tribe.

3. **Only borrow clothes. Then return them quickly.**
   Fake it for a season if you need to. Esther was undercover for a season. Saved her people from impending genocide. Then, returned the borrowed clothes. Moses, a Hebrew, lived as an Egyptian throughout his childhood. Yet, returned this disguise and came to his true self and delivered his people from bondage. Sometimes you have to do what you have to do. Borrow those clothes. But, never accept them as your own. Return them quickly.

4. **Don't buy clothes just because they are on sale.**
   Many of us have bought things we did not need, like and that did not fit us, just because the original price was lowered. Authenticity never goes on sale. Transparency cannot be found on the clearance rack. Being your true self...is going to cost you something. Pay it!

> **Prayer:** "Organic, Authentic, Genuine Spirit, Give me the courage to wear my own clothes today. Amen."

THE INNER KINGDOM

July 10

Trusting Your Own Inner Voice

Affirmation
"Today I will honor my own voice and trust that it has the divine guidance that I need."

Anyone who has ever worked in construction before knows that until you get down to a layer that's solid, you'd better not start pouring concrete or building anything on top of it because you'll just have to rip it out and start again sooner or later. When you don't dig deep enough to hit bedrock, you get cracks in your foundation.

When putting that in the context of your life, you've got to find a way to get to the place where you can hear your own voice, which often means shutting out all the other voices around you. Once you can hear it - you have to listen.

Hearing and listening are two different things. You can hear something and not really pay attention to it. You can hear something and then ignore it or discount it. But listening to something means you absorb it and allow it to guide your actions.

In the course of growing up (which is a lifelong process), we've all had some missteps because we're human. We've all listened to the wrong advice before. But hopefully, we've learned from those mistakes and have used each of them to get more closely aligned to our own inner voice and guidance - that core layer within us that cannot be moved by the opinion or advice of anyone else - and to trust it more and more.

> ***Prayer:*** *"God of Conviction, help me to listen to the voice of my own inner guidance which comes from my divine higher self. Amen."*

Challenge Your Mind. Channel Your Power. Change Your Life.

July 11 — THE INNER KINGDOM

Freedom From Form

> *Affirmation*
> *"Today, I affirm that I am not my race, gender, sexual orientation, religion, political party or country of origin. I declare my freedom from form."*

So many times, we accept definitions of ourselves that are really not WHO we are. These definitions may assist in describing what, where and when. But, they do not sufficiently define WHO. Race, gender, age, sexual orientation, religion, country of origin are all a part of what, where, when, and perhaps even how we experience life. However, WHO you are is above these labels, definitions and temporary forms. You are the formless, normless, ageless, shapeless, nameless, blameless, shameless, label-less, skinless, sinless, endless, eternal spiritual being having a momentary expression in the physical, material world. Why does this matter? On the surface, celebrating race, culture, religion, gender, sexual orientation, country of origin is fairly harmless. And yet, when there is a subtle separation, defining or labeling of the human family there will inevitably be a presence of, and tendency toward, "otherness." From this otherness caste systems form, hierarchies are enabled and violence becomes a probability. Allow me to share one of my favorite quotes regarding living above form:

> *When you call yourself an Indian or a Muslim or a Christian or a European, or anything else, you are being violent. Do you see why it is violent? Because you are separating yourself from the rest of mankind. When you separate yourself by belief, by nationality, by tradition, it breeds violence. So, a man who is seeking to understand violence does not belong to any country, to any religion, to any political party or partial system; he is concerned with the total understanding of mankind.* ~ Jiddu Krishnamurti

Prayer: *"Formless Spirit, awaken my vision. Open my eyes to my eternal self and soul. Grant me the grace to live above form. Amen."*

THE INNER KINGDOM

July 12

A Vision of Love

Affirmation

"Today, I bring all of me to God...I bring my pain and my past, my filters and my frustrations, my lenses and my losses. As I bring them all out, I know I will be able to see them more clearly. On this day, I choose to see them and not see life through them! On this day, I choose to create my life through the Vision of Love and not through any filter of pain. Bad things have happened to me. However, I am not the things that have happened to me! I am an eternal Spirit having a temporary human experience."

In 1990 Mariah Carey exploded onto the music scene with her hit song "Vision of Love." I can remember the first time I heard her voice. Like most of the world, I was captivated and moved. One line in this song still resonates with me: "I visualized the love that came to be." What a powerful truth. Things that come to be are visualized first. This principle works both positively and negatively. Most of us have had an experience in our past that caused us a tremendous amount of pain and sorrow. When the event, loss, relationship, sickness is finally over, we are shocked to see this very thing show up in our lives again and again. This is not a simple matter of bad luck, a curse, being snake-bitten or the devil being "busy." We subconsciously create our future experiences using filters of past hurts. Fear, jealousy, pessimism, suspicion, superstition all help to create a filter through which we see the world and unknowingly manifest our reality.

Let go of the past and any lingering filters hanging around in the back of your subconscious mind. You are not the thing that happened to you. What didn't kill you made you stronger. What didn't break you taught you how to bend. Your past failures are now your present wisdom. Consciously choose to see and create life through a new Vision of Love, not an old filter of pain. Today is a new day. Visualize love and watch it come to be!

Prayer: *"God of Vision, remove any filter of pain and give me a vision of love. Empower me to visualize and then create love, peace and joy. Amen."*

Challenge Your Mind. Channel Your Power. Change Your Life.

July 13

THE INNER KINGDOM

Why Do You Call Me Good?

> **Affirmation**
> "Today I know that the same spirit that was in the historical Jesus, lives in and works through me, and so I can confidently say: I am the Christ."

The concept of goodness can be very subjective because people have lots of different ideas about what *good* is. One of the first questions to be asked is, "in comparison to what?" It really depends on what your baseline is.

Also, we use the term *good* in such a broad sense. For example, what one person would consider a "good" meal, movie, song, or idea can be vastly different from what someone else would consider those same things. In that context, it has to do with someone's taste or personal preference. So, we need a little better gauge when trying to define what goodness is.

The best way to measure a person's goodness is to determine how well their character and actions align with God-likeness. The part of us that is divine is what makes us good.

The more we wake up to our Christ nature - moving and working in, through and as us - the more goodness we begin to see in ourselves.

> **Prayer:** "God of our Sovereign Nature, help me today to find my own divine nature through the Christ that is within me and to align with it in all that I say and do. Amen."

THE INNER KINGDOM

July 14

Is It Working For You?

Affirmation

"Today, I am aware that there are many ways to find peace. Everyone's path is different and no two journeys are exactly the same. I will not spend my life arguing with others about their chosen path. Instead, I will ask myself the only question that really matters: Is It Working For Me?"

Some people find peace through religious literalism (adhering to a strict code of behaviors and rituals). Some find peace through meditation. Yet, others find peace by serving others. Whether a person finds peace through deep study or physical exercise, always be aware it is their path, and their peace. The personal path to peace is not a "one size fits all." Projecting your path onto others is a sure way to keep peace at a distance and encourage people to practice social distancing with you. Some people need closure. Others need a new landscape. Assuming that everyone must walk the same path or connect to Source using the same method, in the end, only threatens your own peace as you will struggle with the frustration of wondering why they don't realize how right you are. The reality is…the only universal truth that applies to universal truth is allowing each person their own universal truth. Learn to respect other people's journeys and you will inevitably find peace for yourself.

Arguing over who is right, whose perspective is the most accurate, whose path is the straightest, will ultimately only serve to create a chasm between family and friends. The only question we should concern ourselves with is: IS IT WORKING FOR ME? And, what works for me may not work for all those I love. Arguments over right and wrong will never be satisfied. Furthermore, knowing what works for me in this season may not work forever or even in my next season. Allow people their own path to God. And, encourage them to change at their own pace and in their own space.

Prayer: *"Universal God, I am aware there are many ways to connect to You. Today, I will allow everyone to find their own connection. Amen."*

Challenge Your Mind. Channel Your Power. Change Your Life.

July 15

THE INNER KINGDOM

Sound Doctrine

> *Affirmation*
> "Sound Doctrine is not tainted by culture, subject to gender, influenced by race, partial to any era of history or area of the world. Sound Doctrine is not hostage to opinion, conscious of geography, biased to politics and never speaks from prejudice. Sound Doctrine does not choose sides, have favorites or show partiality. Sound Doctrine is timeless, universal and exists above humanity's attempt to create God in its own image."

One of my mentors passed along a piece of wisdom to me over 20 years ago that still resonates with me. He said, "Any doctrine that is worth keeping will accomplish three things: 1. Bring glory to God, 2. Create peace on earth, and 3. Foster goodwill between men." When Jesus was born, an angel laid the foundation for Sound Doctrine by announcing, *"Glory to God in the highest, And on earth peace, goodwill toward men."* (Luke 2:14).

Does the doctrine of hell and eternal torture bring glory to God? Does the promotion of one religion as supreme above all others create peace on earth? Does favoring one sect of God's children over another foster goodwill between men? I would hope the answer to all three of these questions would be "No!" So, Sound Doctrine must be accepted as being sound on more of a foundation than because some man from a specific culture and geographical area of the world claims God told him his race was chosen, that God favored the firstborn son over the others and that God permitted slavery as long as you didn't enslave your own race of people. Arriving at Sound Doctrine requires common sense, critical thinking and an ability to find objectivity above the temptations of cultural and tribal influences. Sound Doctrine begins with one idea: God is love.

> **Prayer:** *"Timeless Truth, equip me to bring You glory, empower me to create peace on earth and enable me to foster goodwill between men. Amen."*

THE INNER KINGDOM **July 16**

How to Clean Up Negative Self-Talk

Affirmation
"Today I will clean up my negative self-talk."

Think of all the church songs you've heard all your life telling you how sinful you are and calling you a wretch and a worm. After a while, all that actually sinks in. Throw in all the unrealistic portrayals of life you see on television and in the movies and it can be a recipe for disaster if you don't realize that most all forms of media are just one giant advertisement aimed at convincing you how much better your life could be if you would just buy more stuff.

The information you consume on a daily basis, whether it's entertainment or news, forms the basis for what you value, how you feel about yourself and others, as well as the constant self-talk that goes on in your mind. That's why it's important to make sure what you watch, read and listen to contains a good balance of positivity and negativity.

You can't avoid negativity entirely. It exists. But you can certainly control the amount of time you dwell on it, and you can make a conscious decision to pay attention only to what is relevant to you.

So much of our information intake is on subjects that do not directly affect us and that we can do absolutely nothing about. Spending too much time consuming this type of media is unhealthy because it leads to unnatural fear, anxiety as well as powerlessness.

Being more discriminating about what information you take in and focus on will do a lot to clean up your negative self-talk.

> **Prayer:** *"God of Discernment, help me today to distinguish between information that is relevant and necessary for my life and that which will only cause negative self-talk. Amen."*

Challenge Your Mind. Channel Your Power. Change Your Life.

July 17

THE INNER KINGDOM

My Happy Place

> **Affirmation**
> *"Today, I choose to be happy. I believe I deserve to be happy. And, I am actively seeking my happy place as my eyes, ears and mouth are only open to information that will bring happiness to me and through me. I will choose my words, my thoughts, my deeds and my friends wisely…making sure they are all in harmony with who I am."*

Everyone wants happiness. Everyone desires to be at peace. Miss America knows to talk about world peace. But, what are the choices we make every day to make peace and create happiness in our lives? There are several ways we create happiness. Consciously, and unapologetically, choose to be around happy people. It takes an immense amount of mental strength to maintain happiness when you spend your time around unhappy people. Unhappy people never find happiness and don't want you to. Even on the occasion that happiness finds them or when good things unexpectedly arise, unhappy people will inevitably find a way to be skeptical, unimpressed and cast a sarcastic, negative light on everything good.

It sounds simple, but often some of the negative people of lower vibration are our family members. Release the guilt. Win the battle over obligation. And, spend your time around people of high energy and good vibrations. Once you establish your circle of friends, filter the information that comes your way. There is always a "Debbie downer" lurking in the shadows waiting for the first opportunity to bring you the news and gossip of the day and to convince you the glass is indeed half empty. Be courteous and gracious. Then, end the conversation as quickly as possible. These people are energy thieves. Misery loves company. Don't align yourself with people who feel their calling is to be the bearer of bad news. Choose happiness today. Choose to be around happy people. Filter the information coming your way. Get happy, stay happy, and see what happens!

> **Prayer:** *"God of Joy, I know that Your joy is my strength. Today, I will protect my joy by guarding my heart, mind, ears and mouth. Amen."*

THE INNER KINGDOM

July 18

The Power Of I Am

Affirmation
"Today I am aware that only I can say 'I Am.' The world I create begins with 'I Am' so I will be mindful of what I attach to 'I Am.' My 'I Am' is more powerful than anyone's 'you are.' No one's 'you are' could ever create my life unless their 'you are' becomes my 'I Am.'"

Isn't it amazing that you are the only person who can say "I Am?" No other person can say "I Am" for you or even about you. The best others can do when speaking about you is use the words "you are." And, the beautiful truth is that when they say "you are" it has absolutely zero power over you. Throughout our entire earth journey people will say "you are" in an attempt to criticize, demean or diminish us. However, they will continue to be unsuccessful as long as their "you are" statements never become our "I Am" statements. God, the "I Am that I Am" models this for us when He refuses to give Moses any other words or names after "I Am." Never give your "I Am" power away to anyone else's definition about you or labelling of you. "I Am" is all you need to harness the power of your divine creativity. And, "I Am" is yours and only yours.

You are made in the image and likeness of God. This means, you are not dependent on anyone or anything outside of yourself to create for you. Your "I Am" does not wait on anyone, blame anything or even ask permission. "I Am" is now. Once you awaken to the power of your "I Am" you will become more mindful not to project any negative "you are" statements onto others. You will especially not project "you are" onto God, the "I AM that I AM!" Sticks and stones may break our bones, but words will never hurt us…unless, those words become our beliefs. Negative people use negative words. Let them talk. Their opinion of you is none of your business. All that matters is what you think and say about yourself.

Prayer: *"Power of I Am, awaken me to the power my 'I Am.' Help me be aware of the power of my words about me. Amen."*

Challenge Your Mind. Channel Your Power. Change Your Life.

July 19

THE INNER KINGDOM

Dealing with Traffic

> *Affirmation*
> "My happiness is not at the mercy of traffic or any other external condition. I will take a deep breath, be grateful that I have transportation, and rest in the knowledge that trouble, and traffic, don't last always."

Road rage. High blood pressure. Frustration. Impatience. Meanness. We have experienced all of these maladies while sitting in traffic. If you live in or near a large metropolitan city you can find yourself in traffic on any day, any hour and any street. If traffic is a reality that we cannot always avoid or escape, how should we approach it?

1. **Allow traffic to reveal who, and what, you do not want to be.** If you see something hostile or angry, really look at it. Ask where it comes from? Is it a feeling of lack? A projection of being slighted or disrespected? Is it an opinion of being more important than others? Endeavor not to be the car who waited for the last minute to get over. Conversely, set your intention not to be the car who refuses to let someone over. The collective findings are numerous. The individual lessons are many and readily available.
2. **Assume best intention.** Do not allow yourself to believe that every other car, and persons driving those cars, are out to get you and take something from you. Each car is being driven by someone created in the image and likeness of God. What humans do is not always who we are. Be mindful that we all have good and bad days.
3. **Take the high road.** If there is an elderly person driving slowly, be empathetic and patient. If there is someone in a hurry, move over from the passing lane and allow them to go by.
4. **Find serenity!** Listen to some beautiful music. Take the chance to learn a new language. Call a loved one or friend that is on your heart. Traffic is not going away. Use the time to find serenity. Use the car as your classroom. Take a deep breath!

> **Prayer:** "Longsuffering Creator, grant me the patience to deal with traffic, the grace to assume best intention and the empathy to make the expressway a better place. Amen."

THE INNER KINGDOM

July 20

Wielding Power Lightly

Affirmation
"Today, I am fully aware of my power. I will walk in it with both confidence and humility. I will use my power for good and not use it to cause hurt or to subjugate or subordinate others."

In a world full of hierarchical power structures there will be times when we find ourselves in positions of power and other times when we need assistance. How should we handle the times when we may have some sense of advantage on others?

There are different types of power: physical, mental, financial, positional. Hopefully, physical power is not something we ever use to harm others. But, abuse of power becomes more nuanced when we consider it positionally, or even mentally. Let's make this practical. How should an employer treat an employee? How should a pastor handle the perceived power of the pulpit? How about a parent and a child? How should a winning team treat its opponent? All of these power dynamics help to reveal the true character of an individual. The way we handle power says so much about who we are.

How should we manage our power as customers and consumers? I often watch as patrons in a restaurant or grocery store make the wait staff and employees run all over the place in an effort to prove that "the customer is always right." Is there a way to get good service while respecting those who serve us? Perhaps when scripture says *"be faithful over a few things"* (Matthew 25:23) we could apply this to power. One image that comes to mind is of King Arthur and the "Round Table." The creation of a round shaped table is so there will be no specific head of the table. In essence, everyone and every voice is welcomed at the table. When we wield our power lightly, we become truly powerful.

Prayer: *"God of Power, thank you for entrusting power to me. Strengthen me to use it wisely and to wield it lightly. Amen."*

Challenge Your Mind. Channel Your Power. Change Your Life.

July 21

THE INNER KINGDOM

Listen to Your Body

> ### Affirmation
> *"Today, I am aware that no one knows my body better than me. I am not my body. My temporary body houses my eternal spirit. However, I am in this body for now. And, I choose to treat it with respect and care for it as it facilitates my earthly purpose."*

Each moment of each day our bodies are talking to us. Our bodies tell us when we feel well. When we are at homeostasis in and with our bodies we feel calm, our heart rate is steady, our breathing is peaceful and even our minds experience a sense of rest. Our bodies also speak through pain. When our noses run it may signal coldness, an immune deficiency or even the presence of pepper. When our throats are sore, we may be getting a cold or even talking too much. When we have a headache, we can be dehydrated, sleep deprived, or even experiencing high blood pressure. When we feel swollen, our bodies may be telling us we have digested too much sodium.

I have an irregular heartbeat. It has been called a murmur, a mitral-valve prolapse and an arrhythmia. When I am too sedentary my heart begins to lose rhythm. In other words, my body actually alerts me when I need to exercise. All of our bodies talk to us constantly and in unique ways. Listen to your body. It knows when it needs to move, drink, eat, sleep. Be aware of what your body is saying to you and don't ignore it. If you take care of it, it will take care of you.

> **Prayer:** *"Incarnate God (Jesus), today I give thanks for the body that houses my spirit. Help me set my intention to listen to it when it talks to me. Amen."*

THE INNER KINGDOM

July 22

Spiritual GPS... My Internal Navigation System

Affirmation
"Today, I am at peace with my internal navigation. I am in the body, but not at home in the body! My spiritual Global Positioning System (GPS) is greater than my physical senses. I am present with my navigation when I am fully awake to my spirit and when my sense is greater than my see. My saying is greater than my seeing and my knowing is more powerful than my hearing."

What is spiritual GPS? This innate, internal navigation is also known as intuition, premonition, inner knowing, gut feeling, the inner voice or a *"still, small voice."* (1 Kings 19:12) And, the good news is that everyone has it. We are all equipped with an internal guidance system that warns us of danger and confirms deep "knowings." It can push us forward into an open door and hold us back from an opportunity that is not a vibrational match for the life we are creating. So, how do we hone this gift?

First, don't ignore it. Welcome it. Acknowledge it. Listen to it. Feel it. Next, surrender to it. Trust your sense more than your see. Lean to your inner knowing more than your outer hearing. Finally, take an inventory. Be open to recalibrate if you miss it while being aware when you were accurate. Ask yourself the question: "How often has my Spiritual GPS led me astray?" Before long you will notice that you have sharpened a skill and developed a gift capable of saving your life and bringing abundant life.

Prayer: *"Omniscient Mind, awaken in me today my internal GPS. I am ready to listen and willing to follow. Amen."*

Challenge Your Mind. Channel Your Power. Change Your Life.

July 23

THE INNER KINGDOM

It's IN There

> **Affirmation**
> *"Simba, Luke Skywalker, Neo, Bruce Leroy, the Tin Man, and I all have something in common. We are looking for something without, that can only be found within. Today, I choose to see Mufasa, to feel the force, and to see the chosen one within me! It's in there!"*

There is an old Ragu spaghetti sauce commercial where a husband asks his wife if the Ragu sauce has tomatoes, oregano, garlic, onions, etc. The wife finally screams, "It's in there!"

In the movie "The Lion King," Simba looks into the water and sees Mufasa in his own reflection. In "Star Wars," Luke is searching for the power he experienced in Obi Wan and discovers the force within himself. In "The Matrix," Neo finally believes that he is the one Morpheus perceives him to be. In Motown's "The Last Dragon," Bruce Lee-Roy will either be killed by Sho Nuff or awaken to the truth that he is the master. In "The Wizard of Oz," Lion wanted courage, Tin man wanted a heart, Scarecrow wanted a brain. And, they all found these attributes within. The rock group America later revealed that "Oz never gave nothing to the tin man that he didn't already have." Whitney Houston sang that she "found the greatest love of all" inside of herself. If what we are searching for is within why do we spend so much time and effort searching without?

Jesus reminds us the Kingdom of God is within. (Luke 17:21 KJV)
Paul declares Christ in us is the hope of glory. (Colossians 1:27 KJV)

> **Prayer:** *"Power Within, give me the strength to believe that the same power that raised Christ from the dead is in me. Grant me the insight to see Christ in me, the hope of glory. Allow me to awaken to the Kingdom resident within me. Amen."*

THE INNER KINGDOM

July 24

Recognizing Happiness, Not Chasing After It

Affirmation

"Today, I will neither chase after happiness nor run from unhappiness. I will choose happiness by forgiving and not holding grudges. I choose to heal and not nurse old wounds. I choose to experience happiness now, not after some future event. As I intentionally create my life I am manifesting a life that I do not have to escape from! In this way I am choosing to recognize the happiness that is always available…the happiness that is within. Amen."

Everyone chases after happiness, not noticing that happiness is right at their heels. (Bertolt Brecht) When we allow the ego to persuade us to believe that all we are is the sum of our experiences, memories, pains, failures and bad choices, we project happiness into the future and place happiness at the mercy of ideas like closure and apologies. We are not our story. We are not the things that have happened to us. We are the observing Presence that is aware of these events, yet not defined nor confined by them.

There is a beautiful life of simplicity calling out to those who will listen. It invites us to live the life we were born to live, not the life our neighbor is seeking to achieve. Simplicity invites us to pursue the things we value most, not the values of billboards and magazines. It invites us to remove the distractions that keep us from living and enjoying life to the fullest. When we stop chasing the world's definition of happiness, we begin to recognize the decision to experience happiness has been right in front of us all along.[*]

Prayer: "Ever-Present Joy, enable me today to see that my happiness is one choice away, one moment away. Grant me the courage to choose happiness. Amen."

---

[*] Joshua Becker, becomingminimalist.com

Challenge Your Mind. Channel Your Power. Change Your Life.

July 25

THE INNER KINGDOM

Life's Changing Seasons

Affirmation
"Today I understand that while what I do may change, the divine nature of who I am is always constant in my life."

Often we find that our purpose shifts and changes over the course of the years. Sometimes we're supposed to do something only for a season and then when it has been accomplished, we move on to our next purpose.

Let's take, for example, being a mother. There is no higher calling and purpose in the world. But at some point, no matter how many children she has, eventually, they all become adults, and although she will always be their mother, her purpose in their lives as well as the focus of her own life shifts into something other than what it once was.

Don't be afraid of the shifts. Know that throughout your life the one constant is you. You are a divine creator and you have the ability to continue from purpose to purpose for as long as you live. Just because one phase of your life ends, don't believe your only option is to be "put out to pasture." Don't get stuck. And most importantly, don't allow your peace, happiness or self-esteem to be tied so securely to one purpose that you are destroyed when it is no longer there.

Prayer: *"God of shifting seasons, help me to recognize my power as the divine creator of my own reality. I know that I may have many purposes over the course of my life, and that each one will serve the ultimate purpose of my calling. Amen."*

THE INNER KINGDOM — July 26

We Don't Get What We Want. We Get Who We Are.

Affirmation

"Vibration is happening around and through me at all times, whether I am aware of it or not. I know the truth, that I am a vibrational being in a vibrational universe. I am also awake to the universal law that I attract people, relationships, experiences, opportunities and things to myself according to my level of vibration."

We all want a loving spouse, loyal friends, obedient children, understanding co-workers and a gracious boss. The difficult truth is wanting something does not create it. We must learn to manifest our desires by shifting our thoughts and raising our vibration to match the level of what it is we want. Otherwise, we will continue to want things and be frustrated that we don't receive them.

We don't get what we want, we get who we are. This statement can either arouse a great deal of optimism and hope or become a heavy burden of guilt and despair. If our lives are full of loneliness, lack and disloyalty we are only experiencing the level of vibration we exist in or we are merely manifesting who we are in our daily lives.

"Birds of a feather flock together…" "Whatever we sow, that will we reap…" "The apple doesn't fall far from the tree…" "An object in motion stays in motion unless acted upon…" "Like tends toward like." These colloquial, religious, philosophical and even scientific sayings are all pointing us to the idea that we get who we are. This knowledge can cause a great deal of heaviness. However, instead of living in guilt and regret, which do not produce positive change, accept this truth, own what you are creating and who you are, and raise your level of vibration to shift who you are. Then, as you begin to like yourself, or who you are, you will notice that you attract who you are to yourself.

Prayer: *"Ultimate Reality, I will raise my vibration to righteousness, peace and joy and watch as all good things are attracted to me. Amen."*

Challenge Your Mind. Channel Your Power. Change Your Life.

July 27

THE INNER KINGDOM

Listen to the Still Small Voice

> ***Affirmation***
> *"I declare today that as much as lies within my power, I will pay attention to the whispers so I don't have to deal with the shouts!"*

When something catastrophic occurs, in retrospect you can usually see the warning signs and realize that you should have, or at the very least, could have seen it coming. Not that you're always responsible for it or that you caused it, but that it could have been predicted.

When it involves someone other than you, someone you love and are close to, sometimes even if you see it coming and know what will very likely happen if their course doesn't change, there's often very little you can do about it because you can't control their actions.

But when it's your own life - you can. Too many times we have these earth shattering moments simply because we refused to listen and pay attention to the still small voice that was nudging us to go in a different direction or to stop a certain activity or change something about the way we were handling a situation way back down the line before we passed the point of no return.

Is it possible to learn all your lessons in a gentle way rather than having to deal with a tragic situation? Maybe. Maybe not. But your chances of that increase greatly by controlling what you can, which is yourself and how you listen to what the still small voice of Spirit is telling you so you won't be caught off guard by things that could have been prevented.

> **Prayer:** *"God of the Still Small Voice, help me to be sensitive to you before it takes a tragedy to teach me a valuable lesson. Amen."*

THE INNER KINGDOM

July 28

Soul Prosperity

Affirmation
"Today, I am aware of the truth that I will prosper, and be in good health, as my soul prospers. Therefore, I will facilitate thoughts that support a prosperous soul."

Wherever you travel. Whatever the political climate or social structure. Whatever the religious culture. All people want to prosper and be healthy. I want to prosper. I hope we all want to be in good health. How do we realize this blissful utopia? The soul is the key.

"Beloved, I pray that you may prosper in all things and be in health, just as your soul prospers." (3 John 2)

Notice, the soul both invites prosperity and brings health. The condition of the soul is directly connected to prosperity and health. When Jesus asks *"What will a man give in exchange for his soul,"* (Mark 8:36-37) He is asking what is your mind worth to you? *Soul* in the Greek is *psuche* – meaning mind. Psuche is where we get the related terms psyche, psychology, psychic, psychiatry. All dealing with the mind. With this knowledge, we can see that prosperity and health are relative to the condition of the mind.

Consider this line of thinking: if guilt, condemnation, and unworthiness are central to the message of the current Evangelical Christian expression, do these ideals create a peaceful soul? If not, we must find another approach that facilitates the conditions for a prosperous soul, that creates a prosperous life and a healthy body. There may be times when you are in a spiritual environment, but your soul is not at rest. Don't suffer silently, wondering where health and prosperity are hiding. Find a place where your soul can prosper. And, watch as what is within, manifests itself without.

Prayer: *"Soul of the Universe, I desire prosperity and health. Strengthen me to align my thoughts and my mind with my desire. Amen."*

Challenge Your Mind. Channel Your Power. Change Your Life.

July 29

THE INNER KINGDOM

The Difference Between Faith and Faithfulness

> *Affirmation*
> "Today I know that having faith and being faithful are two different things. Both are required to create the reality I want for my life."

We often think of faith as believing in something we have no evidence for; something invisible; something that hasn't happened yet; may or may not ever occur or even be real or true. It's ethereal. It cannot be touched or nailed down. It's not solid.

But when we think about the word faithfulness or the concept of being faithful, the first words that come to mind are reliable, consistent, and stable, which would seemingly all be the exact opposite of the root word. A faithful friend is one you can always count on. This presents a dichotomy of sorts.

But these two very different concepts actually work together quite well. When you have a dream that hasn't yet shown up in physical form, it requires faithfulness on your part in order for it to become a reality.

The book of James in the Bible reminds us that *faith without works is dead*. Showing up consistently, putting in the necessary work and remaining faithful over any dream you have in the faith realm is essential to its coming into fruition.

Most of the time we see people being recognized for their accomplishments only after they have put in years of work. We see the result, but have little to no concept of what it took for them to get there. Rest assured, in every case, faithfulness on their part was required.

> **Prayer:** *"Faithful God, help me to be consistently faithful over the plans and dreams I have for my life. I know this is the path to seeing them fulfilled. Amen."*

THE INNER KINGDOM

July 30

The SPECK and the PLANK

Affirmation
"My life is too powerful and purposeful to waste it searching for the speck in my neighbor's eye. I will not make a habit of committing the spiritual sin of judging others. Instead, I will focus my mind on fully connecting with the unconditional love of God. Once I have been baptized in love, I will overcome my need to judge. God's love will enable me to see others through the eyes of love…only then will I be able to compassionately offer them help and restoration without judgment."

Jesus asks a very thought provoking question:

"why do we spend our time and energy searching for the speck in someone else's eye without considering the plank in our own eye?"
(Matthew 7:1-5; Luke 6:41-42)

A speck is a small thing. However, a plank is a much larger thing. In essence, Jesus is saying our desire to judge is the bigger issue here. The smaller issue is whatever another person may be struggling with in their own life. Unfortunately, many people focus more on another person's speck (their sin) than on their own plank (judgment of others).

We are encouraged to get rid of the plank (our desire to judge others) and then we will miraculously be able to see clearly and bring healing to others (help them remove the speck). Assisting others on their journey toward renewal and restoration can only be done with love and compassion.

Prayer: *"Spirit of God, let me see through eyes of love today. Grant me the strength to build up, not break down. Give me the courage to restore, not condemn. Today, I surrender my need to judge others and open my heart and mind to be filled with Your love. I want to see others as You see them! Amen."*

Challenge Your Mind. Channel Your Power. Change Your Life.

July 31

THE INNER KINGDOM

Why Is This Happening... Again?

> **Affirmation**
> *"Today, I will see what I have created, not be surprised by it and consciously create the life experience I desire. Nothing is happening to me. All of life is happening through me. I am awake to my divine capacity to create. And today, I will create consciously."*

There are three different levels of awareness from which we create life. We create our lives consciously, subconsciously and unconsciously. How do we know which level of creative awareness we are operating from? To be honest, most people create life from the middle, or from a mixture, of all three levels of awareness (even those who are self-aware and self-actualized). When things show up in our lives that completely shock us and catch us off guard, we are likely creating unconsciously. If we continually ask the question, "why is this happening to me?" we are probably creating life unconsciously. If we ask the question, "why is this happening to me AGAIN?" we are definitely creating life unconsciously. Most of the time we create life subconsciously or from the middle ground of our conscious awareness. Subconscious creativity is a bit like driving on cruise control. We are aware. We are involved. But, we are also allowing the machines, mechanisms and daily environments to drive. In subconscious creativity, when events or situations arise we are not shocked and we actually have some level of remembrance with our choices and thought life that invited this experience into our reality. When we create consciously we are not caught off guard by our life reality. Rather, we are fully awake to what we think, completely connected to what we choose, and when our outer world begins to reflect our inner thoughts we are not surprised because we have already received the RSVP that these things were going to show up. We are more powerful than we have ever imagined. When we create consciously we are harnessing our God-given ability and right to operate in divine creativity.

> **Prayer:** *"Conscious Creator, awaken me today to create my life from a conscious mind. I desire to be fully awake. Amen."*

THE BEGINNER'S MIND

August 1

RenewING My Mind

Affirmation
"Today, I agree to the renewING of my mind...which is a constant and ongoing process. Faith comes by hearING, not by having heard. Similarly, I am transformed by the renewING of my mind, and not by any renewED mind or mindset. I am an eternal spirit having a temporary earthly experience and fleeting human expression."

"*Faith comes by hearing...*" (Romans 10:17). On the surface this seems simple. All we have to do is listen to the words of the Bible being taught and we will have faith. However, on a deeper level, faith (or faith-ing) is the result of an ongoing process of continually hearing. The ING on the word hearING suggests this may not be a one-time thing. Just two chapters later we stumble across this ING principle again – "*be transformed by the renewing of your mind*" (Romans 12:2). The transformation happens, not from a renewed mind, but from a renewING of the mind.

Jesus struggled to teach this ING principle to the Pharisees and religious order of His day. He often said to them "*you have heard of old, but I say.*" In other words, you are living in the past and I am speaking to you now. Your faith has been stunted because you exist on what you heard, what you read or what was said. They struggled to live in the present moment...in the hearing, the saying, the renewing. When it comes to spiritual growth, one of the most detrimental habits hindering expansion is living in the past while attempting to create the present. Jesus gives us a clue when He taught that "*man should not live by bread alone but by every word that proceeds from the mouth of God.*" In other words, God is still speaking. Are you hearing?

Prayer: *"Holy Spirit, I set my intention for hearing and renewing. I am available for a fresh daily bread and an organic living word from You. I surrender to the truth that I cannot live organically in spirit while eating only religious preservatives and leftovers. Amen."*

Challenge Your Mind. Channel Your Power. Change Your Life.

August 2

THE BEGINNER'S MIND

Become Like a Child

> *Affirmation*
> *"Today I will be open to see a different story unfold from the one I expected."*

Have you ever wondered why children seem much happier than adults most of the time? Why they tend to laugh more? It's because there's still a little mystery in their lives and they are very comfortable with not knowing everything. Children generally take life as it comes and adjust accordingly.

Parents say, "Get in the car." The kids rarely know where they're headed or what they'll do once there, but that seldom bothers them. Kids are very content to live in the present moment. They remain open to all possibilities and still have a sense of wonder and awe about the most common things; things adults barely notice.

Adults should take a lesson and try to incorporate a little of this childlike anticipation into our daily lives. "What's going to happen today?" is a question that should be asked with a feeling of joy, not dread.

Try to remain open to the possibility that the person we're always having an issue with might have changed since we saw them last. Or how we've changed since then might cause us to experience them in a totally different way. That distasteful chore might now hold some pleasure. When you live your life in anticipation of the positive, there's a much greater chance that's what you'll experience!

> *Prayer:* "God of Wonder, let me be grateful for the quality of anticipation and childlike wonder. Help me expect the best outcome possible in every situation I face today. Amen."

August 3

THE BEGINNER'S MIND

The Beginner's Mind

Affirmation

"Today I celebrate the BEGINNER'S MIND. I am the knowing and the unknowing. I am believing and disbelieving. I am learning and unlearning. In this present moment I surrender to the process of being transformed by the renewing of my mind."

Jesus introduced a concept to the religious order that didn't sit very well. He told them they *"must become like little children"* in order to enter the kingdom of God. They struggled to accept this teaching as they had worked tirelessly to be perceived as experts in their field. They had memorized laws, perfected rituals and become masters in their religion. Now Jesus has the audacity to suggest they voluntarily take a demotion, unlearn some of what they had spent years studying. And further, become open, curious and inquisitive? Like children? Unfortunately, they could not humble themselves to this place of openness. It seems they possessed zero capacity to celebrate the Beginner's Mind. Consequently, they were unable to believe, receive, or even perceive, the teachings of Jesus. Why? Because when you believe you have learned it all, there is no available space for new learning. In essence, you become a "know it all." There is also quite a bit of ego wrapped up in this resistance. Mastery brings with it benefits: better titles, reserved seating, higher salaries. Those who grow accustomed to the kickbacks of mastery are unwilling to take a demotion in the name of expanded consciousness. So, it was the uneducated, the unlearned, the untrained who received the message of Jesus. He even chose disciples who were young and inexperienced so He wouldn't have to wallow for years through the deep mud of religious indoctrination. Let's make the decision to leave some available space for God to continually bring us new and fresh revelation. Today, let's become like children. And, then stay that way.

Prayer: *"Daily Bread, I'm open and available for fresh manna and a living word. I'm not a 'know it all' and want to celebrate the Beginner's Mind. Give me the courage to become like a child. Amen."*

Challenge Your Mind. Channel Your Power. Change Your Life.

August 4

THE BEGINNER'S MIND

Taking On the Mind of Christ

Affirmation
*"I now take on the Mind of Christ and become
the hope of glory."*

Are you ready to take on the Mind of Christ? If so, there are three basic steps.

1. Change your beliefs about yourself. Know that you are worthy to embody the same Christ Spirit that was in Jesus of Nazareth.

2. Realize the Christ Mind is already within you and has always been with you. You just have to do the work to remove everything that's *not* it from your reality.

3. Just say *yes* to the Christ Spirit, and continue walking toward the truth of who you are.

Jesus is not going to do all our work for us. Jesus of Nazareth has already done his job. He came, he taught, he delivered his message and he died to fulfill his mission. He embodied the Christ Consciousness by *becoming* the Christ.

But now, according to the Bible, he sits at the right hand of the Father, waiting for us to do the same. He is waiting for us to wake up to the Christ within *US*, which is the hope of glory!

Prayer: *"Hope of Glory, help me wake up to the Christ within me today so that I may be a vessel of your glory here on earth. Amen."*

THE BEGINNER'S MIND

August 5

Empty Your Cup

Affirmation
"Today, I am willing to empty my cup, clear my mind, release old wine and ancient wineskins that would keep me from hearing and receiving what the Spirit is saying. I am willing to detach from the known and be open to the unknown. I have heard of old, but I am willing to hear today."

There is a common story in Buddhism of a young scholar seeking wisdom from an older Zen master. The young scholar sits with the master and goes on and on of his understanding of Zen. As he talks, the older master begins to pour him a cup of tea. When the tea reaches the top of the cup he continues to pour and even allows the tea to spill everywhere. The young scholar tells the master that he is spilling and that the cup cannot hold anymore tea. The old master says to the young scholar, *"You are like this cup. You ask for teaching but your cup is full. Before I can teach you, you must empty your cup."*

The most famous martial artist of my generation, Bruce Lee, used this philosophy to create a new and more advanced form of martial arts. Many martial arts purists did not believe you could combine new moves and unknown maneuvers with the old trusted methods. Their cups were completely full and there was no room for anything new. When criticized by these traditionalists, Bruce Lee said to them, *"Empty your cup so that it may be filled; become devoid to gain totality."* Every off season, Kobe Bryant, 5 time NBA champion, NBA MVP and top 5 scoring leader in NBA history, decided to learn new moves. Tiger Woods, arguably the greatest golfer of all time, continues to tweak his swing. The Apostle Paul described this philosophy as *"counting it all loss"* and admitting that he had *"not yet attained."* Jesus encourages us to become like little children. Experts become masters as they remain open and continually make the choice to empty their cups.

Prayer: *"Eternal Word, I empty my cup, celebrate the Beginner's Mind and make room for more. I will empty my cup. Fill my cup Lord! Amen."*

Challenge Your Mind. Channel Your Power. Change Your Life.

August 6

THE BEGINNER'S MIND

A Prison of Our Own Making

Affirmation
"In the Kingdom of God there is neither male nor female."

Just because we have the power to create our own reality doesn't mean we always use it to create things that are beneficial to us. That comes only with maturity. Unfortunately, sometimes what we create, either consciously or unconsciously, are prisons for ourselves and for each other.

One prison we've created collectively involves the rigid stereotypes of the masculine and the feminine and the valuing of one over the other. Pretty much every institution in Western culture, from government to religion to sports to music, the film industry, etc. over the last few thousand years has systematically worked to either erase entirely or to seriously diminish or dismiss feminine power and the feminine perspective of the world.

It's referred to as *The Patriarchy*. The thing about this prison that most people don't understand is that it doesn't just affect women. Both men and women have suffered from the creation of this mental prison of a male-dominated world view. Some feminists would disagree, but it's the truth.

Men suffer just as much from this imbalance in society because it necessitates them cutting a part of themselves away. As we know, God is ALL. His light is not complete without his darkness; his masculine is not complete without her feminine. Each of us has masculine and feminine characteristics and we are also incomplete without both. When either is out of balance, in an individual or in society at large, we all suffer.

> **Prayer:** *"Mother God, help me to remember that we are all feminine as well as masculine and that one without the other is incomplete. Help me to embrace all of myself today and to honor all of my characteristics equally. Amen."*

THE BEGINNER'S MIND

August 7

I Am Not My Beliefs

> ### Affirmation
> *"Through this awakening process I have realized I am not my beliefs. I am a spirit capable of considering, having and even changing beliefs. I am at peace being surrendered to the process of the Holy Spirit guiding me into all truth, even if all truth is different from my present truth."*

Christ may be a Solid Rock on which we can stand, but His journey toward higher truth was fluid. The strength of Jesus is hidden away, not in His rigidity, but in His flexibility. On one occasion He attempted to teach a rigid, inflexible religious leader named Nicodemus the recipe for spirituality:

> *"That which is born of the flesh is flesh, and that which is born of the Spirit is spirit. Do not marvel that I said to you, 'You must be born again.' The wind blows where it wishes, and you hear the sound of it, but cannot tell where it comes from and where it goes. So is everyone who is born of the Spirit."* (John 3:6-8).

This doesn't mean we are to be *"blown about by every wind of doctrine"* (Ephesians 4:14). It does mean we must not be so stuck in what God has said that we miss what God is saying. Many times Jesus would begin a teaching by saying, *"You have heard it was said of old, but I say to you."* Those weakened by loyalty to what was said could not summon the strength to hear what God was saying. We must be cognizant that faith comes by hearing, not by having heard.

The tallest buildings in major cities are built with a flexible design. These skyscrapers actually sway back and forth with the wind. Palm trees, planted by shorelines that are regularly visited by hurricanes and heavy winds, can literally bend over and touch the ground without breaking. Whether it is a building, a tree, our bodies, or our spirits, flexibility signals strength while rigidity invites weakness.

> **Prayer:** *"Wind of the Spirit, I am not fragile. I am flexible. I invite You to blow truth to me and through me. I can handle it. Amen."*

Challenge Your Mind. Channel Your Power. Change Your Life.

August 8

THE BEGINNER'S MIND

True Humility

> ***Affirmation***
> *"I am who God says I am. And God says I am good. I know that I am created by God, creative like God and creating as a god. And today I create good things from a space of worthiness."*

People often think of being humble as being unassuming, which, for some reason, is only a short hop in our minds to being unworthy. But these two concepts are not the same at all.

Unassuming means to be "modest, lacking arrogance, pleasant and polite." *Unworthy*, on the other hand, means "not deserving of effort, attention, or respect. Having little or no merit."

True humility, however, is agreeing with what God says about you. Think about how much audacity it takes to disagree with the one who created you, yet we do it all the time - every time we think of ourselves as unworthy. It's actually not humble to think less of yourself, but rather the ultimate demonstration of your pride; believing you know better than God.

God created you as a perfect being, in His image and likeness; a little god, if you will, who is completely worthy. Unworthiness is a man made perception. We've been taught that our worthiness depends on how hard we work or how much we produce. But it's really the other way around.

We must feel worthy first. Then we can speak and act and accomplish things from that place of knowing who we are and what we deserve.

> **Prayer:** *"Worthy God, please show me my worthiness today and help me to agree with you about who I am. Amen."*

August 9

THE BEGINNER'S MIND

Eating The Question

Affirmation
"Today, I will relax into the mystery. I will be at peace with the process of answering questions and questioning answers. I will celebrate truth as a journey, and not as a destination. And, I will eat the question knowing it may be my connecting point to a new dimension and a higher elevation."

The Hebrew children have been delivered out of the bondage of Egypt and rescued from 400 years of enslavement. They are now free. But, afraid, unsure, in a strange place and having to learn new ways of being and doing. They have a pillar of fire to warm them at night, a cloud to shade them from the heat of the day and water coming out of rocks to satisfy their thirst. Their food is also a mysterious provision. It is called "manna," which is more of a question than just a word. Manna means "what is it?" So in essence, each morning, in order to survive, they must eat the question. Similar to our journey toward liberation, there is a connecting flight between bondage and freedom. They departed from Egypt, had a layover in the wilderness, and eventually arrived in the Promised Land. But, in order to make it to the promise they were forced to eat the question.

What are the questions we are presented with as we connect from one season to another? Why did my marriage fail? Why don't my children respect me? Why am I always disappointed? Do I need more money or more money management? Who is to be blamed? Is it working for me? The questions can be many and not so easy to eat and digest. The Hebrews didn't particularly like eating the manna, the question. They asked Moses to take them back to Egypt, where they would be in bondage again, but also have bread, pots of meat and not have to eat the question. Yet, until they, and we, eat and digest the questions, we will continue to remain in the wilderness. This is our journey. Eat the questions or go back to bondage. Questions are answers in seed form. And, they hold the key to our Promised Land.

Prayer: *"Eternal Mystery, thank You for freeing me from the bondage of my past. Strengthen me to walk into freedom. Amen."*

Challenge Your Mind. Channel Your Power. Change Your Life.

August 10

THE BEGINNER'S MIND

Spiritual Baking

> **Affirmation**
> *"Today my goal is inspired action."*

Learning how to create and manifest things in your life is a lot like following a recipe. One of the things you must learn is that the order in which you do things matters. When cooking or baking, the recipe begins by giving you a list of all the ingredients you need and how much of each. But it doesn't end there. Then it goes through the steps. It tells you what to put in first, when to stir, and what temperature to set the oven, etc. The point is you can't just dump all the ingredients into a pot or dish all at once and think you're done.

Similarly, in terms of creating and manifesting, the order also matters. The word *inspire* comes from *in-spirit*, meaning to have spirit come through you. Inspiration is the necessary first step to create anything.

Because we've been conditioned to believe that action and thinking are far superior to and more valuable than being and feeling, we tend to put more emphasis on those qualities and want to act first.

But the inspiration (which is a feeling) must come first. THEN you can take whatever action is required because only then is it *inspired action*. Uninspired action is like a cake that has not been baked long enough with a couple of ingredients added in the wrong order or in an incorrect amount.

Everything that manifests in the physical world is created in the invisible realm of energy first. Feeling as if what you want is already accomplished is always the essential FIRST ingredient!

> **Prayer:** *"Source of Inspiration, help me understand today that in the creation process, action is meaningless without inspiration. Amen."*

THE BEGINNER'S MIND

August 11

Dust in the Wind

Affirmation
"Today, I will be aware that my physical form, and the material world in which I live, are temporary. I will be mindful to cherish each day and honor every moment."

The rock group Kansas wrote a song entitled "Dust in the Wind." The song's theme is a reminder of the impermanence of life. The apostle James describes the human lifetime "like a vapor" appearing for a moment and then vanishing away. (James 4:14) The difficult reality is that we will all die. To be clear, our physical forms will die…leaving only our spirits. Krishna reminds us "*all that lives, lives forever. Only the shell, the perishable, passes away. The Spirit is without end. Eternal. Deathless.*" (Bhagavad Gita) So, we have a tension between mortal and immortal, permanent and impermanent, eternal and temporary.

Let's find the beauty in it all:

1. We are only temporarily dust, material, physical, earthly. We are eternally spirit. Our bodies are indeed dust in the wind, merely vapors. Yet, our spirits are unending.

2. As our bodies are passing away, let us set our intention not to define ourselves by physical categories like gender or race. Refuse the temptation to be tied to temporary labels while in this momentary physical form.

3. Enjoy every day to the fullest. This earthly life is short. Don't waste one moment with lower vibrations like bitterness or regret.

4. Let us build our hopes on things eternal, our spiritual essences.

   Prayer: *"Endless Mind, I give thanks for my eternal spirit. And, I choose not to place more importance on a temporary expression than on my eternal existence. Amen."*

Challenge Your Mind. Channel Your Power. Change Your Life.

August 12

THE BEGINNER'S MIND

Saving by Playing Part I

> **Affirmation**
> *"Today, I will value a playful approach in connecting with God. I choose to serve others, worship God, love myself and practice spirituality from a playful attitude."*

In Christianity, the commonly held doctrines of salvation are that Jesus saves us by blood, sacrifice, dying, resurrecting, ascending, interceding. The salvific methodologies associated with Jesus are both sacred and serious. In the study of Krishna, the Hindu savior figure, we find that one of the ways Krishna saves His adherents is by playfulness. In Sanskrit the word is "lila" or divine play. Krishna saves us through divine play by teaching us to relate with divinity in a less formal, less fearful, more playful way. This may sound sacrilegious to some as sainthood has never been achieved by playfulness (although St. Francis of Assisi did play with animals). Playfulness can be associated with distraction, selfishness, a lack of seriousness, an absence of devotion to neighbor and also with a lack of focus on calling or purpose. I'd like to challenge this idea by considering these questions:

1. **Can we prosper and be in good health without play?** Are we dishonoring God when we play Legos with our children? Ride bikes? Is God only honored as we are correcting and instructing our children?
2. **How do we serve others without play?** Is calloused, insensitive, exhausted service to others (all can result from a lack of play) our highest and best?
3. **Is seriousness more spiritual than play?** Is there a hierarchy where prayer and fasting sit atop the supposed lesser expressions of joy and peace? Is the kingdom of God seriousness, heaviness, and solemnity or is it righteousness, peace and joy?
4. **Can we truly love God without playfulness?** If our relationship is only driven by the fear of being cursed? Missing heaven? Is this love? Or is this fear?
5. **Can we fathom being at peace with God today?**

> **Prayer:** *"Playful Presence, today I choose to relate to You in awe and in love. As I pursue peace I will connect to You out of joy and devotion, not from fear. Amen."*

THE BEGINNER'S MIND

August 13

Saving by Playing Part II (Jesus At Play)

Affirmation
"Today, I am open to seeing a different perspective of Jesus. I am also available for a connection with God that encourages relationship, not fear."

Jesus was born into an environment of death threats, Roman oppression and religious rigidity. He narrowly escaped being executed as an infant, was eventually crucified by Roman officials and seemed to be perpetually in a struggle with the religious order. Sounds like Jesus needed to play. And, He did!

Jesus was not foreign to "lila." He had a playful side. Jesus first miracle was not healing the sick, raising the dead or feeding the hungry. His first miracle was turning water into wine at a wedding. The wedding party already had wine. They just drank it all. And, Jesus provided them with more. Jesus related the kingdom of God to little children playing and taught that if we do not learn to play as the children we cannot enter the kingdom. Jesus recreated, relaxed, refreshed in Bethany with His closest friends Lazarus, Mary and Martha. Furthermore, Jesus was unconcerned and unimpressed with long prayers and the serious formalities of religious expression. He cautioned us to not be overly preoccupied with ritual, robes and religious titles. (Matthew 23:5-8)

When we connect to this lighter side of Jesus, perhaps we can conceive or relate to God, not from fear and awe, but from love and devotion. When we learn to be playful we signal to the universe that we are not only saved from God's wrath, but safe in God's love.

Prayer: *"Joyful Spirit, today I will play in Your presence without fear or reservation. Amen."*

Challenge Your Mind. Channel Your Power. Change Your Life.

August 14

THE BEGINNER'S MIND

Is It True? Is It Necessary? Is It Kind?

> **Affirmation**
> *"Today, I will be mindful to only speak words that are true, necessary and kind. I will use my words to create life and not death. I will speak high vibratory words and avoid words of lower vibrations."*

Have you ever been exposed to someone whose words seem to always be heavy, harsh and hateful? I try my best to avoid these people. And, when I must encounter them, I "agree with them quickly" (Matthew 5:25) and "ease on down the road!"* How can we be certain that we are not creating death with our words? "Before we speak we should ask ourselves three questions: Is It True? Is It Necessary? Is It Kind?" (Sadhguru)

Speaking truthfully keeps us from causing drama and steers us away from people questioning our character. However, sometimes the truth is not necessary in a particular situation. Only Captain Obvious speaks the truth when every other person knows it should be unspoken. Occasionally something can be true and necessary, but not spoken with kindness. Practicing the wisdom of kindness is what enables us to always be truthful, yet diplomatic with our timing and tone.

> **Prayer 1:** *"God, grant me the senility to forget the people I never liked anyway, the good fortune to run into the ones I do, and the eyesight to tell the difference. Amen."* **

> **Prayer 2:** *"Let the words of my mouth and the meditation of my heart Be acceptable in Your sight, O Lord, my strength and my Redeemer."* (Psalm 19:14)

---

*   Michael Jackson, Diana Ross, Ease on Down the Road, The Wiz. 1978.
** Ben Witherington, The Senility Prayer

FULLY AWAKE 365

THE BEGINNER'S MIND

August 15

The Beauty In Mystery

Affirmation
"Today I am willing to say, 'I don't know' - and that's beautiful."

There is great beauty in mystery. Life gets very boring when we get stuck in the same old stories we tell about ourselves and others, or when we create an atmosphere where we think we must know everything, or as much as we can know, beforehand in order to enjoy an event.

Sometimes we just need to ask ourselves the question, "What's the harm in not knowing?" And if we really want to get philosophical, we can ask, "Why do we think of it as higher or better to know something than to not know it?"

When you get right down to it, needing to know or thinking knowing is better than not knowing is a very ego and fear based way to live. We think the more details we know about a situation, the more we can control it. The same goes for our relationships with others. We pride ourselves on how well we know someone.

But have you ever thought about it this way – when you define someone, you also confine them to the story of them you've created. And when you do this, you aren't really experiencing all of who that person is or allowing them to grow, change and evolve.

Learn to be open and leave a little room for the mystery of what you might not know about them or of who they have become since you last saw them. If you don't, you might be missing a beautiful opportunity.

> **Prayer:** "God of Beauty, help me get comfortable with the mystery of life. Help me to allow others the room they need to grow and evolve into the fullness of all you have created them to be. Amen."

Challenge Your Mind. Channel Your Power. Change Your Life.

August 16

THE BEGINNER'S MIND

Room to Grow

> *Affirmation*
> *"Just as a fish will only grow to the size of an aquarium, my mind will only expand to the size of its container. I will not allow the growth potential of my mind to be stunted by any limitation of race, religion, country, or culture. Today, I choose to live above label and free from any container. Today, I choose the mind of Christ!"*

Have you ever been to a pet store and seen a large fish in a small aquarium? Sometimes the fish has lived its entire existence in that same small space. Other times, someone bought that fish and realized it's capacity and growth potential was more than they could handle and brought it back in desperation to the place they purchased it as a last resort. There is an old adage that a fish will only grow to the size of its container. In my 20's I got into tropical fish. One of the fish (called an Arowana) that I thought was especially beautiful was actually from the Amazon River. My Arowana grew to be almost two feet long. I was so proud of how big and beautiful he was. Until one day, I visited the Tennessee Aquarium and saw an Arowana in an aquarium about the size of my house. This Arowana was almost as big as me! I was both amazed and humbled. Obviously, I had limited my fish's growth potential by placing him into a container that didn't allow him to flourish and thrive. Yet, with my limited perspective I was living in pride.

Have you placed your mind into a container? Were you born into an environment that limited your potential? What are the boxes, boundaries, borders or barriers we place around our minds? Is it religion? Or only reading one religious book? Is it a boundary of color, culture or country? Make the choice today to never place your limitless, endless spirit into anything limiting. And, then give that same freedom to others.

> **Prayer:** *"Spirit of Limitless Expansion, give me courage to live outside of religious systems or finite structures that would hinder my spiritual growth and awakening. My mind is open. I am ready to expand. Amen."*

THE BEGINNER'S MIND

August 17

God Wants US to be Happy

Affirmation
"Today I know that suffering is not necessary for me to be holy, and struggle is not required for me to receive good things."

Who has convinced us that life must be hard and that struggle is required in order to have good things come to us? The Bible clearly states in Luke 12 that it's *the Father's good pleasure* to give us all things that pertain to life and happiness. And in John 10:10, Jesus said, *"I have come that you might have life and have it more abundantly."*

So why do we feel the need to add on to the end of every request we make, *"if it's God's will?"* What is it that has made us believe it would ever be God's will for us to suffer, not have the things we need or to be unhappy?

If you've ever believed that, or if anyone has ever told you that, let me make it clear to you right now - it's *always* God's will for us to feel good and for good things to come to us.

But so often we choose to suffer, either because we've been taught that it makes us more holy or because it comes to us as the consequence of our own unwise decisions.

Let's be clear that God places no value on our suffering. God wants us to be happy - ALWAYS! Happiness is not something we earn with our good behavior. Neither is it something we reach out and pull to us. It's ever flowing, just like a river. All we have to do is step in!

> **Prayer:** *"Source of Joy, help me understand that it is never your will for me to suffer and that happiness is always available to me. Amen."*

Challenge Your Mind. Channel Your Power. Change Your Life.

August 18

THE BEGINNER'S MIND

Clearing Out Space

> **Affirmation**
> *"Today, I am ready to clear out space and provide God room to create new life. I will not force new wine into old wineskins. I readily invite the Holy Spirit to guide me into all truth, new truth and higher truth."*

Genesis 1:1 *"In the beginning, God created..."* The 5th word in the Bible is *"created."* Created in Hebrew is *bara* – meaning to carve away, reshape and clear out space. So, this text (originally written in Hebrew) should read, *"In the beginning, God carved away, reshaped and cleared out space."* If God was clearing out space, reshaping, this means there was something to reshape...something in the way needing to be cleared out. You can't reshape, carve away or clear out something that is not there. With this knowledge, we can now say this text should read, *"In a beginning, God carved away, reshaped and cleared out space."* Now it should make more sense to us when the very next verse says, *"the earth was without form and void."* In a beginning, or the Genesis account of this specific beginning, God was reshaping and clearing out space, not just to create, but to re-create or create again! And, in order for God to bring order to chaos, light to darkness and design to void, there had to be a clearing out of the old to create the new.

When we experience God's love and begin the journey of awakening to the Christ Mind, the Genesis process of creation, re-creation and reshaping begins within us. We must be willing to clear out old thoughts, reshape our hearts and carve away the old mind to make room for the new man. Unfortunately, most Christians are like concrete...all mixed up and permanently set. We desire a new start and for God to re-create in us a clean heart and renew a right spirit within us. The challenge is that we must be willing to clear out space (or release old thoughts) for God to re-create a new life, a new mind, a new consciousness within us.

> **Prayer:** *"Re-Creating Spirit, reshape, clear out and carve away anything that keeps me from my highest and greatest good. Amen."*

THE BEGINNER'S MIND

August 19

Hitting the Reset Button

Affirmation
"Hitting the reset button is good for my body, my mind and my spirit."

Being exhausted has become a recurring theme these days for most of us. I challenge you to start paying attention to how many times, in your daily conversations, people mention how tired they are. I guarantee it will be a lot. When something becomes pervasive in society, it's good for us to stop and ask ourselves why. Why are so many people so tired so much of the time?

One of the main causes is that we haven't learned when to just stop and hit the reset button. All of us need to do this from time to time. And we shouldn't think of it as something we do only when we feel we've messed something up or made a mistake. It needs to be a part of our regular routine because it helps to keep our channel clear so energy can flow through freely.

Making sure there is a good balance between times of high energy and hard work and times of rest and relaxation in your life at regular intervals is key. If you don't allow yourself a time of rest after a time of activity you become out of sync energetically. This puts your body into dis-ease, which often leads to disease.

Nature shows us through its 24 hour daily cycle that the times of light and darkness are equal. We should take this as a signal that we need just as much *down time* as we spend working. That's tough to accomplish in our present work-centered culture, but finding time to hit that reset button will ultimately help you be even more productive.

Prayer: *"Source of Rest, help me remember to refresh myself today. Amen."*

Challenge Your Mind. Channel Your Power. Change Your Life.

August 20

THE BEGINNER'S MIND

The Sin Against the Holy Spirit

> **Affirmation**
> *"Today, I will welcome the Holy Spirit into my life by allowing It to have Its way. I am open to hearing all truth, even the truth of myself. I am aware that the Holy Spirit has been sent to me to lead me into all truth. I will not restrict It from operating in my life by declaring that I already have all truth."*

I was raised with an abiding and ever-present fear that I would sin against the Holy Spirit. Jesus taught that if we did sin against the Holy Spirit, it would be an unforgiveable sin. Needless to say, as a preacher's kid, I was leery of "playing church" or pretending that I was speaking in tongues as I perceived this might be sinning against the Holy Spirit. As I grew in knowledge and had experiences with the presence of the Holy Spirit I began to open up to a greater understanding. Not only did I sense the presence of the Holy Spirit, I began to receive new revelations and awaken to deep mysteries I had never known or heard before. I realized the purpose of the Holy Spirit in my life was to guide me into green pastures, new ideas and hidden truths of spirituality, and of myself.

It came to me, if the Holy Spirit was sent to guide me into all truth, then the sin against the Holy Spirit was not playing church. The sin against the Holy Spirit was perceiving that I already had all truth. I began to say things like "I don't know." Amazingly, as I detached from the known, a steady knowing flooded my daily experience. As I allowed the Holy Spirit to operate fully by creating space in my mind, new thoughts and quantum revelations became common place. Further, I realized that sinning against the Holy Spirit was only unforgivable, not because God wouldn't or couldn't forgive it, but because a "know it all" doesn't possess the capacity to see the error of his "know-it-all-ness." Therefore, the condition cannot be changed, or "forgiven," because there is no awareness that there is a condition. Empty your cup, create space, and experience a constant flow of truth from the Holy Spirit.

> **Prayer:** *"Holy Ghost, have Your way! I give You permission to guide me into all truth, this day and every day. Amen."*

August 21

The Optimist and the Pessimist

Affirmation
"Today, I will avoid extremes and find a balanced approach to life. I will begin today creating the life I desire to experience by starting where I am in this moment."

Is there a middle ground between the hopeless romantic and the dyed in the wool pessimist? Extreme optimists always see possibilities and potential in everything. Pessimists will endeavor to find the bad in something that is inherently good. Is pragmatism the answer we seek? Not necessarily. Pragmatic, practical thinking can limit our ability to dream and imagine a better life experience. Pragmatism alone cannot deliver us safely to racial harmony and religious coexistence. Many of us dream of beginning a business. Yet, we can become stagnated by the fear of failure. One rational approach to dreams is to begin where you are. Be faithful over a few things. Grow where you are planted. Do the best with what you already have. Crazy faith might seem glamorous, but stewardship of what God has already blessed us with might be the achievable action for the present moment.

If the dream is to own a salon, is the first step buying or leasing commercial space? Or could it be offering your service to those in your family and circle? Buildings are expensive and require upkeep. And, that may be the eventual destination. But, beginning where you are with what you have is always available…today…in this moment. Overly optimistic people have a tendency of grasping at whatever sounds good. This results in falling for "get rich quick" schemes and passing fads. Truly pessimistic individuals become paralyzed with waiting on God and excuses. Consider these questions that might help us find a balance: Can we be hopeful people who also have a retirement plan? Can we believe in divine healing while living a healthy lifestyle of disease prevention? Can we be big dreamers who are happy to begin small? I believe the balance presents us with power and purpose.

Prayer: *"God of Balance, help me to see the possibilities and the pitfalls. And, navigate my soul to a place of wisdom, balance and action…today! Amen."*

Challenge Your Mind. Channel Your Power. Change Your Life.

August 22

THE BEGINNER'S MIND

I Am The Path to Happiness

> **Affirmation**
> *"I will not put qualifications or conditions on the source of my happiness. I will not wait until something happens or until I reach a certain place to be happy. I create my own happiness.*

"It's not easy to find happiness in ourselves, and it is not possible to find it elsewhere." This quote by Agnes Repplier is telling us that when your only choice is between impossible and difficult - you're going to choose difficult no matter how hard it seems because you literally have NO other choice.

Just like when you're hungry enough your food preferences fall by the wayside, if your desire to be happy is strong enough, you will stop putting conditions on how it comes to you. When you're starving, all food - ANY food - is good. When you really want to be happy, you'll find a way.

It's like this: you see an option and you think, "Oh, this is too difficult. Let me move on to the next one." But then the next option is impossible. All of the sudden, the first option doesn't seem so bad anymore. It's amazing how much easier things seem to get when you realize you have no other choice. If it's difficult to find happiness inside yourself, but impossible to find it anywhere else - if you want to be happy - you're going in!

> **Prayer:** *"Giver of Life, help me to know that the path to happiness lies inside me and only inside me. Even though finding happiness within is sometimes a difficult path, I will walk it because I WANT TO BE HAPPY! Amen."*

THE BEGINNER'S MIND

August 23

The Certainty of Uncertainty

Affirmation
"Today, I am certain that certainty is uncertain. I will be flexible, malleable, versatile, agile, and mobile as I celebrate the certainty of uncertainty."

Business models shift. Our cheese gets moved. The Stock Market rises and falls. Relationships begin, shift, flourish, and then sometimes they end. If change is the only constant in the universe shouldn't we be approaching life from uncertainty rather than certainty? When we get locked into a belief, or business model, we become rigid and stagnant, unable to shift, unwilling to evolve, ill-equipped to adapt and incapacitated to adjust. As much as we desire certainty in every area of our lives, uncertainty seems to be the common experience most of us must face.

Yet, I perceive there to be some beautiful uncertainties of which we can be certain. What is certain?

I will remain open.
I will be flexible.
I will always have available space for Spirit to shift and shake anything that needs it.

So, the outcomes and variables are consistently uncertain and unpredictable. But, it is in the approaches of openness and flexibility where we can find some level of certainty. As we become comfortable in uncertainty, we will realize a powerful certainty of always being relevant and even revelatory wherever, whenever, however, whatever and with whomever!

Prayer: "God who WAS, and IS, and IS TO COME, today I give thanks for a progressive, organic, fresh revelation and revolution of approaching life from flexibility rather than rigidity. Amen."

Challenge Your Mind. Channel Your Power. Change Your Life.

August 24

THE BEGINNER'S MIND

Baby Steps

Affirmation
"Practice makes perfect."

Because you are made in the image and likeness of God you have the same ability He does to create. However, you're not born knowing how to create on the same level as God because you are literally (physically, mentally, and spiritually) a baby. And what do babies do? They grow. You grow up here on earth. That's how it works.

The purpose of incarnating as a human is to experience life, which involves some experimentation - specifically with our ability to create. We don't come here knowing everything already. God is aware of this. Using the common model of God as our parent, look at it from a human perspective. When your toddler is first learning a skill, you, as a loving parent, don't expect the child to get it 100% right the very first time, or even the first few times. The fact that it takes your child repeated attempts to learn something new doesn't make you love him any less or think she is stupid.

Learning to create is a process, and just like anything else you have the ability to do but have not mastered just yet, it requires practice. God put all of us here to experience life and to experiment with our ability to create. He's good with your failed attempts - those things you call mistakes. You're the one who allows them to make you feel unworthy. He knows you're just growing up!

Prayer: *"Patient God, help me to see myself as you do and know that my mistakes help me to grow. Help me to be patient with myself as I experiment today with my ability to create. Amen."*

THE BEGINNER'S MIND

August 25

No Male. No Female.

Affirmation
"I am open and available to see a bigger vision and version of the awesome God of the universe. God is neither male, nor female. God is Spirit. And today, I will worship in spirit and in truth."

The Apostle Paul has an amazing revelation: *"there is neither male nor female in Christ."* (Galatians 3:28) For this period of time this was a very bold statement. Paul was challenging Greek and Roman household codes, questioning cultural norms and challenging the accepted order of how society was to be structured. Although Paul offers this disparate view of God, Christ and religion, he also continues to struggle with the application of this progressive, egalitarian idea. This is not all that uncommon. Many times, humanity gets a revelation of truth before it surrenders to the application of that truth.

If we set our Bibles and our dogmas aside for just a moment we can have a conversation that is a little more accommodating of reason. Sometimes a mental breakthrough comes to us via common sense questions. Like: Is God a male? We call God Father, but is God actually male? Or is God a Spirit that we try to understand in human terms of gender? A spiritual approach to God allows us a different perspective. God is neither male, nor female. Further, God is not black or white, American or Mexican. Even further, God is not a Christian. When we surrender to the basic idea that God is Spirit, a whole new universe opens up to us.

Prayer: *"Genderless Spirit, thank You for allowing us a greater glimpse of Your immeasurable, indescribable, undefinable essence. Amen."*

Challenge Your Mind. Channel Your Power. Change Your Life.

August 26

THE BEGINNER'S MIND

Transactional vs. Unconditional

Affirmation
"God's love is unconditional."

People have different kinds of relationships with each other, one being *transactional*, where conditions are present and everything between them is treated as a transaction: "I'll give you this or do this for you only if you give me that and do that for me in return."

Many people have this type of relationship with God. The transaction we're taught is: If I get up on Sunday morning, come to church and give God praise and my tithe, then He will bless me. Or, if I am good and I follow all the rules someone else handed me and made me repeat over and over as a child until I memorized them, then I will be protected, get my prayers answered, and go to heaven when I die. But if I don't - the deal is off! And what I get in return is a life of misery at the end of which I am sent to hell forever.

It is amazing how many people still believe this even though it is in direct contradiction to the many places in the Bible where God's love is described as unconditional. A relationship based on unconditional love could not be further from one that is transactional which requires us giving something in equal measure or of equal value in order to earn God's love and protection.

A transactional relationship requires two parties, so in order to believe in this type of relationship with God you must see God as separate from yourself. The more you accept your own god-likeness, the more this belief dissolves as you realize you are one with God.

Prayer: *"God of Oneness, help me understand that I don't earn your love by being good or giving you anything. Amen."*

THE BEGINNER'S MIND

August 27

Walking Your Talk On-Line

Affirmation
"Today I will walk my talk in all areas of life."

You can say anything you want to, but no one will believe the things you say unless they see those words backed up by your actions. One place it's hard to do this is on-line, which is where we all spend increasingly more of our time these days. It's easy to hide behind the anonymity of a screen name and to sit behind a keyboard and type out things you would never dream of saying to someone if you were looking them in the eye.

If it's your goal to be on a spiritual path, and to live on the highest level of consciousness you can, you can't compartmentalize your life into "real life" and "on-line life." You must hold yourself to the same standards and principles at all times.

You can't put your *spiritual hat* on only in certain situations, for instance when you are at church, or in yoga class or some other spiritually minded gathering and then conveniently take it off and put it to the side when arguing with someone about politics on Facebook, allowing yourself to devolve into aggressive language and name-calling.

If you're calling people names, either in real life or on-line, you're not living in higher consciousness. Period. It's important to walk your talk… especially on-line, where it's so easy not to. Remember the words of John C. Maxwell: *"Your talk talks and your walk talks, but your walk talks louder than your talk talks."*

> **Prayer:** *"Gracious God, help me today to walk my talk at all times, even when it would be easier not to. Help me not hide behind a screen, but show the same courtesy to people on-line as I would in real life. Amen."*

Challenge Your Mind. Channel Your Power. Change Your Life.

August 28

THE BEGINNER'S MIND

The Higher Octave Part I

Affirmation
"I am limitless!"

An octave is a musical interval embracing eight diatonic degrees, or notes. There are only seven notes in music and they are represented by the first seven letters of the alphabet, so when you play A - G, the following note is just A again, but in a higher octave. It takes eight notes to form a complete scale, so the last note of one octave is also the first note of the next.

When thinking of our lives we can visualize it in the form of these octaves. Most of us are accustomed to seeing the world through the dualistic lens of labeling everything as either bad or good; right or wrong. But a more mature spirituality brings us into the concept of judging things by asking: "Is this working for me?" "Is this for my highest good?" or "Is this the highest response I can give?"

Instead of focusing so much on whether something is right or wrong, you begin to judge your behaviors, characteristics, responses, emotions, and choices in relation to how low or high an octave they're in.

This shift expands your thinking exponentially because while the good/bad and right/wrong polarities are very limiting, thinking in terms of octaves is limitless. There are only so many octaves on physical instruments, but the *concept* of the octave is limitless, continuously repeating itself to infinity.

When thinking in terms of octaves, it's no longer about a single choice between *this* or *that*, but you see that there's always room to go higher, which is a much more appropriate thought process for beings who are constantly evolving.

Prayer: *"Limitless God, help me today to understand that it's not about right or wrong, but about what is for my highest good. Amen."*

THE BEGINNER'S MIND

August 29

The Higher Octave Part II

Affirmation
"Today I will be the pioneer of a different ending."

The process of recreating some aspect of our lives that we find undesirable involves saying, seeing, surveying and shifting. But before we can shift, we've got to understand why we are where we are. What's causing us to live, move and act from a lower octave rather than a higher one? Usually, it's because of a pattern we've developed. Most lower octave behavior comes from patterns of unhealed pain.

Vienna Pharon says: *"Avoiding your triggers isn't the same thing as healing. Healing happens when you're triggered and you're able to move through the pain, the pattern, and the story and walk your way to a different ending."*

That's the shift - being able to have the same experience that previously resulted in a lower octave behavior or emotion, but instead of just avoiding similar experiences in the future, learning to walk your way through them to a higher octave response.

"Every time you are tempted to react in the same old way, ask yourself if you want to be a prisoner of the past or a pioneer of the future." ~ Deepak Chopra

This quote doesn't question whether something is right or wrong - but asks: "Do I want to be a prisoner of a past behavior that isn't working for me, or the pioneer of a new way - a different ending?"

The choice is always yours.

Prayer: *"Higher Self, help me learn how to truly heal rather than just avoid the things that cause me pain. Help me deal with my patterns of unhealed pain so that I can respond from a higher octave rather than from a lower one. Amen."*

Challenge Your Mind. Channel Your Power. Change Your Life.

August 30

THE BEGINNER'S MIND

To Be Poor In Spirit

> **Affirmation**
> *"Today, I set my intention to inherit the kingdom of God as I choose to be poor in spirit. I am open, empty, curious, teachable and available…poor in spirit."*

Jesus warns that a rich man cannot enter the kingdom of heaven. Paradoxically, Jesus also offers a parable on financial investing that is painfully absent a happy Disney ending. Unfortunately, those who are ignorant about banking and gaining interest on their money (or "talents") are cast into outer darkness. This disparity leaves us with a choice of which Jesus to follow. The Goodwill shopping, basement dwelling, video game playing, unemployed starving artist Jesus? Or the savvy business mogul Jesus who is in negotiations to acquire some lending institution? When Jesus blesses those who are "poor in spirit" is He channeling broke Jesus again?

To be poor in spirit is not the spiritual or emotional equivalent of being financially bankrupt. Neither is it a life sentence to the isolated, self-deluded island of false humility. Spiritual teacher, Emmet Fox, has a beautiful take on this teaching. Fox offers that to be poor in spirit is not to be confused with being poor-spirited (or falsely humble). But rather, being poor in spirit means to surrender indoctrinations, to lay down all preconceived ideas when seeking God.

Egoic subtle deception convinces the religious mind that mastery is superior to mystery, that knowing is to be desired more than not knowing and that firm doctrinal etymological foundations are safer, wiser than following inner intuition. Yet, being poor in spirit means we must be open, flexible, available, malleable, even curious. Do you desire to inherit the kingdom of heaven? Make the choice today to celebrate the Beginner's Mind!

> **Prayer:** *"Expanding Universe, awaken the seeker in me. Arouse the inquisitor within. Grant me ample spiritual wealth to be poor in spirit. Amen."*

THE BEGINNER'S MIND

August 31

Not Knowing Why

Affirmation
"Today, instead of asking: What's wrong with me? I will ask: What else is possible for me?"

When we're sick, we often waste a lot of time and energy trying to figure out why - and that's not productive. You don't always need to understand why, or where the sickness came from with your mind because that implies that's where the solution lies. Understanding it on the mental level doesn't do much to stop or heal the condition.

We do not heal on the mental level, but on the energetic level. That can sound contradictory because we're always talking about the fact that if you can *think* yourself sick, you can also *think* yourself well. Thoughts, which take place on the mental level, are important and they create. But healing takes place on a different level entirely. Thoughts are only part of the healing process. They *direct* the energy, but it's on the energetic level that we are healed.

Instead of: *Where did this come from? Why did this happen?* Or *What's wrong with me?* A better question to ask is: *What else is possible here?* This question opens you up to a different state of mind, more possible solutions, or even the resolution to the problem or symptoms.

> **Prayer:** *"God, My Healer, help me to understand that I don't always need to understand sickness on the mental level in order to allow healing on the energetic level. I know all things are possible to him who believes. And I believe my body has the ability to heal itself. Amen."*

Challenge Your Mind. Channel Your Power. Change Your Life.

September 1 — TRUTH IS A JOURNEY, NOT A DESTINATION

The Symbolism of 3

Affirmation
"Today I will pursue peace."

The number 3 holds a good deal of symbolism in the Christian faith; most notably it represents the Trinity. The next most recognizable significance would be the three days between Jesus' death and resurrection.

There is also a wider religious significance in that three of the world's most prevalent religions, Judaism, Christianity and Islam, are descended from Abraham and known as the Abrahamic Faiths.

When Abraham died, his two oldest sons, Ishmael (representing the Islamic faith) and Isaac (representing Judaism) met to bury their father in a cave called Machpelah, which means *the place of coming together*. It's no secret these religions have a history of war between them. The sons were given an opportunity that day to bury their grievances toward each other, along with their father, and to make peace. They could have walked out of that cave united. The thousands of years of bloodshed that followed proved they did not.

However, God is continually giving mankind opportunities to redeem himself. Approximately every 30 years (3 decades) the holidays of Easter (Christianity), Passover (Judaism), and Ramadan (Islam) fall on the same day. The chance for the adherents of each of these religions to stop fighting each other and come together is particularly highlighted at this time.

All of us are being presented regularly with the possibility for peace in our individual lives and in our greater world. It is our choice whether to take it or not. But if we do not, we can rest assured the opportunity will come around again. Why not make the choice to pursue peace today? There will never be a better time.

Prayer: *"God of Peace, help me to gratefully accept the opportunity to pursue peace that is on constant offer. Amen."*

TRUTH IS A JOURNEY, NOT A DESTINATION

September 2

The Dance Between Effort and Ease

Affirmation
"Today I understand that resting is not being lazy; it's being prudent and taking care of my physical temple."

Good yoga teachers will always use a specific strategy in their classes. They will take you through a few challenging poses where you have to expend a lot of energy, maybe get your heart rate up a bit and have to work to keep your balance in order to stay in the pose. And then they'll go into what is called a restful or restorative pose so you can catch your breath and re-establish your center before going back into poses that require more effort.

They call this the dance between effort and ease, and it's also a good way to look at life. You're not always going to be going full steam ahead. So in those times when you feel stuck or like you are in a rut... you might be. But you might also just be in a phase of ease, gathering your strength and preparing for whatever is coming next.

Taking time out to rest now and then is not being lazy. It also doesn't mean we're not doing what we're supposed to be doing. *Resting* is an action. And pacing yourself is an important component of self-care.

To everything there is a season, and a time to every purpose under heaven. (Ecclesiastes 3:1)

> **Prayer:** *"God of the In-Between Times, help me understand that sometimes the best thing I can do for you, myself and others is to take care of myself by experiencing a time of rest. Amen."*

Challenge Your Mind. Channel Your Power. Change Your Life.

September 3

TRUTH IS A JOURNEY, NOT A DESTINATION

The Harmony of Your Heart Space

> **Affirmation**
> *"Today I will recognize that every disharmonious thought I have is actually a lie. I will stay in my heart space and see all situations through the lens of love."*

The mind will never resolve itself through itself. No problem will ever be resolved by creating endless mental labyrinths for it to flow through. If we use mental logic alone to try and figure out our place in the universe while ignoring our heart-centered intuition, all we end up with is confusion, which is all a dualistic system has to offer.

The heart, by nature, is a place of harmony and oneness. We call it the singularity because it is our connection to the source of all consciousness. When we buy into the thought that duality is all there is, we are living in our mind space, from which it is impossible to escape because the mind is its origin.

To resolve dualism and return to oneness you must shift into the heart space because it alone is centered in the non-dualistic concept of love. It takes a mental concept to create fear, which always sets itself against love. Emotional states such as shame, aggression and anxiety dissolve through reclaiming the heart space and taking solace in the eternal quality of love.

That means that the only true reality is that which uses the heart space - love - as its filter, which leads us to a simple yet powerful truth - anything based in disharmony is a figment of our imagination; an aspect of the temporary consciousness that is dualism.

> **Prayer:** *"Source of Harmony, help me today to discern the difference between looking at situations through the dualistic nature of my mind and the harmonious, loving nature of my heart. Amen."*

TRUTH IS A JOURNEY, NOT A DESTINATION

September 4

Finding a Rhythm... Not a Routine

Affirmation
"Today, I give thanks for rhythms that bring joy and health into my life. However, I will not become routine or married to a specific schedule. I will follow, flow and be flexible."

The word routine carries several definitions. One definition suggests there is a similar pattern that repeats at similar times. The other has more of a negative connotation, as in, something has become routine, predictable, boring. In other words, we can have a routine without the routine becoming routine. Even when we follow the same daily schedule we can hold space for an allowance or spontaneity and freshness. Food, friends and even fitness can all find a rhythm without becoming routine. You can eat healthy and also try new seasonings and ways to prepare the same entrees. Friends can find new ways of communicating and sharing sacred moments together. When a fitness routine becomes routine, your body grows immune to it and begins to beg for a shock.

If you repeat the same prayer over and over why not just try saying "God, can we just talk? Today, I just want to share some things with You from my heart." If you wear the same outfit, button your shirt or blouse differently, wear a belt, tuck something in or let something out. Never allow your mind the satisfaction of figuring you out!

Prayer: *"Diverse Universe, today I give thanks for heathy patterns and rhythms that provide me with order and design. However, I will never be married to any schedule or method. I will remain open for new twists and turns. Amen."*

Challenge Your Mind. Channel Your Power. Change Your Life.

September 5

TRUTH IS A JOURNEY, NOT A DESTINATION

The Progression of Righteousness, Peace and Joy

> *Affirmation*
> *"I know that righteousness, peace and joy are a progression in my life. One builds upon the other to create for me a thriving existence!"*

Romans 14 tells us that the components of the Kingdom of God are righteousness, peace, and joy. I believe the order of those attributes are important because they describe the progression. Righteousness, or right living - right standing with God, yourself, and your fellow man - leads to inner peace. Having inner peace leads to a joyful life.

Many people believe it's the other way around and that in order to be at peace your life must be full of joy first, but peace is actually the foundation for joy, and righteousness is the foundation for peace.

When you can lay your head on your pillow at night knowing you have done everything that day from a pure heart to the best of your ability - and if you haven't, you know you have done whatever you could to make amends and have repented (re-thought) your behavior; this is right action (righteousness), then you can wake up every morning respecting, liking and being proud of the person you see in the mirror. This will bring you inner peace.

Some see being in a state of peace as the ultimate goal of their lives, however it's just a step in the process. Peace should be considered a basic requirement that is the foundation for a thriving, joyful existence!

> **Prayer:** *"Progressive God, help us to understand that there is a state beyond peace, and that state is joy, which should always be our ultimate goal! Amen."*

TRUTH IS A JOURNEY, NOT A DESTINATION

September 6

A Difficult Question

Affirmation
"Today, I am not afraid of difficult questions or unexpected answers. I celebrate questions as answers in seed form. My faith is flexible, fluid and forever evolving. I know the truth that ultimately sets me free might initially piss me off."

One of my mentors presented me with a difficult query. Offering me only two options, he asked which one I would choose:

Option 1: "Either God cannot do it, but wants to." Or, Option 2: "God can do it, but won't." Option 1 doubts the power of God. Option 2 questions the character of God.

Let's apply this. Either God cannot solve world hunger, climate change, and bloodshed, but really wants to. Or, God can feed the hungry, rescue the polar bears suffering and intervene in the Russian invasion of Ukraine, but won't. Wow. What options am I left with? Isn't there a third choice?

I am a theologian. Allow me to settle your fears. I am fully aware that we have been given free will and that God does not infringe on our agency to choose. Yet historically, God miraculously intervened for Moses and the children of Israel, freeing them from bondage and feeding them in the wilderness. God also sent a flood (interfered with the earth's climate) to eliminate evil. So, why would God do it then and not now? Aside from the ridiculous answers of "all in God's timing," "it's not my season" and "we don't have enough faith," this question poses a real threat to the character of God.

Good news! There is a third option. But, this option painfully places the answer heavily, squarely, solely upon our shoulders. Here it is: we are made in the image and likeness of God. This means we can feed the hungry. We can reduce, reuse, recycle. We can wean ourselves off of oil dependency. We can find peaceful resolutions to avoid bloody conflicts. But, we choose not to do so, preferring prayer, begging and fasting to "move" the hand of God. Here is the basic truth – while we are waiting on a God up there, God is waiting on us down here. The God without awaits the God WITHIN.

Prayer: *"Divine Presence, help me awaken to Your power in me. Amen."*

Challenge Your Mind. Channel Your Power. Change Your Life.

September 7

TRUTH IS A JOURNEY, NOT A DESTINATION

The Beauty of Duality

> ***Affirmation***
> *"Today I will understand that what I may consider to be a weakness can be turned into a strength if I just change its direction."*

While on the level of Spirit we know that there is only one God and that we are all just smaller expressions of it, as long as we live on the earth plane, we are subject to the duality that exists here. In other words, there are always 2 sides to the coin on this plane.

That's not necessarily bad, however. What we think of as our greatest weaknesses can also be our greatest strengths. For instance, the same mind that is good at figuring out how to look at things differently than others and can find ways around obstacles and seeming impossibilities can either use it to commit crimes and get away with them, or to discover entirely new ways of doing things or come up with new inventions.

Anyone who has the capacity to do great good has the same capacity in the other direction, to use those same skills and talents for evil purposes or to hurt others rather than help them.

No one is predisposed to be either all good or all bad. All of us have the capacity for both inside us. It's always our choice how we use our powerful gifts and to what end we expend our energy. It is duality that allows us to do that.

> **Prayer:** *"Source of Ultimate Creativity, help me to see my skills, talents and gifts clearly. And help me choose to always use them for good. Amen."*

TRUTH IS A JOURNEY, NOT A DESTINATION

September 8

The Middle Way

Affirmation
"I am balanced, stable, moderate and at peace walking the Middle Way. I am not attracted to extremes or gimmicks. Today, I confess that I am clothed in my right mind and seated at the feet of Jesus."

The Middle Way is a Buddhist teaching that encourages balance by avoiding extremes. The Middle Way suggests that we not be overly given to self-indulgence or self-denial; over-eating or starvation; sexual promiscuity or asceticism; hilarity or seriousness. The Middle Way could be described as practicing the wisdom of moderation. I have observed human behavior, as it relates to religious practice, for most of my life. Many I have observed get extremely excited about their relationship with God and attend every church service possible, set early morning prayer times, go on all manner of fanatical fasts depriving themselves of food and any form of fun. These types never successfully find the Middle Way. And, as a result, their extreme lifestyle leads to exhaustion, sensory overload and eventually a strong sense of guilt and self-criticism over their inability to maintain their imbalanced commitments.

On one occasion, one of these fanatical types called me at 3:00 a.m. to discuss a particular Bible verse. I told him my wife and children were asleep and that we could talk in the morning at an appropriate hour. He ridiculed me for my lack of hunger for God. Less than one month later he was done with his unsustainable exuberance and done with church altogether. Twenty-eight years later, I am still walking the Middle Way and growing in Spirit at a steady, consistent and balanced pace. The Apostle Paul asks a question *"you ran well, but what did hinder you?"* Or, you started strong, but then you burned out…or perhaps lost balance? Whether it is exercise, work, spending, volunteer work…there exists a balanced path that allows for stability, consistency and longevity. Find it!

Prayer: *"Sustainer God, teach me the ways of balance. Give me the passion and pace, the wisdom and way, to endure to the end. Amen."*

Challenge Your Mind. Channel Your Power. Change Your Life.

September 9

TRUTH IS A JOURNEY, NOT A DESTINATION

God Honors Our Choices

Affirmation
"Today I recognize that I am created by God, creative like God, and creating as a god."

The biblical account in Genesis tells us that the animals are all named what they are because that's what Adam named them - not God. God gave Adam the power to name them, told him to name them and then honored the names Adam gave them.

This free will and power to choose that God gave Adam has always extended to all of mankind. Here's another example. It wasn't God who demanded the blood of Jesus in order for us to be "saved." *WE* decided that the shedding of blood was necessary for the remission of sin because we all agreed at some point that that was what our truth was going to be. *WE* demanded blood to atone for wrongdoing - not God. And because that was our choice, God honored Jesus' sacrifice. But it was our reality, not His.

The good news is that we still have the power to choose and to create our reality, both as individuals and collectively. If we have in any way created a hell on earth through our choices, we can also go back and recreate a heaven on earth through that very same power. And God will honor it.

Prayer: *"Creative Source, help me today to understand the power I have to create - and also to recreate - my reality. Help me to use my free will and power of choice to create a heaven for myself rather than a hell, and to know that you will always honor my choices. Amen."*

TRUTH IS A JOURNEY, NOT A DESTINATION

September 10

Don't Throw It All Away

Affirmation
"Today I will trust my own inner guidance and withhold judgment."

In addition to rightly dividing the Bible, we must also learn to rightly divide the words and messages we receive from others. People are human. All people. Even preachers, teachers, spiritual leaders, and gurus. You can never and should never believe 100% of anything anyone says because everyone has individual biases, life experiences and lenses that their words and ideas come through.

Just because a person speaks a lot of truth, we must remember that no one is right all the time. We are all fallible. Some personal opinion is bound to come through every now and then, and that's fine as long as you, as the listener, are aware of this.

It's also helpful to remember that all good and true things come from source. When a person is plugged into source and writes an inspired song, book, sermon, etc., any good they've created has come from source. They are merely the vessel through which Spirit flows. So even if later on they turn away from source and allow their ego to take control, and you hear some things about how they are living their personal life that don't sit well with you - know that the good they created when they were creating from source will always be good.

Sometimes when this happens we want to throw away everything they ever did. But that has nothing to do with their inspired work. Our past or future behavior has no effect on our Spirit inspired creations.

Prayer: *"Source of Inspiration, help me to rightly divide every word I hear and every truth I accept. You are the source of all good things. I will not judge the vessel through which truth flows. Amen."*

Challenge Your Mind. Channel Your Power. Change Your Life.

September 11

TRUTH IS A JOURNEY, NOT A DESTINATION

Avoiding the Trap of Literalism

Affirmation
"Today, I am aware that the letter (or literal) kills, but the Spirit brings life. I set my intention to walk by the Spirit."

Bishop John Shelby Spong, revolutionary Episcopal minister and prolific, provocative author, changed my life! I met him several years before he transitioned. He actually sat in on a session I was teaching. I was very nervous with him sitting there. Bishop Spong wrote books like: *Rescuing the Bible From Fundamentalism, Why Christianity Must Change or Die, A New Christianity for a New World*…and many more. One quote from Bishop Spong has taken up residence in my subconscious mind for several years:

> *"Unless biblical literalism is challenged overtly in the Christian church itself, it will, in my opinion, kill the Christian faith. It is not just a benign nuisance that afflicts Christianity at its edges, it is a mentality that renders The Christian faith unbelievable To an increasing number of the citizens of our world."* [*]

Religious literalism flew planes into the World Trade Center Towers and also sparked the medieval Christian Crusades and the slaughter of countless Muslims. When Paul encourages us that the *"letter kills"* (II Corinthians 3:6) he is also suggesting that literal interpretations of scripture kill our spirits, and minds. The Bible is full of love and hate, freedom and bondage, spirit and flesh. How do we present this book to an intelligent person who is aware of its contradictions and of its culturally biased, tainted authorship? We must "rightly divide the Word of truth" away from literalism, toward Spirit. In order for the Christ to be seen in us, let us set our intention to walk in Spirit, not the letter.

> **Prayer:** *"Intelligent Mind of the Universe, as I encounter curious and intelligent people, help me to walk by the Spirit. Today, I let go of the literal mind and make room for the Spirit Mind. Amen."*

---

[*] Spong, Shelby. Biblical Literalism: A Gentile Heresy: A Journey Into a New Christianity Through the Doorway of Matthew's Gospel.

September 12

TRUTH IS A JOURNEY, NOT A DESTINATION

The Higher Octave of Love

Affirmation
"Today I will discern the difference between living in the lower octave of the law and the higher octave of love."

For when we were in the realm of the flesh, the sinful passions (nature) aroused by the law were at work within us, so that we bore the fruit of death. But now, by dying to what once bound us, we have been released from the law so that we serve in the new way of the Spirit, and not in the old way of the written code. (Romans 7:5,6 The Message Bible)

Why does the law arouse our sinful nature, or in other words, why do we have a desire to break the rules sometimes? The answer depends on what level or octave we're on spiritually. Immature people who have not yet learned self-control balk at the law because it won't let them do what they want.

But people who are no longer children, spiritually, who have grown up on the inside, inwardly hesitate for an entirely different reason. Somewhere deep inside they know they shouldn't have to be told what to do because it is in their nature to be God-like. When you fully integrate the idea of being made in God's image and likeness you know you are supposed to be able to govern yourself, co-create your reality, and have the ability to make sovereign decisions over your life.

These two responses look the same, but are very different. They represent the higher and lower octaves of living in love or according to the law.

Prayer: *"Higher Self, help me to live in the higher octave of love on a daily basis. Amen."*

Challenge Your Mind. Channel Your Power. Change Your Life.

September 13

TRUTH IS A JOURNEY, NOT A DESTINATION

Don't Get Distracted

> *Affirmation*
> *"Today I will think before I act and be wise about where I am putting my focus and spending my energy. I will not let the good become the enemy of the great in my life."*

Sometimes we find that "good" can be the enemy of great and we must make a choice between two or more worthy options. If we actually want our work to count for something, the fact that a particular issue is important or righteous might not be a good enough criterion to decide where to put our energy. There are thousands of important and righteous causes, but you as an individual cannot give your focus to all of them.

We often think that focus and distraction are opposites, but actually, the opposite of distraction is attraction, and focus is just a by-product of attraction. When we are attracted to something, it's very difficult for anything external to shift our focus away from it. So what we need to focus on is whatever it is that naturally attracts us and that we have a degree of aptitude for.

Our culture has conditioned us to base what we do on the things that are screaming at us the loudest, but these are often not the areas where we make our best contribution. Focus on those issues that pull you toward them rather than forcing yourself to concentrate on things simply because you think you should.

> **Prayer:** *"God of Focused Attention, show me the best places to put my focus and energy where I will do the most good for the most people. Amen."*

TRUTH IS A JOURNEY, NOT A DESTINATION

September 14

Literally?

Affirmation
"Today, I will venture away from the biblical, religious, literal mind and awaken to spiritual nuance. The student is ready. Teacher appear!"

No one takes the Bible literally. Not one person.

Allow me to explain.

In the Old Testament, a rape victim had no choice as to whether she must marry her rapist. Younger women were considered worth twice as much money as older women. Jesus teaches that a rich man could not enter heaven and then casts those who did not earn interest on their money into outer darkness. Jesus forbids the use of a sword and then tells the disciples to sell everything and buy swords. Jesus announces that He only came for His own people, not those of other cultures and countries. Then, approaches a woman of a different culture and exhorts her that God is bigger than any lines of separation. If a person followed these ideas literally they could only follow half of them while being in opposition to the contrary teachings.

When Jesus says to pluck out your eye if you lust, do we? Do you know anyone who has literally cut off their hand as Jesus instructed? Hopefully not! So, how do we read the Bible if we are not to take it literally? We must ask the Holy Spirit to help us *"rightly divide the Word of truth."* (II Timothy 2:15) Ask God to guide you in finding Spirit and eternal truth in the midst of man's religious and temporary ideas. Let us set our intention to take the Bible seriously and to approach it respectfully and reverently, but not literally.

***Prayer:** "Guiding Spirit, lead me away from literal thinking and to spiritual maturity. I have studied to show myself approved. Enable me to rightly divide the Word of truth. Amen."*

Challenge Your Mind. Channel Your Power. Change Your Life.

September 15

TRUTH IS A JOURNEY, NOT A DESTINATION

Love as Foundation and Filter

> **Affirmation**
> "Today I know and affirm that love is the strongest power in the universe on which I will base all my decisions."

Jesus told us over and over and showed us by His example exactly what our foundation should be, and what we, if we are going to consider ourselves Christ followers, should filter everything in our lives through. It's love - plain and simple. We've made lots of other things our filter that do not create a solid foundation, but the bottom line is if you can't build it on love, it's not a good foundation.

The cross is not the filter. The Bible is not the filter. Jesus (the historical man) is not even the filter. As long as we keep trying to use anything other than love as our filter we will continue to fall short as responsible citizens and as effective spiritual leaders.

It's easy to be discouraged by the state of separation and negativity our world is in at the moment. But the good news is that we can really make a difference. You, as an individual can do so each time you act out of love.

Love carries more power than the negative emotions of hate and fear because it comes from a higher vibration. And because it is the stronger power, it will always win in the end.

It is our responsibility as spiritual people to show love, give love and send love to those who are creating the problems through their negative emotions. Choosing love in every circumstance is not always easy, but it's always worth it because love should always be our filter, and it's truly the only answer.

> **Prayer:** "God, our Foundation and Filter, help us choose love today, tomorrow and always. Amen."

TRUTH IS A JOURNEY, NOT A DESTINATION

September 16

Back and Forth... The Spiritual Journey

Affirmation
"Today, I accept that my spiritual journey might not be predictable. There will be moments when I leap forward and also times when I shrink back. This is my journey. And, I will shift in my own time."

The spiritual journey is not a predictable algorithm. Sometimes we have an *aha* moment, a true breakthrough, and an undeniable awakening that sticks permanently. At other times, we experience two steps forward, a step back, three steps sideways, and a detour into childhood regressive memory that causes us to question everything we thought we knew and held true. The good news is that, on the spiritual journey, there are no prescribed patterns, no universally accepted expectation, and no exterior imposed expectations other than your own.

The apostle Paul taught that if you are in Christ, circumcision of the flesh would be a step backward and completely unnecessary. Then, he forced one of his disciples to be circumcised before an important missionary journey. Paul made the bold declaration that in Christ *"there is neither male nor female...bond nor free."* (Galatians 3:28) Then, he regressed into a teaching that women would not be allowed to speak in church and that slaves should obey their masters as their Christian duty.

This is the unpredictable nature of the spiritual journey. Why? It is very difficult to rid ourselves of a lifetime of conditioning in one moment, or even in one month. Give yourself a break. You did not accept the idea that God was angry and vengeful in one Sunday school class. This was drilled into your head for years. So, it may take more than one yoga session or meditation experience to completely rid yourself of conditionings. Just keep walking. Keep breathing. Keep thinking. Keep questioning. Keep moving forward and back and sideways and know that the Holy Spirit will continue to guide you as you do.

Prayer: *"Spirit without a blueprint, thank you for the steps forward, the breakthroughs upward, and for the patience You show me as I step backward and sideways. I am grateful for the process. Amen."*

Challenge Your Mind. Channel Your Power. Change Your Life.

September 17

TRUTH IS A JOURNEY, NOT A DESTINATION

The Spirit Gives Life

> ***Affirmation***
> *"Today I understand that the letter kills, but the spirit gives life."*

There is a concept in Buddhism that implies the way to end suffering is to eliminate desire and attachment, but it's a little more complicated than that. First of all, if it is true that we are spiritual beings who came to earth in order to have the natural experience of being human, then escaping the very human experiences of having desires and attachments would be counterproductive.

Too many people, in the name of never having to come into contact with suffering, have misused this principle to keep themselves separate from others and have called it non-attachment.

They've convinced themselves that it's just better not to want things or to never be genuinely involved in and committed to relationships than having to deal with the possibility of not getting what they want or having their relationships not go exactly the way they want them to.

In doing this, they've not only misinterpreted what Buddha said, they've robbed themselves and others of the richness of what the human experience was meant to be. Desire is necessary. If we had none at all (the desire to eat for example), we'd die. Desire is necessary to move us forward. Attachment to others is necessary to create families and keep communities together. Avoiding them entirely is not the answer. Learning to rightly divide does not pertain to the Bible only. We must learn to rightly divide and properly apply all spiritual principles.

> ***Prayer:*** *"God of all faiths, in navigating my spiritual path, help me to affirm truth wherever I find it, but also to rightly divide each holy text and apply it to my life in the most practical way possible. Amen."*

TRUTH IS A JOURNEY, NOT A DESTINATION

September 18

7 Universal Timeless Truths

Affirmation

"God is within…not up there, out there, on the way or in the past. I can experience God and live in the Kingdom right now. Healthy religion is simple and universal: Love God, love your neighbor as you love yourself. The reason this is not effective is because it is backwards. I must learn to love myself, then I will be able to love my neighbor, then I will understand how to love God. I will fill my consciousness with good thoughts and be conscious that I am eternally a created, creative and creating being. As I think in my heart, so am I. I will not give my power away or my mind over to any religious leader, pastor, guru or teacher. I give thanks for them all. But, the Holy Spirit will always be the most important Teacher in my life. For the rest of my life, I will rightly divide the Word of Truth…rightly divide my pastors…and rightly divide myself. I am healthy, happy and whole! And, with this new wineskin, I am now empowered to remain this way!"

1. **God is within me** (not up there, out there, on the way or in the past).
2. **Love God, neighbor and myself** (but in reverse order).
3. **Be aware of my Spirit** (prayer, worship, meditate, study, be in service to others).
4. **Fill my temple with good thoughts** (your life is a reflection of your thoughts. Put good in and get good out).
5. **I am Created BY God, Creative LIKE God and Creating AS a god** (I am created in the image and likeness of a Divine Creator and I am creating).
6. **No religious leader should control my life or destroy my faith** (I will respect spiritual guides but never allow them full control of my journey).
7. **If I am not experiencing Righteousness, Peace and Joy I must reexamine my spiritual practice** (nothing else needs to be said)!

Prayer: *"Indwelling Spirit, etch these timeless truths onto my heart and into my consciousness. Lead me into a healthy spiritual practice and into a pattern of growth and fulfillment. Holy Spirit, guide me into all truth. Amen."*

Challenge Your Mind. Channel Your Power. Change Your Life.

September 19

TRUTH IS A JOURNEY, NOT A DESTINATION

True Equality

Affirmation
"Today I recognize that it's my job to recognize and honor both my masculine and feminine traits."

In Western society, especially, we tend to have very rigid gender roles that begin being reinforced at birth. Pink is for girls. Blue is for boys. Girls play with dolls. Boys play with trucks. Boys are not supposed to cry. Girls are not supposed to be smarter than boys and if they are, they're not supposed to act like it. Boys are not supposed to back down from a challenge or a fight. Girls are not supposed to be aggressive or bossy. The same qualities that are praised in males are seen as negative and "unlady like" in females.

Not nearly as much today as in times past, but not so long ago, girls were trained to protect the male ego at any cost. That cost has been high, and both men and women have paid it. Boys have been indoctrinated into these beliefs just as strongly as girls have, resulting in cutting men off from their own emotions, causing them to deny and suppress very important and necessary aspects of themselves.

The entire society has been negatively affected by this imbalance. Yes, men and women are different. Equality doesn't mean identical, but we have reached a point where women have been expected to carry too much of the emotional burden because men are not encouraged to explore or even be responsible for their own feelings, let alone taught how to properly express them. It's time for us to recognize that showing and dealing with emotions is not just the job of women.

Prayer: *"Genderless God, help me to properly balance my masculine and feminine aspects and qualities today so that I am emotionally healthy and whole. Amen."*

TRUTH IS A JOURNEY, NOT A DESTINATION

September 20

CHOOSING to Heal

Affirmation
"Today, I will take up my bed. I will walk down a different street. I will write a new story. I will believe that I deserve peace. I will be made well. I may not know where I am going. But, I know where I am not staying. This day, I will pursue peace as I choose to heal."

In the 5th chapter of John we discover a man who has been lame for thirty-eight years. Jesus asks this man a seemingly innocent question: *"Will you be made well?"* (John 5:6 KJV) Yet, this question can be very offensive to many who live in pain. Let us present the question like this: Will you get up? Get over it? Move on and away from it? Can I take your story from you? Will you write a new one? How much longer will you nurse this wound? In this light, Jesus' question sounds less innocent and a bit more offensive.

After the question Jesus gives an instruction, *"take up your bed and walk."* (John 5:8 KJV) Notice, the lame man could not walk until he chose to take up his bed, move from his environment, leave the place of pain. Similarly, Jesus healed a blind man, but before he opened his eyes Jesus led him out of the city where the blind man had lived for years. Sometimes before we can be healed we must choose to change our location, environment, mindset, story. The excuses are many: I don't want to move. This is my story and I am sticking to it. We all have reasons. And, we all have struggles that can become our stories. The only question we must answer is: Will we be made well?

Prayer: *"Healing Spirit, trouble my water, tear down my resistance, take my pain. I will be made well. Amen."*

Challenge Your Mind. Channel Your Power. Change Your Life.

September 21

TRUTH IS A JOURNEY, NOT A DESTINATION

No Longer Children

> ***Affirmation***
> *"Today I will write the law of love on my heart and become the Living Word of God, eliminating the need to be governed by the written laws and rules of organized religion."*

God is the ultimate example of self-governance, and when we have also learned to self-govern, we become no longer children but "competent ministers of the new covenant" as Paul says in II Corinthians 3. What covenant is he talking about? The covenant Jesus created, based on the Spirit and the law of love in our hearts rather than the old covenant of Moses, based on the written law of the Ten Commandments.

The written law - the container of religion - will always keep us children because it will always arouse in us the desire to break it (Romans 7:5).

The way we lose the desire to break the law is to eliminate the need for it, which we do by learning to self-govern. We eliminate the need for the law by recognizing our own God-likeness which gives us the ability to transcend the written law and become the *Living Word* just as Jesus was.

We need the container of religion with its framework of rules, laws and commandments only until it teaches us to self-govern.

> **Prayer:** *"Spirit of the Living Word, teach me today that the more I live in the law of love and govern myself by that law, the less I will need written rules and the container of religion. Amen."*

September 22

TRUTH IS A JOURNEY, NOT A DESTINATION

Aristotelian Happiness

Affirmation

"I am more than my gender, race, religion, sexuality and country of origin. My happiness is not at the mercy of what I consume, dependent on my career accomplishments, or subject to my contribution of helping others. I am happy because being happy is who I 'BE.' Happiness is my being-ness. Today, I am happy to go higher. I choose to Go HIGHER!"

Almost every strain of philosophy is aimed at finding one thing… happiness. The philosopher Aristotle offered that there were different approaches and levels of happiness. However, his argument was that lasting happiness could only be sustained in the fourth level. Let's see where we land on Aristotle's happiness chart:

Happiness level 1: *Laetus.* In level one, happiness is sought out by way of consumerism. Material objects bring us a temporary joy. But, the shine soon wears off and the newness wanes, leaving us searching for the next object to purchase.

Happiness level 2: *Felix.* This is happiness by comparison. Our ego is stroked momentarily as we feel happy by comparing ourselves to others and by the illusion of being more admired. That is, until someone is more accomplished or admired than us.

Happiness level 3: *Beatitudo.* This happiness comes from doing good for others and making the world a better place. This seems sustainable. Yet, we will occasionally let others down and they will also fall short of our expectations.

Happiness level 4: *Sublime Beatitudo.* This happiness is undefinable. Here, happiness is a state of being independent of things, accomplishments, people or service. It is sustainable because it is not action, but rather essence.

Prayer: *"Sustained, Unspeakable Joy, today I give thanks for my things, for my successes, and for my service to others. But mostly, I am grateful that happiness is who I am and is not connected to what I do or have. Amen."*

Challenge Your Mind. Channel Your Power. Change Your Life.

September 23

TRUTH IS A JOURNEY, NOT A DESTINATION

Unique Instead of Special

Affirmation
"Today I will value everyone's unique contribution to the whole and not bring the specialist mentality into my spirituality."

We live in a world where specialists and experts who know a great deal about very specific subjects are considered smarter and more important than the jack-of-all-trades kind of people.

But who does the cardiologist call when his toilet is backed up and a plumber is not available? That neighbor who is no specialist in any one area, but just has a lot of common sense about house repairs. At that moment, none of his specialized knowledge or ability to perform heart surgery will solve his problem.

The whole concept behind specialists is *being special*. Because our society places such value on it, everyone seemingly wants to be or feel special. The classic conundrum, though, is that if *everyone* is special, then no one actually is. Why don't we try being unique instead?

Being unique basically just means being different, whereas being special is usually thought of as being better or greater. Unique removes the judgment. It merely means that something is unlike everything else.

Especially in matters of spirituality, let's lose the specialist mentality that says only our narrowly focused belief system is valuable or right. When we begin to value everyone's unique perspective and contribution to the whole, we are making progress towards true oneness.

Prayer: *"Inclusive God, help me to remember that the body is made whole by what every joint supplies. Let me strive to be unique instead of special. Amen."*

TRUTH IS A JOURNEY, NOT A DESTINATION

September 24

Freedom From Labels

Affirmation
"Today, I declare and celebrate my personal freedom from labels. No temporary label can define or confine my eternal spirit. I am bigger than any label of race, religion or region. I do not have a need to identify with any label and I also relinquish any right to label others. In Spirit, the only label I carry is love! I am the skinless, sinless, endless, nameless, shameless, blameless, label-less image and nature of God and good in the earth! I believe it! I perceive it. Now, I receive it!"

Before we took on physical form, we were spirit, without skin or sin, name or shame, region or religion, gender or geography. As we emerged into the physical, we took on many labels unconsciously: white, black, gay, straight, male, female, American, Christian, etc. Then, we permitted this labeling to condition us to believe we were inherently different and eventually, inevitably, separate from the rest of the world and especially different from anyone who didn't carry our specific set of labels. Humanity's inability, or unwillingness, to relinquish labels is the reason we fear terrorism, nuclear annihilation and the prospect of race wars. Labels lead to otherness. Otherness leads to separation. Separation leads to intolerance. And, intolerance leads to violence. It all begins with a seemingly innocent label.

There is a higher law, a more perfect way. As Sting says, *"There is a deeper wave than this."* And, as Paul explains to the Galatians and Colossians, in the renewed Christ mind, where there are no labels, *"there is neither male nor female, Greek nor Jew, circumcised nor uncircumcised, barbarian, Scythian, slave nor free, but all are one in Christ."*

> **Prayer:** *"God Without Label, awaken me to never be defined, disqualified or dismissed by any label. The only label I carry, or care about, is Spirit! Protect my love, preserve my life and promote my light without the bondage of any label. Help me today. I want to live without limit, purely in love and completely above label... just like You. Amen."*

Challenge Your Mind. Channel Your Power. Change Your Life.

September 25

TRUTH IS A JOURNEY, NOT A DESTINATION

Doing Your Part

> **Affirmation**
> *"Today I will do my individual part to make the world a better place."*

"Vanity of vanities, all is vanity . . .That which has been is what will be, that which is done is what will be done, and there is nothing new under the sun. Is there anything of which it may be said, 'See this is new?' It has already been in ancient times before us." (Ecclesiastes 1:2, 9 -10)

The writer of Ecclesiastes is telling us it is vanity to believe we can come up with anything that's completely new. That's often the first way we silence ourselves - by believing we don't have anything new or original to say. Well, nobody does... because there is nothing completely new!

Deciding NOT to create something because you don't think it's 100% original in every aspect, whether it's a sermon or a song or a painting, is not a good enough reason. The real beauty comes from your unique interpretation.

Five artists can paint a picture of the same sunset and each will be different because each will see it a little differently. A hundred musicians can write a song about the same subject matter and no two will be alike.

The great thing is that because we all have different tastes and preferences, different types of art forms, etc. will touch people's hearts and speak to them in a way that resonates specifically with them. You never know who your unique interpretation of something will affect in a profound way. You might be the only person to say it the way they need to hear it. So, do your part!

> **Prayer:** *"Source of Individuality, help me to remember that I have a unique perspective and a specific contribution to make today. Amen."*

September 26

TRUTH IS A JOURNEY, NOT A DESTINATION

Run Your Own Race

Affirmation
"I know that God has given me all the tools I need to create for myself an abundant life. I will not depend on a magic prayer to an external being, but will instead recognize the Christ Spirit within myself, which brings me salvation."

In The New Life translation of the Bible, Hebrews 6:19, 20 reads: "...*This hope goes into the holiest place of all behind the curtain of heaven. Jesus has already gone there. He has become our Religious Leader forever and has made the way for man to go...*"

In the *New King James* version, this same passage refers to Jesus as our *High Priest* and a *forerunner*. Interestingly, none of the translations of the scripture seem to call him savior.

What does it mean to be a leader? It means people follow you and you show them the way. You are not the way; you show the way. What about *forerunner*? What function does he perform?

A forerunner is also someone who goes ahead and that others follow behind. The forerunner is the first to finish the race. But once he's done, he doesn't turn around and start pulling all the other runners across the finish line. No. He simply sets the pace and opens the path so that everyone behind can look to him as an example.

Each runner must finish the race. Jesus came to show us how to run our own race, not to run it for us.

> **Prayer:** *"God, our High Priest, help me learn from your example and follow in your footsteps, but always know I have the courage and ability to run the race of life for myself. I will work out my own salvation with fear and trembling. Amen."*

Challenge Your Mind. Channel Your Power. Change Your Life.

September 27

TRUTH IS A JOURNEY, NOT A DESTINATION

Dominate or Tend?

> **Affirmation**
> *"Today, I will be conscious that the Creator has entrusted the creation into my care. I am commissioned to tend the creation, not dominate the creatures."*

In the Garden of Eden metaphor, we find an interesting commission given: *"tend and keep the garden."* (Genesis 2:15) Somehow, corporations claiming to be run by Christian entrepreneurs, have turned tend and keep into dominate and destroy. We are called to care for the earth and for the creatures that exist here with us. If we eat meat, we should do so in a fashion that honors the animal, making certain they were slaughtered without unnecessary trauma. If we eat chicken or eggs, we should research ways to buy responsibly from farmers who do not pump them with steroids and restrict their existence to a small, wire cage. As we consume fish, we can agree to sustainable harvesting that does not mistreat the fish or deplete the species.

Scripture tells us that God will *"destroy the destroyers of the earth."* (Revelation 11:18) As we ponder this idea I believe we will discover that God does not have to destroy those who destroy the earth. Why? We will destroy ourselves.

Let's set our intention today to be aware of our responsibility to tend and keep the earth, and not to rape it of all its resources and mistreat its creatures. The earth is the Lord's! The fullness is the Lord's. The creatures on the earth are the Lord's. Let us remember to treat it, and them, as such.

> **Prayer:** *"Mother Earth, today I will care, tend and keep you in a way that honors You and me. Amen."*

TRUTH IS A JOURNEY, NOT A DESTINATION

September 28

Climb the Right Wall

Affirmation
*"I am a powerful creator because divinity runs through me.
I bless my day and know that it will be successful."*

Have you ever heard that little story about the guy who climbs a ladder, rung by rung, very slowly and carefully, only to realize at the top that he had leaned his ladder against the wrong wall? The moral of the story is: you can put a lot of effort into getting to the top, but if it's the top of the wrong wall, all your work has been in vain.

The universe, as God created it, in its original, pure and uncorrupted state, vibrates on a certain frequency that is actually pretty high. So when we pray and ask for things, if we're praying or asking in a low vibration - like begging - the universe doesn't understand that language because our words are not a match for its frequency. Thus, our words create little or nothing.

You can "pray" in the low vibration of begging all night long for months on end. You can pray so hard you sweat drops of blood. But all that effort won't create what you're asking for because begging is not a vibrational match for the process of creation. It will just be wasted energy, like climbing a ladder leaned against the wrong wall.

When you pray from a position of power, knowing that what you are speaking is already done, your frequency automatically increases. This is how you sync up with the Divine Mind from which all creation emanates.

> **Prayer:** *"Omnipotent God, help me understand that because I am made in your image my words are powerful. I pray in the high frequency of knowing what I say will be done. Amen."*

Challenge Your Mind. Channel Your Power. Change Your Life.

September 29 — TRUTH IS A JOURNEY, NOT A DESTINATION

The IS-ness of God's Love

> ***Affirmation***
> *"I cannot earn or un-earn God's love. God's love is not a response or reaction to anything. God IS love. Nothing can separate me from God's love. Nothing can separate God from being God. And, nothing can keep God from being love. Today, I understand a mystery...that I have boldness in the day of judgment. Because as He is...so am I! Perfect love casts out fear. And today, I will allow my love to conquer any fear."*

1 John 4:8 tells us that *"God is love."* The key word here is *"IS."* Notice, the word here is *"IS,"* not *"DOES."* God doesn't love...God IS love. This means God's love for us flows out of His essence and nature. Love is the essence of God. We may perceive it as the action of God, but it does not come from God as an action. It emits from God as essence. So, God's love to us, and to all, is not an action, reaction or response to anything. This means, we cannot earn or un-earn God's love. God does not give or take away His love from us. The reason we cannot be separated from God's love is because God cannot be separated from God or detoured from being God. God's love is perfect because it cannot be recalled or retracted. And, our understanding of God's perfect love nature is what casts out our fear!

"In this is love, not that we loved God, but that He loved us" (1 John 4:10). We love God because God first loved us. Our love is a response. But, God's love to us is not a response. Our challenge is to learn to love like God... not as a response to love, but because love IS who we are! Jesus challenged the disciples to this level of love by instructing them to love their enemies, not just their family and friends who loved them. In other words, Jesus was saying, don't love as a response to being loved. Let love be your essence. This way, no person and no situation could ever change who you are. In every circumstance, you are always being you. Always being love! Just like God!

> ***Prayer:*** *"Perfect Love, give me the strength to become love. Today, I desire not only to love others. I want to be love. Amen."*

September 30

TRUTH IS A JOURNEY, NOT A DESTINATION

Two for the Price of One

Affirmation
"Today I willingly participate in divinely ordered interactions where I learn my lessons and allow others to learn theirs."

We're all here on earth to learn lessons, but we're not all learning the same lessons at the same time. We are almost always in the process of learning something new, developing an underused ability or talent, or toning down an overused one.

Sometimes we even cooperate with each others' lessons without even knowing that's what we're doing. For example, two people having an interaction with each other can be learning two different things from the same situation.

One person can be learning how to give and the other how to receive. One person can be learning how to stand up for themselves while the other is learning how to surrender; how to lose with grace, or the lesson of retreating in order to fight another day.

Understanding this helps us to be patient with the process. In the end, the pendulum settles comfortably in the center, balance is restored and each person learns the lesson they were meant to.

Prayer: *"God, My Teacher, help me to understand that I am not learning the same lessons as everyone else. I need only play my part in each interaction and not worry about another's lessons. If they are open and receptive, they will get what they need from the situation just as I will get what I need. I trust you today to be the divine orchestrator of my life. Amen."*

Challenge Your Mind. Channel Your Power. Change Your Life.

October 1

No Fear

Affirmation
"I create everything in my life."

I heard a story once of a woman talking about an experience she had while meditating. She was having quite an issue in her life with fear, so she decided she would try to talk to the fear as if it were a person while in meditation.

She asked it, "Why are you here?" And the only answer she got was, "I'm here because you created me." And then she asked it, "Why are you trying to hurt me?" And its reply was, "I'm not trying to hurt you. I'm just trying to survive."

That was a profound discovery for her. Her fear was her own creation. It was her child, as it were; she had given birth to it, had brought it to life, and manifested it with her imagination. Once created, it did what all creations strive to do - live!

In order to survive, it had to be fed. It had to be given fuel. When she realized it was not this evil, external entity out to get her, but merely a creation (of hers) trying to survive, it was completely up to her to continue feeding it, or to let it starve.

We know that we create with our thoughts, but what we might not realize, that once created, we need to learn how to be good parents to our creations because we are responsible for them. The most humane thing to do to those creations that are not serving our highest good is to put them out of their misery, which also ends ours.

We have the power not only to create, but to recreate again and again.

Prayer: *"Creative God, help me to realize that fear is something I can either create or destroy. Amen."*

FULLY AWAKE 365

NO FEAR

October 2

The Knowledge of Good and Evil

Affirmation
"Today I will not eat of the tree of the knowledge of good and evil. Instead, I will know that all things are from God, of God, through God, work for God, consist in God and will return to God. It's all good and all God."

Let's stay right here in the Garden of Eden metaphor. Whether there was an actual garden and a tree of knowledge with literal fruit really should not be our focus. I have witnessed, more than once, people debating whether the fruit Adam and Eve ate was an apple or a pomegranate. The truth is missed when we give our attention to arguing over where the garden was located and if there was actually a talking snake. The truth is in what all of these things represent. The garden is a place of innocence, peace and goodness. The tree of knowledge is the only thing threatening this divinely ordained existence. In this garden, all of the trees were good to eat from. The only forbidden tree was the one that made a judgment about the other trees or truths. Trees represent truths.

So, we could say all of the truths in the garden were good. The tree of knowledge represents the potential for religious division, disunity, dissension, discord and eventually destruction. We can apply this symbolism to every piece of our individual lives as well as the way we experience the world around us. Things happen to us (or through us) every day. They all have purpose (good) and can be significant in waking us up to our divine potential. Judging the experiences of our lives as bad causes a division of our minds, or double-mindedness. Furthermore, judging one tree (or truth, religion, philosophy, etc.) as evil only causes separation, breeds violence and forces us to leave the garden of peace. Unity with ourselves, harmony between religions and being at peace with God all begins with one choice…don't eat of the tree of the knowledge of good and evil.

Prayer: *"Eternal Good, open my eyes to see that all things are working together for my good. Amen."*

Challenge Your Mind. Channel Your Power. Change Your Life.

October 3

NO FEAR

Don't Be Afraid of the Dark

Affirmation
"God is equally the God of the light and of the dark."

The collective unconscious that exists in our present world has conditioned us to equate the darkness with evil, but that's not the truth. It's just a belief that can and certainly should be changed.

From the fairy tales we are told as children to the stories most of us are told from pulpits as adults, we are taught that God is good and is represented by the light. And Satan (or some evil character acting as a stand in for Satan) is bad and is represented by the dark.

But thinking of God as only good and only light is only half of the story. We always say: *God is good all the time.* But that's not really the whole truth. God is *ALL* all the time - which includes both the light and the dark. God is the God of both creation and destruction, birth and death. It is only our conditioning that teaches us to see half those things as good and the other half as evil instead of all of it being created and used by God for our ultimate good.

Think of a dark room. The same things are there whether the light is on or off. You just can't see them when it's dark. And that's where our fear comes in. Actually, the dark is where everything exists equally in its potential form. You can reach in and pull out whatever you want. The next time you are fearful, remember that, and don't be afraid of the dark!

Prayer: *"Source of All, help me realize today that you created all and are present in all. Therefore, I have no need to fear the dark. Amen."*

NO FEAR

October 4

Saved from God by Jesus?

Affirmation
"Today, I will be aware that I am not saved from God by Jesus. I am reconnected to God in consciousness through Jesus. God is at peace with me. And, I am at peace with God."

How many are "saved" by Jesus who never truly feel safe with God? Does Jesus save us from God? For most of my childhood I knew Jesus saved me, and yet I never felt safe. So, I got "saved" again every Sunday night. Then, when I went to school on Monday mornings and saw pretty girls in my classroom, I felt like I needed saving all over again. This type of torture leads to an unhealthy vision of God and to an unmanageable version of religion and reality.

As I grew in knowledge, I began to understand that the primary connection with God is not merely to achieve, or keep, salvation or to "make it in" to heaven, but rather to find peace of mind! I also began to accept the idea that Jesus was not different from the Father, but rather came to show us the Father. The disciples, like many of us, struggled to make the connection that Jesus was the expression, the incarnation of God. So, they asked Jesus to show them the Father. Jesus answered them,

> *"Have I been with you so long, and yet you have not known Me, Philip? He who has seen Me has seen the Father; so how can you say, 'Show us the Father?'"* (John 14:9)

Prayer: *"Incarnate God, today I am saved, safe and sane, as I settle into the knowing that I am not separated from Your love. Amen."*

Challenge Your Mind. Channel Your Power. Change Your Life.

October 5

NO FEAR

The Void Part I

> **Affirmation**
> "Today I will realize the beauty of the darkness and understand that both darkness and light are necessary parts of the creation process."

In the beginning of the biblical creation story there is darkness; an open space; a void. And God spoke into this darkness and created light. Think about how we all begin our human lives - in the darkness of our mother's womb. It's mysterious. Even with all the scientific knowledge we have today, we're still not exactly sure how everything that happens inside that womb takes place.

Our culture tends to view darkness as evil at worst, uncomfortable and scary at best, but it is actually the place of the greatest potential there is. In the light, you see everything as it is. You know what's there. But when it's dark, the potential for anything to be created still exists.

If you cling only to those things you can see in the light because you fear what might be in the dark, you will end up compromising yourself - being less of what you could be because you have given up all the possibility and potential that lies in the darkness of the void; the womb of creation. Light is born of darkness. So don't be afraid of the dark!

> **Prayer:** "God of the darkness, help me not to fear the dark times of uncertainty in my life, but know that it is only a time and a space for creation. Amen."

October 6

NO FEAR

The Void Part II

Affirmation
"Today I recognize the beauty of darkness and understand it as the completion of the light as well as its opposite."

God is often described as light. But God is much more than that. God is ALL. If we truly believe this, we must also accept the darkness, or dark side of God. At first, that concept sounds wrong to our ears because we live in a heavily Judeo-Christian influenced culture where we associate everything good with the light and tend to stay away from the dark because it is uncertain and sometimes frightening. However, because we live in a world of opposites, we can only know light in the context of its opposite - the dark.

In human terms, we also think of God as Father. But what is the other half of that? The feminine. Masculine characteristics are all about what is seen, and solid, and unchanging (represented by the light). Whereas feminine characteristics are changeable, mysterious and flow like water (represented by the dark). In order to create life, we know that we have to have contributions from both male and female. It is the union of the two that accomplishes this.

Once we have shifted our perspective of darkness from one of fear and dread to seeing it as the womb of all creation, we realize that it's just as easy to reach in and pull out joy, peace, love and abundance as it is to pull out the more negative aspects. It all depends on us and what level of vibration we choose to live on. When our vibration changes, our view of darkness does as well.

Prayer: *"Source of All, teach me today that darkness is not wrong or evil, but creative in nature. Amen."*

Challenge Your Mind. Channel Your Power. Change Your Life.

October 7

NO FEAR

Fear: Friend or Foe?

Affirmation
"Today I will not fear."

Fear is an energy, and as such, once created, it can never be destroyed, only transformed into some other form of energy. So getting rid of fear is really not an option. People often talk about conquering or overcoming fear - and you can look at it that way, but that's such an adversarial relationship to set up.

The energy of fighting anything is such a low vibration. But how can *not* fighting fear ever be a good thing? How can we bring dealing with our fear into a higher frequency? Let's begin with its purpose. If everything that's created serves a purpose, what is the purpose of fear; something that seemingly has no positive side or redeeming virtue?

Perhaps it exists to cause us to make a choice about how we're going to live our lives and what we're going to actively choose to focus on. When fear knocks on our door will we hide from it and cower in the shadows? Or will we focus a spotlight of love and truth on it? Will we give in to it? Or remember that the love within us is stronger, and live our lives from the strength of that divine love, which is the highest vibration that exists?

Fear cannot survive in the presence of pure love but it will not be transformed by us man-handling it and wrestling it to the ground, declaring victory over it in some sort of fight. All we have to do is stand firmly in our own divine light and love, never wavering from who and what we are.

> **Prayer:** *"Loving God, help me understand today that fighting fear will not get rid of it, but I can transform it through perfect love. Amen."*

October 8

NO FEAR

Divided by Language

Affirmation
"Today, I open my heart to connect with all of creation. I may speak a different language than a fellow human being. However, we can connect in Spirit."

Arguably, language (not culture, religion, country, gender, race or sexual orientation) is the ultimate dividing line between human beings. Being able to understand each other is the foundation for conversations that allow us to see different perspectives that carry the potential of achieving some level of common ground. Have you ever been in the presence of what seemed to be a very warm, friendly person, but were unable to connect because of a language barrier?

Growing up, I was a fan of the television show Sanford and Son. I loved the banter between Fred, Lamont, and of course Aunt Esther. Occasionally, a white police officer would come by Fred's house. After he spoke, his fellow black officer would interpret to Fred what the white officer was saying. It was humorous as well as telling. We can even speak the same language and not understand each other. This is the beauty of the Day of Pentecost. People from every nation, gathered together, hearing God speak to them all in a way that they could understand. When we speak in Spirit, love, peace, goodwill, we connect with each other in a way that is beyond language.

Prayer: *"God above language, teach me to speak in Spirit so that I may connect with all of Your creation. Amen."*

Challenge Your Mind. Channel Your Power. Change Your Life.

October 9

NO FEAR

The Sacred No

> *Affirmation*
> *"Today I will not be afraid to say no to anything that does not support the authentic life I am creating for myself."*

There should be balance in every part of our lives, and sometimes finding that balance involves saying *no*. It's always good, healthy and productive to accept the present moment as it is. But sometimes, after you've surveyed your present situation and accepted that's where you are, you realize you don't want to stay there. And that's perfectly ok.

Often, the first step to changing your current life circumstance is saying *no*, and doing that appropriately is every bit as sacred, helpful and productive as saying *yes*.

In order to say either, however, you must first find, and then use your authentic voice, which involves realizing who you are at your core. Once you truly know that, it is easier to say no to the things that are not supportive of the life you are creating for yourself. Get in the habit of asking yourself, "Does this support the life I'm trying to create?" If not, just say NO!

> **Prayer:** *"God of the Sacred No, help me to realize that saying no to certain things in my life is just as important to saying yes. Help me to find my authentic voice and then to use it to stay true to myself first and foremost. Amen."*

NO FEAR

October 10

Protected by an Enemy

Affirmation
"I'm at peace with my PAST. The lessons, the hurt, the relationships I've lost and gained have all worked together for my good. I release the hurt. I bless and forgive those who did not know what they were doing. I do not need closure or an apology to move forward with seeking and pursuing peace in my life. I embrace the wisdom I gained from difficult lessons. I know that I will not learn those lessons again. And, I am aware that what threatened me in the past might protect me in the future."

When David fought against Goliath he had only a sling-shot and a few stones. After striking a deadly blow, David went over to the slain giant and cut off his head, using Goliath's own sword. Gruesome, I know. I'm going somewhere. Several years later, David rushes into a battle. In his haste, he fails to take any weaponry with him. When he arrives to the battleground he asks his men if there is anything he could use to fight. One of his captains tells him all of the weapons are already spoken for. However, the sword of Goliath (used mostly as a memorial and symbol of remembrance) was not being used. David grabbed Goliath's sword and went into the battle. Here is the lesson: The very thing that had threatened David's life in the past was now protecting him in the present, and potentially the future.

What threatened you in the past that is now presently protecting you? What former enemy is now a current friend? An accusation? Legal situation? Divorce? Bankruptcy? Pride? Ambition? Along life's journey all of us will experience a brush with devastation, even arrive at the brink of disaster. We'll be threatened by various predicaments and vengeful people. When we come through these anxious encounters we are blessed with a gift. We carry the gift of wisdom we gained with us forever. The very thing that threatened to kill us in our past is now anxious to protect us in our present and future. Let it!

Prayer: *"God of peace and calamity, I will give thanks in everything…for my past enemies now stand watch as my present protectors. Amen."*

Challenge Your Mind. Channel Your Power. Change Your Life.

October 11

NO FEAR

Born to Stand Out

Affirmation
"Today I will understand the difference between belonging and fitting in."

A famous quote by Dr. Seuss is, *"Why fit in when you were born to stand out?"* As humans, we are social animals who, although capable of surviving alone - especially in this day and age - thrive when we cooperate with each other and figure out a way to harness the energy of an entire community. Also as humans, one of our biggest fears is of being alone, and so, one of our greatest drives is to *fit in* so that we will be accepted, valued and loved by our group or tribe.

But we must remember that there's a difference between *fitting in* and *belonging*. Paradoxically, the more you *try* to fit in, the less you actually belong, because the very act of trying to fit in means you *don't* already belong.

When something, a piece of clothing for instance, doesn't fit, you must alter it in some way to get it to fit. In order to fit in, you must alter yourself or become something you are not.

True belonging, on the other hand, never asks you to change the essence of who you are. In fact, it demands that you be exactly who you are and bring your unique gifts and talents to the group so that everyone can benefit from them.

Belonging is being a part of something bigger than yourself while at the same time having the courage to stand alone, belong to yourself first above all else, and to never betray yourself in order to just fit in.

Prayer: *"Unique God, help me be grateful today for all the ways I am unique and different, and show me how to use these for the benefit of my community. Amen."*

FULLY AWAKE 365

NO FEAR

October 12

Getting our Think, Say and Do in Harmony

Affirmation
"Today, I will align my thoughts, words and deeds to be in harmony. As my think, my say, and my do all agree, I will experience harmony and invite peace and happiness into my life."

"*Happiness is when what you think, what you say, and what you do are in harmony.*" ~ Mahatma Gandhi

All of us have been in an environment where we felt like an oddball. Some of us may feel this way in our family relationships. Being a stranger in your own house is a dynamic that creates an atmosphere of disdain and intolerance. Resentment is the ultimate destination when our thoughts and personality are diminished and pushed down. How can we find peace and happiness when we cannot be true to ourselves? We cannot! The courage to be true to our thoughts, authentic with our words, and purposefully intentional with our actions and choices is the only way to realize the inner harmony that manifests the outer peace.

At times, we must speak truth to power. Meaning, even though it may not be popular, truth, justice, and equity must find its voice through ours. However, we cannot perpetually live in environments of stress and strain. How do we find a sanctuary where our think, say and do can work in harmony? At first, that utopia may only exist within us as we remain true to ourselves. However, as our thoughts, words and deeds continue to vibrate in harmony, we will inevitably find our pace, space, vibe and tribe.

> **Prayer:** *"Harmonious Spirit, give me the courage to be true to my thoughts, the strength to speak my truth, and the wisdom to put my thoughts and words into harmonious action. Amen."*

Challenge Your Mind. Channel Your Power. Change Your Life.

October 13

NO FEAR

Learning Proportion

Affirmation
"Strong emotions are only useful as tools for our growth when we learn to use them proportionately."

Feeling the emotion of anger is not wrong in and of itself. It's what we do about it or as a result of it that usually gets us into trouble. If we can learn to feel the anger and then stop instead of reacting immediately, we are more likely to behave appropriately.

Many times we feel anger when we or someone we love has been mistreated. And that anger is a trigger telling us that some level of protection is needed. But it's important to respond not only appropriately, but proportionately so it doesn't get twisted into something destructive or over the top.

For instance, there's a roach in your house. Instead of stepping on it with your shoe you decide to pull out your shotgun. Shooting a rabid dog running loose in a neighborhood where kids are playing and other pets are out is quite a different thing than shooting it because it pooped on your lawn.

We must learn to apply only the force that's necessary to deal with a situation and not let the emotion of anger or any other emotion cause us to go overboard with our response. Let it be a signal that protection is needed, but don't let it spiral out of control into revenge or violence for its own sake.

Strong emotions are voices to be listened to, but softening around the initial impulse to react until you are more fully able to respond proportionately is a vital life skill.

Prayer: *"God of Protection, help me discern what the appropriate and proportionate response is when I am triggered by strong emotions. Amen."*

NO FEAR

October 14

Everything is Spiritual

Affirmation
"Today, I relinquish the need to separate sacred and secular, laughter and prayer, holy and fun. I choose to see everything and every moment as spiritual."

Prayer. Study. Devotion. Worship. Mediation. Service to others. All spiritual. Right? But what about laughter? Joy? Nature? Fun? The song "Bridge Over Troubled Waters?" Are these things not spiritual? Are they somehow less spiritual than church related expressions?

When we finally arrive in the place of peaceful surrender, there is a knowing that *"the earth is the Lord's, the people who dwell in it, and the fullness thereof."* (Psalm 24:1-3 KJV) Here we begin to understand that it's all good and all God. A dog's joyful greeting when you walk into your home after a long day. The laughter shared between two lovely souls. A beautiful Jazz piece written by Thelonious Monk…thank you Jesus…it's all spiritual. Everything is spiritual.

When we see creation in this way we experience the Creator in a more sustainable, experiential, and expansive way. Don't be afraid to celebrate and connect with everything in creation.

***Prayer:** "Creator of All, today I will worship ALL OF YOU! In my prayers, devotion and service to others, I will worship You. When I behold the beauty of nature, the laugh of a child, the smile on a dog's face…I will worship You. Everything is spiritual to me today. Amen."*

Challenge Your Mind. Channel Your Power. Change Your Life.

October 15

NO FEAR

Beyond The Reef

> ***Affirmation***
> *"Today I will feel the fear and do it anyway."*

In the Disney movie *Moana*, the main character is the daughter of the chief who is being groomed by her father to some day rule the people of the island they live on. As she gets older, the people start seeking her out more and more to solve their problems. One day a group of fishermen come to her with the news that they have tried all the usual places, but there are no fish to be caught. Shortly after that, the women tell her the coconut crop has failed, leaving them with no source of food.

Her father has made a rule, for her own protection, that she not go past a certain point in the sea, but she knows she must do so in order to save her people. Her argument is *"But Father, there are more fish beyond the reef."*

So she goes, and indeed, it's not an easy journey. It tests her and pushes her to her absolute limit. There are even times she thinks she's not going to make it back home. But she doesn't give up, and is successful in the end.

Sometimes the things you want in life can be found only *beyond the reef*, outside your comfort zone and will require you to give until you feel there's nothing more to give; to dig deeper than you think is even possible. But when you do, it's such a great feeling that you might never have known if you'd never tried.

> **Prayer:** *"God of Perseverance, help me have the strength and courage today to follow my dreams even when it requires more of me than I think I am capable of. Amen."*

NO FEAR

October 16

Behind the Scenes

Affirmation
"Today, I am aware that God's ways are higher than my ways. I cannot always see what's going on behind the scenes. However, I trust that all things are working together for my good and that I will understand God's plan someday. Until then, I will be of a good report, meditate on positive thoughts and maintain a high vibration. It's all good and all God!"

Whether we are facing a worldwide pandemic like the Coronavirus or struggling through the pain of losing a loved one, all of us have experienced moments where we are left searching for answers. Imagine Joshua's dilemma, being told by God to march around the walls of Jericho (without weapons) playing trumpets and praising God until the walls collapse. Put yourself in Gideon's shoes as he is facing an army of 300,000 men. God tells him all he needs is 300 weaponless men, running around and making noise with lanterns. Consider Moses being commissioned by God to tell Pharaoh *"let My people go"* and then God hardening Pharaoh's heart so that he wouldn't let the people go. Wouldn't it be nice to get a glimpse behind the scenes and into the mind of God?

In Isaiah 45:7 we get a little peek behind the scenes… *"I form the light and create darkness, I make peace and create calamity; I, the Lord, do all these things."* God can and does use what we perceive as evil for good! The walls of Jericho fell. Gideon won the war. Moses and the children of Israel escaped the bondage of Egypt with enough silver and gold to finance their next season. We may not always understand what's going on in difficult moments. However, in time, as we see the beauty of God's sovereignty unfolding, pushing us toward our highest and greatest good, we will be able to accept that God is good and desires good things for us.

Prayer: *"Sovereign God, strengthen me today to walk by faith and not by sight. Even when I cannot see behind the scenes, I will rest in the knowledge that You have wonderful plans for me. Amen."*

Challenge Your Mind. Channel Your Power. Change Your Life.

October 17

NO FEAR

The Treasure You Seek

Affirmation
"I will connect with my eternal, divine nature today."

Scientifically, the bumble bee should not be able to fly because the weight of its body is too much for its small wings to support. But guess what? No one told the bumble bee that, and it doesn't let its mind get involved. All it knows is that in order to do its job, it must be able to fly from flower to flower - so - it flies!

One of the big reasons we struggle within ourselves is because on a purely cellular, energetic level, we know who we are and what we came here to do, but we let our minds get in the way of that, and we give our power away to others who tell us we're not capable of doing what we know we're supposed to.

Our eternal, divine self knows things that cannot be explained on the mental plane and that our mind is afraid of. A famous quote by the poet Rumi says: *It's the cave that you fear to enter that holds the treasure you seek.*

Finding a way to get past our mental fear helps us to strip away the layers that have been covering up who we really know ourselves to be at our core and helps us to remember how to exist in a field of energy and personal power that is far greater than anything the mind can conceive.

That field is where we came from and where we will someday return, but we can and must live in it *now* if we are to do what we came here to do.

Prayer: *"Fearless God, help me tap into my divine power today instead of listening to the fear in my mind. Amen."*

NO FEAR

October 18

Who Created the Devil?

Affirmation
"Today I recognize that a man-made devil can hold no power over those who remain in perfect love."

Whether or not we want to admit it, most Christian churches unknowingly participate in "devil worship" every Sunday. How? Simply by the reverence they give his power. Many Christians are legitimately afraid of "the devil" - and you can't be afraid of something unless you believe it has the power to harm you or that there is a possibility you might be overcome by it. If you know it cannot, there is no fear.

This comes from thousands of years of mankind's dualistic thinking which separates the darkness from the light rather than believing they complete each other. We have separated the two and assigned goodness (God) to the light and evil (the devil) to the darkness. We run from the darkness (devil) because we fear it. But the Bible tells us how to deal with this when it reminds us that perfect love casts out fear.

Although God created the darkness, he did so to serve the light. Darkness is not the equal of light and will never overcome the light. This is made clear over and over again in the scriptures. Understanding that God uses all of it to work out what is ultimately best for us removes the fear of the darkness, and therefore of the entity we have created to represent it - the devil.

> **Prayer:** *"Source that is All, help me to understand that you are the God of both the darkness and the light and that there is no separation in you. I cannot fear a man-made entity known as the devil as long as I am living and walking in your perfect love. Amen."*

Challenge Your Mind. Channel Your Power. Change Your Life.

October 19

NO FEAR

Unexpected Vessels

> ***Affirmation***
> *"Today, I acknowledge that God works in mysterious ways. My systems of thought may not exactly be parallel with God's thoughts. I will allow God to be God."*

Have you ever wondered why God seems to work through the least likely people? What a litany of unexpected vessels and biblical characters we have for our perusal.

Moses, born with a speech impediment, fleeing from a death sentence and as a Hebrew under oppression, delivers his people from four hundred years of bondage and away from the mighty Egyptian empire. David, a lowly shepherd, young and untrained in the ways of war, slays a giant and is anointed King of Israel. Then, revolutionizes temple for generations to come. Rahab, a prostitute, is used by God to hide Hebrew spies, is spoken of in a complimentary fashion by Jesus, and is listed in the genealogy of Jesus. Mary Magdalene, portrayed as a sinful woman caught in the act of adultery, becomes the confidant of Jesus and the first Gospel evangelist. Peter, denies Jesus three times and is then chosen to preach on the Day of Pentecost, the most historic day in the early days of a forming Christian church. Paul (formerly Saul of Tarsus) becomes a voice for Christ even after murdering Christians for their profession of faith.

Is there something in your past that you have thought might disqualify your future? All of us have struggled with not feeling good enough. When those feelings arise, remind yourself of the vessels God has used in the past and surrender to the truth that your future could never be forfeited by your past.

> **Prayer:** *"God of Surprises, I give thanks today that Your Spirit flows around, in, through and as all of us. I may be an unexpected vessel to some, but not to You! Amen."*

NO FEAR

October 20

Focusing on the Good

Affirmation
"Today I will do justice, love kindness and walk humbly before my God." (Micah 6:8)

It's not always the case, but most of the time, you'll find that people are doing the best they can with the information that's available to them, and when they know better, they do better. But getting people to know better is accomplished much more easily when you focus on their good rather than confronting them with their ignorance and demanding that they "do better."

Certain villages in Africa keep order in this way. When any member of the tribe disobeys a rule or does something hurtful to someone else, the elders of the tribe sit the person in the center of the village and the entire village surrounds him or her in a circle.

Each person says something kind about the person or something good they remember they have done in the past. By the time everyone has finished, the perpetrator has usually broken down in tears, apologized for whatever offense has been committed and promised to make restitution.

They don't incarcerate people or string them up with a rope and let their victim or victim's families exact revenge as is the custom in some cultures - an eye for an eye. They simply remind the person of the good inside them - of the God inside them, and help them focus on that.

Prayer: *"God of Divine Justice, help me to understand true justice is more about mercy and less about punishment. Let my goal always be to remind others of the good and of the God inside them, for this will change their behavior quicker than anything else. Amen."*

Challenge Your Mind. Channel Your Power. Change Your Life.

October 21

NO FEAR

Don't Say It

> ***Affirmation***
> *"Today, I will be conscious of the thoughts I think and of the words I speak. I will declare words of power, potentiality and possibility."*

We find several stories in the Bible where God calls on someone for a mission or assignment. Often times in their response we discover a sort of disclaimer or apology because of how unqualified they feel they are for the assignment. Moses alerts God that he has a speech impediment, and that his brother Aaron would be better fit for speaking with Pharaoh. Jeremiah reminds God that he is only a youth and cannot speak truth to the people. Isaiah confesses that he is a man of unclean lips and has been disqualified from speaking for God. In each instance, God responds, don't say that.

To Moses, God says "*I will go with you!*" (Exodus 33:14) To Jeremiah, God says "*Don't say you are just a youth. I will put My words in your mouth.*" (Jeremiah 1:7) To Isaiah, God doesn't say anything. Even better! God takes a hot coal out of the fire and places it in Isaiah's mouth. Then God says, "*I have sanctified your tongue.*" (Isaiah 6:7)

We are more amazing and powerful than we could ever imagine. Whatever faults or frailties we may perceive to have could never stand in the way of Spirit working through us. "Greater is He that is in you, than he that is in the world." God will do "exceedingly, abundantly, more than we could ask or think, according to the power working in us." There is a power working in us that is far greater than anything working against us. Until this revelation takes root in your spirit…Don't say anything!

> **Prayer:** *"Word of God, empower me to see myself as You see me… powerful, more than able, well equipped. And, until I can see me as You see me, remind me to keep quiet. Amen."*

NO FEAR

October 22

Effective Communication

Affirmation
"Today I will be genuinely curious, unafraid and will strive for empathy in my conversations."

Have you ever heard the statement: the best way to avoid a misunderstanding is to have an understanding? That's true. It's always good to remember that people aren't mind readers. We don't and can't know what others are thinking unless they tell us. But it's important sometimes how and what we ask. There's a line between expressing healthy curiosity and being intrusive.

Here are some tips:

1. **Be genuinely curious** - Many people want to talk about the experiences that have shaped them, even if those experiences are painful, but won't unless they're asked. And usually, those who won't talk are the ones who need to most.
2. **Be unafraid** - Don't be afraid to ask the obvious question even if you think it might make you look stupid. Sometimes it still needs to be asked in order to begin communication.
3. **Strive for empathy** - Often the best conversations are when you're speaking with someone who has a completely different story and experience from your own. When you strive for empathy, you're reaching across that difference and putting yourself in that person's shoes. This leads to productive, open hearted communication.

Beginning communication with someone can be intimidating, but also rewarding. The worst that can happen is for them to tell you to mind your own business. The best thing that can happen is they open up to you and you learn something that's helpful in your own life, or you make a new friend. Or perhaps your conversation will lead to them requesting help that they need but have not had the courage to ask for.

Prayer: *"God of Fraternity, help me today be an instrument for effective, helpful communication with my brothers and sisters. Amen."*

Challenge Your Mind. Channel Your Power. Change Your Life.

October 23

NO FEAR

Saving and Spending

> ***Affirmation***
> *"Today, I will endeavor to find a healthy balance between saving and spending. I will set my intention to plan for the future and be spontaneous in the present. I will choose to enjoy my life now and be at peace about what tomorrow may bring."*

Can we find a balance between saving and spending? Many people seem to be caught up in an extreme of either/or…all or nothing. My parents recounted a story to me about a wealthy church member and his financial practices. He was not contributing to the church financially. So, they went to visit him to see if they could figure out where the disconnect might exist. When they arrived at his house, the heat was turned off in the dead of winter, and the lights were off after dark. They jokingly relayed that this millionaire was walking in his cold house with a flashlight. When he died, his children were estranged from him and cared only about what monies they might inherit. Sad indeed. I could also offer a story of a friend who struggled with managing a workable budget. This friend called me one day and said, "God has shown up! I just got another credit card in the mail and I won't have to cancel my trip to Paris." Scary indeed.

If we save every penny we never enjoy our lives, we fail to invest in worthy causes, and we likely will die with our money and no loved ones there to mourn our passing. If we spend every penny we will constantly be in need of God to "show up" and will inevitably live a life of disorder and chaos. Save for retirement. Go on an occasional vacation. Cook most meals at home. And, enjoy going out to eat here and there. Finding the balance between saving and spending might help to maintain your sanity…and your friends and family.

> ***Prayer:*** *"Trustworthy God, thank you for giving me the power to get wealth, and for granting me the wisdom to manage it. Strengthen me to be a saver and a giver. Amen."*

October 24

NO FEAR

Our Love Affair With the Supernatural

Affirmation
"Today I will look beyond the 3-dimensional reality of my five senses and connect with the supernatural force that is God."

The word *supernatural* has a very broad meaning, but technically, it refers to any manifestation or event attributed to a force beyond scientific understanding or the laws of nature.

Once we reached the point in history where we had scientific explanations and technological solutions for the inexplicable events and unsolvable problems that confronted and confounded Medieval man, the expectation was that belief and interest in all things supernatural would diminish in favor of logic and rationalism. But that hasn't happened.

Seemingly, the more we go down the road of technological advancement, the more we need the supernatural. Why? Because it is inherently timeless and cross-cultural. What other concept shares those characteristics? Eternity.

We are still interested in the supernatural because our spirits are eternal, and somewhere deep inside, we are aware of this. We long to return to a place that is timeless and where all people and cultures are one. That's heaven. That's being one with God, our creator.

That's where we came from before we entered our earthly bodies and it's where we will always be drawn back to. It is a place beyond time and beyond all our scientific, rational explanations. And that's why interest in the supernatural will never disappear.

We instinctively know there's something more. There is something beyond our present reality. And we want to be a part of it.

> **Prayer:** *"Timeless God, help me not get so invested in the rational world of things I can see, hear, taste, touch and feel that I disregard the unseen realm, for that is where you dwell. Amen."*

Challenge Your Mind. Channel Your Power. Change Your Life.

October 25

NO FEAR

Disappointments, Expectations, and Projections

Affirmation
"Today, I will not project my happiness onto future events. My only expectation of the future is to be fully awake and firmly aware of the power that only exists in the now."

How many of us have been plagued with a lifetime of disappointment? Does it feel like a pattern? One disappointment after another? Disappointments come from projecting expectations onto the future events. Sometimes those events are societal, social, corporate events. Other times, future events are affected by specific individuals in our lives on whom we project our expectations. When happiness is at the mercy of anything, or anyone, outside of ourselves, we will be continually disappointed. People will let us down. Events do not always turn out to be what we thought they might be. Furthermore, when we place the expectation of happiness outside of the now and present moment we are setting ourselves up for a let-down.

Jesus encouraged the disciples not to give an overabundance of thought to the future:

> *"Therefore, do not worry about tomorrow, for tomorrow will worry about its own things. Sufficient for the day is its own trouble."* (Matthew 6:34)

People will let us down. We will let others down. Events will not be as grand as we imagined they would be. Plans will be changed or even cancelled. The only expectation we should be projecting into the future is that we will be strong enough to adjust to our new reality and awake enough to create the reality we desire.

Prayer: *"Ever-Present Peace, give me the wisdom to never surrender my happiness to anything outside of myself, to anyone other than me or to any time other than right now. Amen."*

NO FEAR

October 26

Daring to Do the Impossible

Affirmation
"Today I will dare to believe I can break through the energetic barrier that surrounds the idea that something is impossible."

Everything is energy. And everything has an energy to it; an energy that surrounds it - especially things that people feel are impossible. The energy associated with the statement: "this is impossible" is very strong. But once one person actually does it, this seems to break the energetic barrier and lots of people then begin to do it because the energy of *impossible* has magically dissolved.

Ever since 1886 professional runners had been chasing the goal of running a mile in less than 4 minutes, but no one could do it. Then in 1954, British runner, Roger Bannister, crashed through the barrier, breaking the *impossible energy* that surrounded it and paving the way for many other runners to do the same, which they have - over and over since then.

Most interestingly, Bannister did it in a way that was counterintuitive to how all the experts believed it could be done. He didn't follow any of their suggestions.

Sometimes all it takes is one person to be that lone wolf, that unconventional thinker who doesn't accept the limitations everyone else is willing to accept in order to break through an energetic barrier and do something others think is impossible.

If you have the courage and the tenacity to be that one person, you can redefine what is possible, not only for yourself, but for everyone else as well.

Prayer: *"Empowering God, please help me to know that the Christ in me can do the impossible! Amen."*

Challenge Your Mind. Channel Your Power. Change Your Life.

October 27

NO FEAR

Dealing With Loss

> ### Affirmation
> *"Today, I am aware that I will deal with grief in this lifetime. I am grateful for the many voices and opinions offering me a way to grieve. However, I must grieve in the way that works for me."*

If we are fortunate to live long enough, we will experience the misfortune of losing a loved one. A big part of being a minister is assisting families in times of death and loss. I have facilitated hundreds of funerals. The one common denominator is that no two funerals are exactly the same. The prayers may be similar. The scriptures may be identical. The songs may even be exactly the same. However, the people who are grieving are all very different.

We all grieve. However, there is no such thing as "one size fits all" with grief. Every person grieves differently. Some people grieve immediately when a loved one passes. Others are not quite ready to grieve. Some people are very emotional at funerals and family gatherings. While others are very introspective and quiet. Some experience emotions of deep sorrow and loss. Still others become angry and wrestle with unanswered questions.

People are always ready to offer their opinions. And, most really mean well. But, when the service is over and they have all left the repass, you are left alone to grieve. Do it your way! Feel it. Resist it. Magnify it. Deny it. There are ways that seem healthier than others. Yet, each person must decide how to grieve. The only question that ever matters is…Is This Working For Me? Join a grief recovery group. Go on a long vacation. There many approaches. Find what works for you and retain your agency by creating your own grief recovery plan.

> **Prayer:** *"Comforting Spirit, thank you for abiding with me in my time of grief. Give me the courage to walk the path of loss in a way that cultivates my highest and best self. Amen."*

FULLY AWAKE 365

NO FEAR

October 28

Living in Integrity

Affirmation
"Today I will act from a place of integrity and encourage others to do the same."

Integrity is one of those words we say a lot, but do we really know what it means? Could we articulately define it if asked? According to author and researcher, Brené Brown, integrity can be broken down into 3 simple concepts.

1. Choosing courage over comfort
2. Choosing what's right over what's fun, fast or easy
3. Practicing your values, not just professing them

Let's break those down a little further with some specific examples. It's not always comfortable to stop someone from telling you something you know they shouldn't be sharing with you because it violates someone else's confidence, especially if it's a juicy piece of gossip you'd really like to hear. But the courageous thing to do is to stop it in its tracks.

It's also not comfortable to stand up for what you know is right when no one else around you seems to be doing so. It's more fun to run with the crowd, or take the easy way out. But deep inside, living in your integrity means doing and saying the right thing - even when you're the only one.

What about your values? You say you value helping those in need. So... have you ever volunteered at a homeless shelter? You say you value your family. Do you spend the majority of your free time with them? Or engaging in activities with friends instead? Living in integrity is *practicing* your values, not just professing them.

> **Prayer:** *"Source of Integrity, help me to understand that my relationship with others as well as the respect I have for myself is built largely on my personal integrity. Give me the courage today to choose integrity above all else. Amen."*

Challenge Your Mind. Channel Your Power. Change Your Life.

October 29

NO FEAR

No Weapon

> ***Affirmation***
> *"What has not killed me has only made me stronger. The pressures in my life have only served to reveal my inner power. What my enemies meant for my demise, God has used for my good. Every failure and mistake are now important pieces of my wisdom. There are no weapons formed against me. There are only opportunities to grow and evolve."*

There is a scene in the movie *The Matrix* where a young child is effortlessly bending a spoon using only his mind. Neo, the main character and protagonist, asks the child how this is possible. The child responds, "Try to realize the truth…there is no spoon." In other words, I have power over this spoon because I know it doesn't exist. In spiritual terms, the material world is an illusion and at very least temporary or passing away. What if we could apply this same principle when dealing with perceived evil in our lives?

God enlightens Isaiah to this concept, *"See, it is I who created the blacksmith who fans the coals into flame, and forges a weapon fit for its work. And it is I who have created the destroyer to wreak havoc; no weapon forged against you will prevail"* (Isaiah 54:16-17). So, God created the creator of the weapon, the user of the weapon and indirectly the weapon itself. What does all of this mean? Maybe the truth is…there is no weapon. Perhaps what we have perceived as weapons in our lives were actually God ordained catalysts pushing us into our next season? The devil tested Jesus in the wilderness and Jesus came out of this testing stronger and prepared for His ministry. Paul had a *"thorn in his flesh"* that he called a *"messenger of Satan."* This thorn enabled Paul to remain humble enough to continue authoring the majority of the New Testament. What if the things we have been cursing are actually working together for our benefit?

> **Prayer:** *"God all by Yourself, I give thanks in everything knowing all life and existence flows from You. No weapon can prosper against me because there is no weapon. Amen."*

October 30

Have the Conversation

Affirmation
"Today I will have the courage to have conversations with people rather than rushing to judgment."

It's surprising how often we expect people to read our minds and know exactly what they did that hurt us. But the mature thing to do instead is to let them know what they've done to cause you pain - even if you think they should know - and go from there.

Did they say or do it jokingly? Is it possible they didn't mean it the way you took it? Perhaps they don't even realize you were offended. Ask them. It's amazing how quickly a simple, direct question can clear things up sometimes. Often, how someone reacts to you in the moment has nothing to do with you and everything to do with what's currently going on with them. If so, a conversation is an open door for them to talk about it with you.

In the absence of having a conversation, go to their history. Look at their track record of past behavior with you. Does this seem like something that's in their nature to do or say? Have they ever treated you this way before? If not, you can probably dismiss it pretty quickly.

If so, all the more reason to have a conversation and say something like, "This has become a pattern with you and it's really hurtful to me." Once you've made that clear to them, it's their decision whether they continue the behavior or change it. But if it's never brought to their attention, they can never change it.

Prayer: *"God of Harmonious Relationships, help me to have kind and loving conversations with those who hurt my feelings, giving them a chance to make things right and adjust their behavior if necessary. Amen."*

Challenge Your Mind. Channel Your Power. Change Your Life.

October 31

NO FEAR

The Thing I Feared The Most

> ***Affirmation***
> *"Today, I will be aware that my thoughts become my reality. I will bring my thoughts into captivity by resisting lower mentalities of fear and scarcity and by resting in the higher modalities of love and joy."*

"What Job feared the most came upon him." (Job 3:25 KJV) The story of Job is full of loss, sickness, betrayal and misfortune. Job's epic is so well-known that even people who do not attend church refer to their own difficulties as "the trials of Job." Yet, many times we fail to remember that all of Job's trials ultimately brought him to greater blessing, deeper awareness and more authentic relationships.

Attempts to avoid evil can range from refusing to watch a horror film to not walking under a ladder. Today's devotion is not about promoting scary movies or belittling superstitions. Today is about being aware of the power of our thoughts. What we think about, we bring about. If we are constantly thinking about not thinking about something, aren't we thinking about it? What we resist persists. What we fight we ignite. Whatever we make the issue becomes the idol. How do we escape the repeating cycles brought about by thought resistance?

We simply relax! Relax knowing that God is good. Relax in the truth that there is only One Power in this universe and it is working in, through, for and as us. Relax and watch a scary movie, or not. Relax and be aware of thoughts of fear and lack, and then let them pass through you. Relax when you cough or feel achy knowing that it may be a cold or even Covid or that it might just be a scratchy throat. But, be diligent to not allow your thoughts to become persistent anxiety.

> ***Prayer:*** *"Manifesting Thought, empower me with greater awareness of my thoughts. Enable me to manifest love and joy by relaxing and taking a deep breath. Amen."*

GRATITUDE

November 1

The Pee-Pee Prayer

Affirmation
"Today, I will think and thank from a higher vibration. I will think first, thank second and only ask as a last resort. I will count it all joy when I remember where God has brought me from. I will live, think, thank and speak from a place of power. As I give thanks IN all things, I am also declaring my healing FROM all things, and then navigating my way THROUGH all things!"

One of my mentors is famous for saying, "a thinking man is a thanking man." In other words, when we stop to think, we all have something to be thankful for. How do we live in a vibration of thanksgiving and approach life with an attitude of gratitude after we lose a job? Endure a painful divorce? When we have more bills than money? There are different levels of gratitude. At times, we must give thanks for life's journey, even when some of the pieces of our journey may be temporarily out of sync. I have noticed when I give thanks in one area of my life it becomes contagious and begins to affect other areas of my life. This is how vibration works. When you begin to raise your vibration in one area of your life it has a powerful effect on other areas of your life. So, get happy and see what happens! Or, don't wait 'til the battle's over…shout now!

I also like to give thanks for small things or things that might be easily taken for granted. Every morning I try to wake up in gratitude. When I wake up, I give thanks for being alive. I give thanks for being in my right mind. I give thanks for my lungs and for the breath in my body (especially after I brush my teeth). It may seem strange, but each morning when I use the restroom, I give thanks that my kidneys are working properly. Dr. Michael Beckwith talks about this in his book *Spiritual Liberation*. He refers to this as the "Pee-Pee Prayer." Sure it sounds silly. Yet, it is a good way to begin each day with thanksgiving rather than in stress, worry and anxiety.

Prayer: *"Fountain of Blessings, thank you for breath, life, health, strength and for a sound mind. Amen."*

Challenge Your Mind. Channel Your Power. Change Your Life.

November 2

GRATITUDE

The Butterfly Effect

> **Affirmation**
> *"Today I will share God's love with everyone I encounter. I will practice random acts of kindness in order to begin a contagion of goodness and grace."*

If you've never heard of the butterfly effect, it's basically the idea that very small things can have a big effect in a complex system. An example would be the flapping of a butterfly's wings beginning a chain of events that eventually results in a typhoon halfway across the world.

Frequently, we don't think what we are doing counts or makes much difference because it's so small. But we so often underestimate the value of one simple act of kindness and the lasting effect it can have on a person's life.

An unsolicited favor, a phone call, or even just a smile can make someone's day and help lift the burden they may be carrying. Kindness is contagious. We never know what one gesture, no matter how small we think it is, may inspire. Don't ever let the size of your gift stop you from doing something for someone. Little is much, if it's done with love. We are all extensions of God's love, grace and kindness here on earth.

> **Prayer:** *"God of small moments, help me to be your hands extended today and share whatever I have, although it may be little, with others. Amen."*

GRATITUDE

November 3

Honoring Our Ancestors

Affirmation
"Each day is a gift from God. As I honor each day, each moment, each breath I am consciously living in gratitude. The best way for me to honor those who have transitioned too early is for me to make the most of my time on earth. I will honor the people in my life who have passed away by gleaning wisdom from the lessons they taught me through their journey."

At some point during our earth journey, we will attend a funeral, memorial service or home-going celebration and grieve the loss of someone we knew and loved. Unfortunately, there are times we say goodbye to someone who we perceived passed away too soon or left unfinished business undone and purpose unrealized. We walk away feeling not only the grief of losing a loved one but also struggle with the regret that this person may have never fulfilled their life's destiny. There is an old saying "The graveyard is the wealthiest place on earth." In other words, many people with endless potential carry this wealth with them to the grave.

How do we honor their deaths? More importantly, how do we honor their lives? What if their lack of accomplishment, their mistakes and missteps, their incomplete journeys and the wealth they carried with them to the graveyard can actually serve a greater purpose? More than dedicating buildings to them or hanging their pictures in hallways, we can honor their lives and their deaths by soaking in the lessons they taught us. You may say "I don't remember them ever specifically teaching me any lesson." However, their successes and their failures are the unspoken lessons they leave to us as an inheritance and as an assignment. As we navigate our journeys using the wisdom of the lessons they left for us to utilize, we are bestowing upon them the highest of all honors.

Prayer: *"Giver of Life, enable me to honor all life by learning, and then living, the lessons left to me by my loved ones and ancestors. Today, I honor their passing by my living. Amen."*

Challenge Your Mind. Channel Your Power. Change Your Life.

November 4

GRATITUDE

What We Know Is What We Owe

Affirmation
"Today I understand that what I know is what I owe."

Many philosophers say our curiosity is what separates humans from the rest of the animal kingdom - our ability to wonder about things like where we came from, what our purpose is while we're here, how we're supposed to treat each other, and where we're going when we leave here.

One of the questions we inevitably ask ourselves as we journey through this life is: *What do we owe our fellow human beings? Our creator? What is our part to give?*

Returning to our comparison to animals, most of them spend the majority of their time and energy getting what they need in order to survive. But the absolute beauty of nature is that each animal serves its own purpose and performs certain functions that contribute to the ecosystem that surrounds it.

But this is not something they contemplate. They just follow their God-given instincts and their contribution is automatic. We, however, can make conscious choices about our actions. And we can also step back and see the bigger picture of history as a whole and realize that there were those who came before us who passed the baton to us. And at some point, we, too, will pass the baton. We will not get it all done in our lifetime.

Whatever knowledge we have acquired through our life lessons, that's what we owe to the big picture of life - to pass on to those coming after us. It's our responsibility to share the part of this life we know best. That's how we make our mark on the world.

Prayer: *"Eternal God, help me know how to both receive knowledge from my predecessors and share it with my descendants. Amen."*

November 5

GRATITUDE

The Courage, Challenge, Charge and Choice to Live Authentically Part I

Affirmation
"Today, I will awaken the courage, accept the challenge, receive the charge and make the choice to be my true, authentic self… no matter how many people it upsets."

How many of us have made the choice to live inauthentically at one time or another? Is there any nuance between selling out and being *"all things to all people?"* (I Corinthians 9:19-23) And, where is the line of demarcation? What is the impact if, and when, you grew tired of the façade? There are people who consciously practice being authentic. There are people who consciously choose to be disingenuous. Then, there are the rest of us who are authentic on some days and not so authentic on other days.

The prospect of living in perfect authenticity can make us feel both hopeful and fearful. Hopeful because being real is craveable, valuable. Fearful because living authentically can be a huge undertaking, shifting, shaking, and even shattering what we have accepted as our norm. Let's take one bite of this elephant by developing a working definition of authenticity:

> *Authenticity is the daily practice of letting go of who we think we're supposed to be and embracing who we are.* [*]

If we want friends we must be friendly. If we want authentic friends we must become authentic ourselves. Refuse the fear. Shun the shame. Forego the guilt. Do you. Be you. No one else can but you!

> **Prayer:** *"Authentic Spirit, strengthen me to be exactly, authentically, unashamedly, unapologetically, who You created me to be. Amen!"*

---

[*] Brown, Brené. The Gifts of Imperfection.

Challenge Your Mind. Channel Your Power. Change Your Life.

November 6

GRATITUDE

The Courage, Challenge, Charge and Choice to Live Authentically Part II

> *Affirmation*
> *"I am ready to bravely own my story. I accept myself, my imperfections and my uniqueness. I will find the courage to be vulnerable, honest and open."*

In Brené Brown's book *The Gifts of Imperfection*, we discover a ubiquitously recurring theme in each lesson: what we perceive as an imperfection, mistake or misstep, can be transmuted into gifts. These gifts are courage, vulnerability, compassion, empathy and connection.

When we embrace our story, and muster the courage to share it, we unearth a wealth of natural resources within. In these vulnerable moments, we tap into compassion for others who may be struggling with shame and guilt from their past mistakes. This compassion opens and facilitates the space necessary to make connection with others.

This recipe of authenticity nurtures new, real relationships that are built and sustained through honesty and openness:

- *Cultivating the courage to be imperfect and to allow ourselves to be vulnerable.*
- *Exercising the compassion that comes from knowing that we are all made of strength and struggle.*
- *Nurturing the connection and sense of belonging that can only happen when we believe that we are enough.*

We have all struggled with guilt, shame and embarrassment from our less than best moments. When we own our story, we invite a new experience of life, we discover the amazing gifts hidden within our imperfections.

> **Prayer:** *"Sovereign God, today I give thanks for the gifts that are revealed even in my shame. I am grateful that all things are working together for my good. Amen."*

GRATITUDE

November 7

Living Our Love

Affirmation
"Today I will make it a point to take more notice of people in need, and do what I can to bring a moment of joy into their lives."

Recent studies coming out of Great Britain have shown that there are as many as 9 million people in that country alone, many of them elderly, who admitted they regularly go for as long as a month at a time without having a conversation with another human being. In fact, in 2018, the United Kingdom appointed as a legitimate governmental office, the Minister of Loneliness because it was considered to have risen to the level of a public health crisis. And this was BEFORE the pandemic.

Sometimes we need to check in with ourselves and just ask, "Am I being a good neighbor?" "Am I even behaving as a decent human being?" If the answer is not a resounding yes, then we should all recommit ourselves to making it a goal to simply check in more frequently with those around us.

Let's determine to look up from our phones a bit more often and speak to a stranger, even if it's just the briefest of greetings or a smile or making eye contact while passing. Let's not be a part of escalating the loneliness crisis. Let's live our love.

Prayer: *"God of Compassion, help me to be your hands and feet, your arms and heart in physical form on this earth. Help me share the love inside with those around me who need it most today. Amen."*

Challenge Your Mind. Channel Your Power. Change Your Life.

November 8

GRATITUDE

Flattery and Criticism

> **Affirmation**
> *"Today, I will wear people's flattery, and their criticism, like a loose garment. Their flatteries touch me, but they do not cling to me. I feel their criticisms, but they don't restrict my movement. I will navigate them all while remaining fully awake."*

Whether we want to or not, we all deal with criticism. Occasionally, criticism comes from a cherished friend or caring loved who deeply cares for us and wants us to grow into our highest and greatest good. Nothing to fear here. Give thanks for it and ask the Holy Spirit to help you apply what is useful. Other times, criticism comes from a mean-spirited competitive enemy disguised in friendly clothing. Sneakily, people use criticism to prey on our insecurities and gain our ear as some sort of needed guide coaching us with tough love into their picture of who we should become.

Flattery is a little more deceptive as it goes down more smoothly. Criticism is a jagged pill, difficult to swallow. Flattery is a subtle intoxicant, lulling us into places, and aligning us with people, we would have never considered while sober. Flattery feeds the voracious ego and offers us what we're hungering for. And, then exposes the predictable, tolerable daily routines with our loving families and trusted friends, that may lack a daily "blowing smoke up your skirt" session. I have watched criticism stymie powerful people. And, I have witnessed it save people's lives, marriages, business and callings. I have watched flattery destroy good-hearted preachers and crush innocent-minded parishioners. Wear all of it like a loose garment. It's touching you, but not tethering you. It's close, but not clingy. Allow it to be respectfully purposeful, without become restrictively paralyzing. And, when either comes your way, take a self-inventory of your own weaknesses and insecurities, and be sure a wolf in sheep's clothing is not preying on you.

> **Prayer:** *"Protective Intuition, alert me to hateful criticism and alarm me to harmful flattery. Today, I need Your help and protection. Amen."*

GRATITUDE

November 9

Agape and Eros

Affirmation
"Whether I am a male or a female, I know both Agape and Eros are necessary for my wholeness and well-being."

One of the ways to look at the difference between masculine and feminine energy is by the two concepts: *agape* and *eros*. Agape is feminine energy that reaches out horizontally, while Eros is masculine energy that is vertical. Agape is receptive and laid back. Eros is aggressive, driven and action oriented. In our lives, we need to utilize both.

Comparing it to a building, Agape would be the foundation and Eros everything that sits above ground. In order to have a balanced and successful life, we can't spend all our time resting and relaxing. If we did, nothing would ever be built above ground level. But on the other hand, there's a limit to how high you can build a building before it starts to tip over unless there's a sufficiently deep and wide foundation underneath it.

Engineers building skyscrapers understand this, but very few of us know how to translate this principle into our everyday lives. We have valued competition (eros) over cooperation (agape) for so long that we've gotten way out of balance.

We push ourselves so hard to achieve and get ahead that we neglect properly caring for foundational issues. Eventually this will cause the building that is our life to come toppling down.

To remedy this, we've got to begin putting a little more emphasis on the feminine quality of Agape. No matter how high a building is or how impressive it looks above ground, if the foundation isn't solid, it will eventually crumble.

Prayer: *"Mother God, help me today to pay as much attention to my foundation as to the parts of my life that are visible. Amen."*

Challenge Your Mind. Channel Your Power. Change Your Life.

November 10

GRATITUDE

No Small Contributions

> *Affirmation*
> *"Today, I will offer help to others and to causes that align with my level of consciousness. I know that my contribution will not change the world by itself. However, it does, and I do, make a difference."*

"No one is too small to make a difference." ~ Greta Thunberg

Social injustice. The climate crisis. The disparity of wealth. Incurable diseases. Hunger and the lack of clean drinking water. These are some really big problems facing the global human family. Actually, issues like these that plague so many seem insurmountable, unsolvable. They even arouse feelings of hopelessness and powerlessness. Often times, people see the size of the obstacle and just decide that their small contribution cannot really change anything, and they allow apathy to get the best of them.

I heard a beautiful story about a little girl who was walking near the ocean. The sand was covered with thousands of starfish that had beached themselves and were dying. She was overwhelmed with compassion and began to throw some of the starfish back into the water. Her father was watching this scene. He approached her and said, "Sweetheart, there is no way you can save all of these starfish. There are just too many. I am not even sure you can make a difference." The little girl then picked up another starfish and threw it back into the water. She looked up at her father and said, "Maybe you're right. But, it made a difference for that one." Our individual contributions may not shake the earth. Yet, if we can help somebody, as we pass along, then our living will not be in vain!

> **Prayer:** *"God who can make little much, as I offer my time, talent and treasure to missions of love and to those in need, use me as a vessel to make a difference somehow, somewhere, for someone! Amen."*

GRATITUDE

November 11

To Each His Own

Affirmation
"I know that everybody grows in their own space and at their own pace."

When we pass by an elementary school, we often remember those days when we were learning the basics like not talking when the teacher is talking, keeping your hands to yourself, standing in line, and raising your hand for permission to go to the restroom. All these lessons are necessary and age appropriate for young kids.

But how ridiculous would it be for you, as an adult, to try to walk back into one of those classrooms, sit at a little desk and have a peanut butter sandwich and a carton of milk for lunch. You don't fit there anymore! And hopefully, you've learned all those lessons and moved on.

However, also hopefully, you realize that there are still children who need the lessons that school teaches. Therefore, you have no desire to go burn down the building!

As we grow and mature spiritually, we must know when it's time to move on from the primary school level lessons and graduate into higher forms of spiritual practice. But when we do, there's no need to destroy whatever practice we first connected to God through.

If you first learned about the love of Jesus and memorized the Ten Commandments in the Baptist church but have now graduated beyond that, there's no need to tear down all the Baptist churches or tell the people still practicing that form of religion that it's wrong. If it's still working for them… let them be.

Learn to grow gracefully.

> **Prayer:** *"God of Understanding, help me to be thankful for the spiritual road that led me to where I am today, to know when to move on, and bless rather than judge those coming behind me. Amen."*

Challenge Your Mind. Channel Your Power. Change Your Life.

November 12

GRATITUDE

The Righteous Pit

> ***Affirmation***
> *"Today, I will remember where God has brought me from. I will seek to be righteous, not through judgment, but by being cognizant of the restorative power of my Creator."*

"Listen to Me, you who follow after righteousness, You who seek the Lord: Look to the rock from which you were hewn, And to the hole of the pit from which you were dug." (Isaiah 51:1) These are the words of the prophet Isaiah. In this teaching there are two basic ideas:

1. Remember your Creator.
2. Remember where your Creator has brought you from.

The result of following these two suggestions is the achievement of righteousness. Isn't it strange that Isaiah does not offer behavioral codes for attaining righteousness? No specifics about clothing, food, or sexuality are offered. Isaiah simply says look to God and to your failures of the past, then you will be righteous. Wow! So, self-righteous attempts to justify ourselves by judging others is not an ingredient in the baking of the righteousness pie.

Here is the beauty in all of this. God does not remember our past mistakes. The Bible says God casts our sins into a forgetful sea and then removes the sin from us a far as the east is from the west. (Micah 7:19) However, when we feel the need to levy criticism onto others, Isaiah encourages us to remember our missteps.

> **Prayer:** *"Forgetful God, today I am grateful that You do not remember my sins. Today, I will walk in righteousness as I look to You, and as I remember where You have brought me from. Amen."*

GRATITUDE

November 13

Ask and You Shall Receive

Affirmation
"Today I know there is something more valuable to ask for than material things. Wisdom, knowledge and guidance are the greatest gifts I can receive from God."

The Bible says, "Ask and it shall be given to you." Many people interpret this scripture in the context of material things, but it can also mean knowledge, more specifically, guidance. Think about it. Who would turn someone away who came to you honestly asking for your guidance?

If your child came to you and said, "Is there anything you think I should know today, Mom? Is there anything you think I should be aware of today, Dad? Can you see something I don't see right now that will help me in the future?" Most of us would not refuse such requests.

Why would God be any different? Sometimes we don't see certain things coming in our lives simply because we haven't asked for guidance. If you take the time on a regular basis to just check in and say, "Hey God, is there anything in my life I should be doing differently? Is there anything in my heart that's no longer serving me that I've held on to for too long that I need to get rid of? Is there anything at all I could be doing a better job with?"

If you go to God with that attitude, it is assured you will receive an answer. You may have to get still enough and quiet enough to hear the answer, but you will receive it!

Prayer: *"God of Protection, help me understand that your guidance is ever available to me. All I need to do is ask. Amen."*

Challenge Your Mind. Channel Your Power. Change Your Life.

November 14

GRATITUDE

Divine Connections

> *Affirmation*
> "Today, I am open and available for Divine Connections. I welcome relationships that bless me with loyalty, honesty, inspiration, vision and power. I will be receptive when a Divine Connection speaks a divine correction or difficult truth to me. And, I will be grateful when a Divine Connection affirms who I am."

Have you ever met someone and immediately had a strong sense that you had known this person your entire life? Or maybe even in another lifetime? Meetings like this are divinely appointed as they are Divine Connections. Said differently, the vibration you send out will attract people to you who operate from the same vibratory pattern and live on the same frequency. Once you tap into that wavelength, you begin to channel people of like mind. Most of us have family, friends and acquaintances we have known for a lifetime, and yet, have never felt as closely connected to them as we do to a Divine Connection we have known for a few hours. The defense mechanisms in us seem to resist giving in fully to these newly discovered Divine Connections as we are programmed to protect our hearts and are trained to be leery of trusting a stranger that we have only just met. There is nothing wrong with these protective measures as we have learned to trust in them to keep us safe. And, a truly Divine Connection will not be scared off by any sense of hesitancy. What God has joined cannot be separated.

Divine Connections offer us a powerful opportunity to grow, give and gain deeper understandings of others, ourselves and the nature of who we truly are, and are becoming. Divine Connections bless us with revelation, elevation, motivation and occasionally correction. When a Divine Connection humbly offers a divine correction, don't be offended or afraid. Digest it and give thanks for someone the Universe has sent to help protect you from yourself and any potential blind-spots.

> **Prayer:** "Divine Connection, thank You for every Divine Connection. I give thanks for connection and remain open for correction. Amen."

GRATITUDE

November 15

Walk Through the Door

Affirmation
"You don't have to see the whole staircase, just take the first step." ~ MLK

Sometimes a door will appear in front of you and you can't really see everything that's on the other side of it, but something in your gut is saying, "Just walk through the door."

At that point, your logical mind, your ego (which is always in need of assurances) might jump in and try to stop you by saying things like: "Hold on a minute! You have no idea where this door leads. There is no five year plan attached to it. It's dark and a little scary on the other side."

And yet, that little voice inside, that still small voice, is saying, "Just walk through the door."

Sometimes, even after you walk through and you're able to look around a little - you still don't understand because it doesn't look like what you'd always dreamed of. It's not what you had in mind when you were setting your intentions for creating your future.

But maybe, after just a few more steps in, BAM! Another door appears and you walk through *that* one. Suddenly you see in reality what it was you had envisioned in your mind and you say, "Ah! I'm here!"

And that process might have to repeat itself a couple of times. It might be the second or even the third door you walk through. But eventually, it will be the one you dreamed of. And you will look back and realize you would have never gotten to the place you are now if you had never listened to your inner voice and walked through that very first door.

Prayer: *"Intuitive God, help me to learn today to follow the still small voice of my inner knowing. Amen."*

Challenge Your Mind. Channel Your Power. Change Your Life.

November 16

GRATITUDE

Learning Tolerance

> ***Affirmation***
> *"Today, on the International Day For Tolerance, I will allow space for others to express themselves freely and live their lives without the burden of my judgment or condemnation."*

As I am writing today's devotion I am wearing my coexist t-shirt. I love the diverse religious, scientific and philosophical symbols collaborating to make up the coexist sign and artistic slogan. Yet, coexistence is not necessarily oneness. Coexistence, and tolerance, simply suggest that we learn to adopt an approach to live peacefully with people of disparate ideals than our own. I often welcome people to our spiritual community by saying "Spirit and Truth is a place where you are celebrated, not tolerated." After all, who really wants to be tolerated?

Tolerance, although seemingly a lower, elementary expression of oneness, actually serves as a foundation for the higher realms of openness and learning. How can we celebrate what we cannot initially tolerate? We may not completely understand, or agree with, another religion or culture. However, if we can set our intention to allow diversity of expression, we are taking the first, necessary step that has the power to lead us to spiritual oneness. Harmony is what makes music so beautiful. Achieving harmony does not mean we sound the same. Harmony means we sound together!

> ***Prayer:*** *"Limitless Expression, help me stir up the gift of tolerance within me. I desire to see one human family living in peaceful harmony. Grant me the courage to take the first step, tolerance! Amen."*

November 17

GRATITUDE

What We Can Learn From Plants Part I

Affirmation
"I know that life is more than just the pretty parts. I will be patient with myself at all times and trust the process of my own growth."

When strolling through a garden, the beautiful flowers are usually the first thing that catch our eye. But just like in life, there's more to a plant than just the pretty part. The actual flower comes and goes, some types bloom only for a few short weeks, and others have no flower at all.

But just because a plant doesn't happen to be in bloom doesn't mean it's dead or isn't serving a purpose. It just means that at this particular time there is no bloom present. Even though the flower may be the prettiest part, it's not the most important; and its presence or lack thereof doesn't determine the overall health of the entire plant.

The lesson we can learn from this is that things are not always as they appear on the surface, and just because your life is not exactly *coming up roses*, as it were, at the moment, doesn't necessarily mean that something is wrong.

It might mean you are in a dormant phase outwardly while much work, evolution and growth is taking place under the ground (or inwardly) in your root system. Learn not to judge your own life or the life of others only by what is showing on the outside. Flowers are indeed beautiful, but they are only part of the story.

Prayer: "Source of Beauty, help me learn and understand that beauty is more than skin deep. What goes on inside me can create as much beauty as what shows on the outside. Help me to be patient during times of inner growth. Amen."

Challenge Your Mind. Channel Your Power. Change Your Life.

November 18

GRATITUDE

What We Can Learn From Plants Part II

Affirmation
"Today I will thrive like a happy, healthy plant!"

There is much wisdom to be gained from nature. For example, how plants survive and thrive presents a great model for us as humans. A plant is made up of many different parts, the three main ones being the roots, the leaves and the stem. Each part has a set of unique jobs to do to keep the plant healthy.

Comparing it to our lives as humans would go something like this: the roots are our belief system, the things we are taught that we then can choose to either discard or hold on to as truth for us. It provides for us nutrition, as it were, from the soil of the traditions and wisdom laid down by those who came before us.

Although strong, roots are also flexible, as our beliefs should be. They are ever evolving and adapting as our environment changes - sometimes growing in an entirely new direction - as we discover which beliefs work for us and which don't.

Leaves represent the love, guidance and friendship we take in on a horizontal level from those around us. And of course, the sun is representative of the light of God, shining down on us from above.

The stem is our open channel, through which flows the energy we receive from all directions - below, our beliefs, which are our roots; horizontally, our relationships with others; and above, the glorious sunlight that is God's presence.

> **Prayer:** *"Source of Life, help me honor all the parts of my system that keep my life in balance. And help me to always have a clear channel through which the life force I receive from all directions can flow freely. Amen."*

GRATITUDE

November 19

The Walking Bible

Affirmation

"Today, I will be the hands of God extending to a hurting world. I will allow the Word to become flesh and dwell in me. I may not read the Bible to someone or inspire them to read it for themselves. But, I will be as a walking Bible, a living epistle, being read by all men and graciously offering God's love to all."

My grandfather was a preacher. A very unique one. His nickname was "The Walking Bible." On one occasion, a local journalist came to hear him speak and then wrote an article about the experience. The writer reported my grandfather had quoted over 300 different bible verses from memory during one sermon. When I would hear my family referring to him as "The Walking Bible" I always understood it in this context…memorizing Bible verses. It wasn't until later that I had a deeper understanding that we all must become "The Walking Bible." This is not to suggest that we all commit to memory the entire Bible or even specific scriptures. It is to suggest that we are all "Walking Bibles" and should embrace and accept the truth that we are the only Bible some people will ever read.

Our love, our light and our lives are the only Bible some people will ever experience. Paul said we are *"living"* and *"written epistles…read by all men."* Our presence becomes the Bible. Our actions become the chapters. Our words become the verses. Our light must shine so brightly that it reflects the love of God in every environment we frequent. Preaching on a street corner takes courage, and a touch of crazy. However, the greatest sermon we could give is to become an extension of God's love in our daily relationships. There is an old saying that has become somewhat cliché, "People don't care how much you know, until they know how much you care." Talk the talk. Walk the walk. You are the Word become flesh.

Prayer: *"Living Word, let Your light wake in me, Your love work through me and Your Word walk as me. Let my walk be louder than my talk. Amen."*

Challenge Your Mind. Channel Your Power. Change Your Life.

November 20

GRATITUDE

Heart Health

Affirmation
"I will look at life today through the lens of unconditional love in order to keep my heart healthy and strong."

Following your heart is superior to following your head because whereas the mind is anchored in duality and is constantly judging between two or more things as better or worse, the heart has only one job - to love. The heart is anchored in oneness and unity and is therefore a better guide than your brain or your logic.

In order for that to be completely true, however, you have to have a healthy heart (emotionally speaking). A weakened or diseased heart is not good to follow. So what keeps your heart from being strong and healthy?

There is a long list of negative emotions that could be the cause, but they are all rooted in one emotion - fear, which is the root of all negative emotions. Many people believe hate is the opposite of love, but in reality, fear is love's opposite. When you allow too much fear to live in your heart, it gets polluted and becomes weak.

You can look at the world through the lens of fear and scarcity where you believe there is only so much love to go around, which means the more someone else gets the less there is for you. Or you can look through the lens of love and abundance where you know there is an endless supply of love and that people are basically good.

Fear closes your heart down and love opens it up. It's that simple. Which lens will you look at life through today?

Prayer: *"Source of Unconditional Love, help me see today that in order to follow my heart it must be healthy and strong. Help me understand that love is limitless. Amen."*

GRATITUDE

November 21

Thank God My China Cabinet Is Clean

Affirmation
"Today, I will be aware of what I create and of any projecting my creations onto an external power. I will be grateful for Divine help and intervention while remaining awake to the truth that I am created by God, creative like God, and creating as a god."

After a series of home renovations my wife and I were exhausted dealing with dust and debris everywhere. Once our china cabinet was finally clean and recognizable once more, my wife said, "Thank God my china cabinet is clean." Almost immediately she paused and asked out loud, "What did God have to do with my china cabinet?" It was a moment of realization that God is not always involved in everything we create. Both mundane and difficult moments alike seem to garner God blame. I remember when Nascar legend Dale Earnhardt died tragically during a race. I was confused by so many fans blaming and questioning God for his death. When cars race at 200 miles an hour within inches of each other…is it God's fault when they crash?

Several of the founding fathers of America were deists…George Washington, John Adams and arguably Thomas Jefferson. A deist believes in a Creative, Divine Source of all life. Yet, they believe once that Source created the earth, it left us to our own devices, to navigate our own journey, to figure it out on our own. To be clear, I don't subscribe to this completely and welcome Divine Intervention! However, I do believe deism offers a balance between Divine china cabinet intervention and world-shaking events. Perhaps we might find a middle way where we are fully aware of our power to create and also open to help from the Divine?

Prayer: *"Divine Presence, I know You are evenly present throughout the universe. I feel You! I am grateful for Your help and also appreciative for Your allowing me to learn how to navigate my own creativity. Amen."*

Challenge Your Mind. Channel Your Power. Change Your Life.

November 22

GRATITUDE

Prodigal

Affirmation
"I remember who I am."

When you have created a situation or condition for yourself that you don't want, hopefully, you will come to yourself and realize it like the Prodigal Son in the biblical story. But that's not always the case.

After eating a few meals of pigs' food, the prodigal realized that's not what he was supposed to be eating and the hog pen was not where he was supposed to be living. He had created a condition for himself he did not want and took steps to change it.

Adam could have come to himself in much the same way in the garden after eating of the forbidden tree, but he didn't. You see, Adam could not let go of his unworthiness long enough to come to himself. And that's actually the *original sin* we inherited from Adam - the inability to come to ourselves and remember our worthiness in the midst of a less than desirable situation.

Adam said, "I'm naked and ashamed." And God replied, "Who told you that?" I can imagine the further conversation being something like: "Of course you're naked. That's how I made you. Your nakedness is beautiful and natural. It's only your misperception that nakedness is something to be ashamed of that is making you feel unworthy to be in my presence. I'm good with your nakedness, and I'm good with your failed attempts at creating your life. You call them mistakes. I call them practice."

So do you want to be like Adam or the prodigal son? Until you can let go of your unworthiness long enough to come to yourself and remember who you are, you will continue to eat the pig slop.

Prayer: "Merciful God, help me remember who I am and what I deserve today. Amen."

GRATITUDE

November 23

An Attitude of Gratitude

Affirmation
"Today, and every day, is Thanksgiving and I will intentionally attract peace and joy by vibrating in gratitude. As I give thanks for small blessings I will undoubtedly attract, manifest and realize larger blessings."

In the 100th Psalm David encourages us to enter God's presence (or "gates") with thanksgiving. (Psalm 100:4) Many church goers are not aware of this, but this verse has dictated the flow of worship services for hundreds of years. Taking a cue from the tabernacle of Moses, thanksgiving, or praise, happens in the outer court or at the beginning of the service. Then, as a reward for expressing gratitude, admittance into God's presence is granted and worship then takes place in the inner court. This methodology proposes that if we maintain a vibration of gratitude, sensing or realizing the presence of God will be the ultimate result. What if we could apply this construct to our everyday lives?

Instead of practicing gratitude once a year on Thanksgiving, or once a week during worship, we can actually live in a space of gratitude. How? Many times, gratitude loses momentum because we allow it to be placed on layaway, waiting for everything in our lives to fall into a perfect, peaceful place. Things beyond our control, like the weather, traffic, the moods of others, the choices of loved ones or even genetic health challenges can hijack our gratitude. Instead of helplessly watching gratitude fly away as quickly as it landed, we can practice gratitude in the small things. When we wake up we can give thanks for life, for health, for another day, for breath, for conscious awareness. When gratitude is maintained in the small things it has a way of finding its way into bigger things. Start today!

Prayer: *"Gracious Lord, I will be mindful to give and live in gratitude. Thank you for the breath in my body, the blood in my veins and the consciousness in my spirit. Amen."*

Challenge Your Mind. Channel Your Power. Change Your Life.

November 24

GRATITUDE

Pay It Forward

> ***Affirmation***
> *"Today, I choose to Pay It Forward to others and to my future self. Future generations, and the future Me, depend on the seeds I plant today. As I Pay It Forward to others, I am also investing into myself, as I am interconnected to all of the human family. As Christ Paid It Forward to me, I will Pay It Forward to every child of God! Amen."*

To Pay It Forward means to do a good deed for someone today knowing that in the process of sowing and reaping, action and reaction, or karma... that good deed will continue to be paid forward to others and eventually find its way back to you. Or perhaps, someone already paid it forward to you and you are simply paying it forward to someone else with gratitude. In a sense, when you bless someone else you are blessing yourself. Dr. Martin Luther King, Jr. once declared that we are all intrinsically connected in an inescapable web of mutuality... *"what affects one directly, affects us all indirectly...injustice anywhere is a threat to justice everywhere."*

My son was playing in his first college basketball game in Kentucky. This particular college arena had an enormous picture on one of the walls of identical twin brothers running a relay race. One twin was handing the baton off to the other twin. It looked as if the same person was handing something to himself. In essence, that's what we do every day. We pay it forward to our future selves by the choices we make today. We sow seeds of love and inclusion and kindness that impact someone somewhere and make the world a better place to inhabit. And, when the world around us is more loving, we reap the harvest.

> ***Prayer:*** *"Magnificent Mother, I am overwhelmed by what You have freely given to me. As I bless others, I am paying it forward with a heart of thanksgiving. And, I am paying it forward to my future self. Grant me an opportunity today to Pay It Forward in some way. Amen."*

GRATITUDE

November 25

Remember Who You Are

Affirmation
*"I am a small piece of the All; the I AM.
Today I will remember who I am."*

When dropping kids off at school or a friend's house, it's common for parents to say something like: "Remember who you are" - which is shorthand for: "Behave yourself and don't forget everything we've taught you here at home when you walk out that door into a different environment."

I can imagine God saying that to us as we're leaving the realm of Spirit - our home - to be born into the very different environment of our life here on earth.

Remembering who we are involves us knowing who we are to begin with, which is more difficult than it sounds. Very early in our lives we are told that our name, our family, our life story, our job, our race, our religion, and our gender are all expressions of the "I" we are supposed to be. But those are nothing but labels. And labels are nothing more than a brief experience within a tiny band of frequency in the universe that we call "the world."

The more you subdivide your sense of "I" with these labels, the further away you move from the greater, eternal, infinite "I" that you were when you were born. In reality, there is only one "I" - the ALL that ever was, is, and ever can be. Each of us is just a unique point of attention of that "I."

The more we self-identify with labels, the smaller we become. The more we are able to drop our labels, the more we can simply say *I Am that I AM*, because that is who we truly are.

Prayer: *"Great I AM, help me to remember today who I really am and to behave accordingly. Amen."*

Challenge Your Mind. Channel Your Power. Change Your Life.

November 26

GRATITUDE

Calling the Qualified? Or Qualifying the Called?

> **Affirmation**
> *"Today, I am qualified and called. I am qualified as I am made in the image and likeness of Divinity. And, I am called because I choose to respond to my divine purpose for being on the earth."*

There is an old church cliché that God "doesn't call the qualified. God qualifies the called." The beauty in this idea is that anyone can fulfill a purpose in the Kingdom of God. All that is required is a willingness. The ugliness is that this statement has been used to insult the educated and downplay the need for preparedness. Is there a middle path that we can find here?

There is nothing more qualifying than a person who is willing and eager to pursue a life of ministry / serving the greater good of humanity. A great attitude makes up quite a bit for lack of knowledge and expertise. Yet, education, training, experience, wisdom, work-ethic, are not lesser ingredients. Perhaps a balanced approach to this idea is that we must do the best with what we have (prepare ourselves the best way we can according to the opportunities that are available to us) and surrender to the Holy Spirit helping, leading, guiding and making up for whatever credentials we may lack.

Consider this verse: *"Therefore take up the whole armor of God, that you may be able to withstand in the evil day, and having done all, to stand."* (Ephesians 6:13) Notice, the stand portion does not happen until we have DONE ALL. The armor of God is a metaphor for preparedness of spirit. God calls the qualified and the unqualified, alike. And, we are all called!

> **Prayer:** *"Qualifying Presence, thank You for calling me, and all of humanity, to work in the kingdom. Today, I am qualified and called. Grant me the strength and endurance to prepare myself for this work. Amen."*

GRATITUDE

November 27

The Purest Love

Affirmation
"Today I know that I am responsible for keeping my own emotional cup full. I cannot and do not expect others to fill it for me."

"Try not to confuse attachment with love. Attachment is about fear and dependency, and has more to do with love of self than love of another. Love without attachment is the purest love because it isn't about what others can give you because you're empty. It's about what you can give others because you're already full." ~ Yasmin Mogahed

When you are attached to someone through dependency on them and the thought of losing them (either physically through death or losing your relationship with them through them leaving you or rejecting you) causes you to go into fear, that's not love. We often mistake it for love, but it's not. That's a false notion we've been given by Disney, Hollywood and The Hallmark Channel.

We've been conditioned to believe that the statement, "I can't live without you" is a loving one, or one that conveys the depth of our love for someone else, but it is actually a very selfish statement that puts undue pressure on another person by making them responsible for our well-being, which they are not.

When you make someone else responsible for your happiness, you are handing your personal power and sovereignty to them.

The higher octave of that statement is the last line - the purest love is not about what others can give you because you're empty, but about what you can give others because you're already full.

Prayer: *"Source of Pure Love, fill me with so much love today that I am able to give to others rather than expecting them to fill up the places in me where love is lacking. Amen."*

Challenge Your Mind. Channel Your Power. Change Your Life.

November 28

GRATITUDE

Unguarded Moments

> ***Affirmation***
> *"I am not who I am while I am on my best behavior. My essence is revealed in unguarded moments…when I am unaware of the presence of others and when my reactions are unplanned and not premeditated."*

One of my basketball coaches was fond of saying "you are who you are when no one is watching." This both troubled and challenged me. Who are we when no one is watching? Who am I in unguarded moments? Perhaps we are not our worst impulse neither are we our highest vibration. There have been some times in my life when I have reacted in childish ways. There have also been very stressful moments when I have responded with calmness and kindness. Which one am I? Who are you?

We could all reflect on our best and worst days…on our highest and lowest selves. Could it be that we are not necessarily either? If we can take a step back we might be able to see that we are not an accumulation of our behaviors but the observing presence of ourselves. We are the awareness that we are either responding from love or reacting out of fear. From this perch, we can detach from both guilt and self-righteousness. And, we can see that as we become self-aware, as we "know thyself," * we become the unlimited potential to awaken to our divinely creative likeness.

> ***Prayer:*** *"Observing Presence, help me be aware of my highest and lowest self. Give me the courage to see all of me. And, grant me the strength to continue the journey toward greater awareness and awakening. Amen."*

---

* Quote from Socrates.

GRATITUDE

November 29

A Double Portion

Affirmation
"Today, I welcome a double portion in my life by giving thanks for the positive and the negative. I will not be blinded by denial or burdened with delusion. Instead, I will endeavor to be fully awake, strive to repeat successes and remain open to learn from any missteps."

There is a story in the Bible of an older prophet, Elijah, mentoring a younger prophet, Elisha. As Elijah reaches the end of his life he asks Elisha what he wants him to do for him before he dies. Elisha answers, *"I want a double portion of your spirit."* Elijah replies, you'll have the double portion *"If you see me when I go."* On the surface, this seems pretty simple. If Elisha remains loyal and subservient to Elijah, stays by Elijah's side and is physically there when he transitions, Elisha will receive the double portion. This interaction has been skewed and twisted to embolden older leaders to manipulate younger leaders into inordinate and undying loyalty for generations. Elisha actually ended up performing twice the recorded miracles than that of Elijah. However, the mystery of the double portion is deeper than tallying miracles.

The mystery is hidden in Elijah's words, *"If you SEE ME when I go."* Elijah was a powerful prophet. Yet, he was burdened with imbalance, rage and fear. One day, he is cutting off the heads of 400 false prophets. The next day, he is running scared, hiding from a woman. Elisha's receiving of the double portion relied upon his willingness to see all of Elijah…good, bad, strength, weakness, spirit, flesh…all of it. Most of us are blessed with mentors who assist us on our journey. Sadly, most mentees become either highly critical of, or blindly loyal to, their mentors. The result of this imbalance is receiving only a single portion. Yet, the double portion exists in the middle; being fully able to give thanks for strengths while remaining completely open to see weaknesses. Review it all. Rest in the middle. Repeat the good. Refuse the bad. Receive the double portion.

Prayer: *"Awakened Vision, grant me a double portion. Give me eyes to see it, openness to survey it and courage to shift it. Amen."*

Challenge Your Mind. Channel Your Power. Change Your Life.

November 30

GRATITUDE

Life as a TV Show

> *Affirmation*
> *"Today I will take a step back and be the observer of my life. I know there are more points of view than mine alone."*

I binge-watched a show once where the writers masterfully weaved together several smaller stories within the bigger, main story, intricately connecting all the characters and their stories to each other.

As the tale unfolds, the audience is able to see the story from each character's point of view, and thus develop a sense of compassion for all of them. They are all dealing with some pretty deep life issues. Inevitably, when some of them come into conflict with each other, because the writers have done such a good job showing that every character is multi-dimensional (no one is all good and no one is all bad), the audience is left not really knowing whose side to be on.

It's so much easier to be objective, understanding, and to have compassion for everyone involved when you're on the outside looking in (watching a TV show), but in real life, you're *in* the show. You're one of the characters. And unless you consciously decide to step outside yourself, as it were, and become the observer, you will only ever see *your* side of the story.

It's also easier to be defensive, angry, overly sensitive and hurt when you're on the inside looking out, because you're not seeing the situation from the perspective of the bigger view and you don't know everyone else's story.

Love never chooses sides. Love finds common ground. Love dares to see from another's point of view.

> **Prayer:** *"God of My Reality, help me today to see the whole picture and to find common ground with everyone I interact with even when it is difficult. Amen."*

FULLY AWAKE 365

PURSUING PEACE

December 1

Choose Peace. Seek Peace. Pursue Peace.

Affirmation

"Today I choose peace by seeking it and pursuing it. I acknowledge I am an active participant in creating my peace and not a helpless victim waiting for someone to speak peace to me or create peace for me. I will maintain a high vibration by avoiding lower vibrations (and crazy people) whenever possible. I am aware that seeking revenge and harboring unhealthy thoughts can transform me into the thing I resent. I am not the thing that happened to me and I will not smell like it for the rest of my life. I am aware that peace is not the absence of chaos as I can choose to create peace in the midst of a storm. My mind is clear. My heart is healthy. And, my life will reflect my thoughts! In this moment, I choose peace!"

The Bible instructs us to *"Seek peace and pursue it"* (Psalm 34:14 / 1 Peter 3:11). Interesting verbs…seek and pursue. These are not passive words. To seek for something is literally to *go on a quest…searching*. To pursue means *striving to gain*. With this understanding we can surmise that peace is not something that happens by accident. Peace does not fall into our laps or leisurely stroll into our lives. Peace doesn't happen by chance. Peace happens by choice!

How do we choose peace? There are many ways we can choose peace every day. One way we choose peace is by being aware that peace is not the absence of chaos. Life is stressful, complicated, tense. No surprise. So, peace must be a premeditated choice. Mentally choose peace in advance of any situation or conversation that could potentially steal your peace. Choose your vibration and don't allow anyone to lower it. Fly above the turbulence by maintaining a great attitude. Seek Peace. Pursue peace!

Prayer: *"God of peace, I know that You will keep me in perfect peace as I choose, seek and pursue peace. Whatever storm or drama I am in will never be in me. The world didn't give me peace and the world can't take it away. Today, I am at peace as I maintain and keep my peace. Empower me to keep my peace by not giving it away. Amen."*

Challenge Your Mind. Channel Your Power. Change Your Life.

December 2

PURSUING PEACE

The Peace of God and Your Piece of God

> **Affirmation**
> "The Peace of God is bigger than my piece of God as the Peace of God surpasses all understanding and surpasses my specific understanding. I will not allow my piece of God to keep the Peace of God from becoming a reality among the global human family. I will let there be peace on earth. I will let it begin with me. And, I will consciously create peace by not allowing my piece to prevent peace!"

The ego is to be blamed for so much of the separation, disunity and violence that has existed between different religions, and human beings, for as long as there has been recordable human history. One religion's piece of God perpetually gets in the way of the Peace of God. From the three Hebrew children being forced to worship King Nebuchadnezzar's god, to Jewish Pharisees sending Jesus to the cross over religious differences, to the Christian's crusading and forcing Muslims to convert to Christianity, our history as a species is replete with one religion's piece of God preventing peace between all of God's children.

Somehow the Universe keeps presenting us with the opportunity to learn this same lesson (the lesson of tolerance and co-existence) over and over. Yet, we keep refusing the learning. Time and again, millennia after millennia, war after war, we continue to resist the lesson and insist that our specific piece of God is really the answer to finally experiencing the Peace of God. Once everyone believes exactly like us, uses our name for God, reads our specific Holy Book, worships like us, there will be peace on earth? Hold your piece of God close to your heart. And, never forget the spiritual tradition that introduced you to the Creator of the Universe. Yet, allow all of God's children the same right. Perhaps when all the pieces of God can agree to this Golden Rule, we will finally have the Peace of God.

> **Prayer:** "God of All, as Your child, I give thanks for my piece of You. Today, my piece won't prevent peace between all of Your children. Amen."

PURSUING PEACE

December 3

Living Peaceably With All Men

Affirmation
"Today I know that it is possible to rise above how others might treat me and to return good for evil."

A particularly beautiful interpretation of the Golden Rule is that it is a unilateral moral commitment to the well-being of another without the expectation of anything in return. The word *unilateral* means "one way" - in other words it is when you've reached a place in life where your behavior is not dependent on the behavior of others.

It is when you have surpassed the level of transactional relationship where you are good only to those who are good to you and instead, you radiate the good inside you always, no matter how you are treated.

Living like this is easier said than done, especially when someone has taken a shot at you or hurt you in some way. Are you able to live like this when life gets real?

Most of us are not at the place where we always return good for what we perceive as evil. We do not turn the cheek in every case. And that's ok as long as we are constantly working toward it. Having that as a goal - aiming for but missing the mark - is better than never even trying.

The key is in living life with your arms metaphorically wide open rather than in "put up your dukes" defense mode. This is made a little easier when we remember the admonition to live peaceably with all men as much as lies within our power. It's not always within our power to succeed. But it's always within our power to try.

Prayer: *"Peaceful God, help me today learn to drop my defenses and let your love and the peace that passes understanding into my life. Amen."*

Challenge Your Mind. Channel Your Power. Change Your Life.

December 4

PURSUING PEACE

Pursuing Peace Without _____

> *Affirmation*
> *"Today, I will PURSUE PEACE without a promise, a prophecy, or a plan. I will PURSUE PEACE without permission, projection, panic or provision."*

A play on words. Of course. We already know that peace is within. So, why should we pursue it without. But for today, I would like to highlight some things that might get in the way of our pursuing peace. Remember, peace is a choice. Peace does not happen by chance. Let us set our intention together to Pursue Peace Without:

A Promise – we do not need promises that can be broken
   (*"faith is the substance of things hoped for, the evidence of things not seen."*) (Hebrews 11:1)

A Prophecy – no need to wait on a prophecy or a prophet
   (*"the Word is nigh thee, even in your heart and mouth."*) (Romans 10:8, Deuteronomy 30:14 KJV)

A Plan – no vision board or blueprint necessary
   (*those of the Spirit are "like the wind" not knowing where they are going.*) (John 3:8)

A Projection – no waiting, wishing or wondering. Peace is possible in this now moment
   (*"why worry about tomorrow? Sufficient for the day is its own trouble."*) (Matthew 6:34)

A Provision – just start walking toward peace and away from chaotic dysfunction
   (*Abraham had no land, no map, no child, no security…he just started walking.*) (Genesis 12)

A Panic – there is peace in my pace
   (*"God is perfecting those things concerning me."*) (Psalm 138:8)

Anyone's Permission – the only permission I need is mine
   (*"Today is the day of salvation."*) (2 Corinthians 6:2)

> **Prayer:** "Peace Within, today I will pursue peace without the interferences of waiting, wishing and wondering. Amen."

PURSUING PEACE

December 5

Single-Minded and Stable

Affirmation
"I know that a double minded man is unstable is in all of his ways! There is no duality in this universe; there is only ONE power...ONE God...ONE Mind. And, that power is working IN, THROUGH, AROUND, FOR and AS me! I will own my creation and allow irritating people and situations to be the spiritual sandpaper smoothing my rough edges."

I grew up on a steady diet of "devilology." That is to say, my church and religious experience was founded on the devil as much as it was on God or Jesus. The devil seemed to somehow be responsible for every bad thing that grown adults consciously created. Financial irresponsibility, relationship failures, unruly teenagers, unfaithful spouses, mechanical problems, inclement weather, political turbulence...everything was to be blamed on the devil and attributed to spiritual warfare or some invisible battle happening in the unseen world.

Far be it for me to take anyone's devil away from them. My goal is not to eliminate the devil - it is to empower people. And, we cannot tap into our God-given strength while giving all of our power away. The best way to become powerful is by not giving it away. When we attribute our own poor choices to a devil or anything other than ourselves, we are subtly, and perhaps even subconsciously, throwing our creative capacity in the trash.

Believe in the devil. Don't believe in the devil. That's your own spiritual journey. If it's working for you, work it. However, double mindedness and devil blaming leads to instability and powerlessness. Own your creation. Wake up to your power. Rest in the truth that all creativity comes from God.

Prayer: *"One Power of the Universe, grant unto me stability and single-mindedness. I know all things were created by You, for You and exist in You. Give me wisdom in what to create and courage to own it. Amen."*

Challenge Your Mind. Channel Your Power. Change Your Life.

December 6

PURSUING PEACE

Gentleness Part I

Affirmation
"Today I will recognize the power of gentleness."

Many of us are accustomed to thinking of strength as being the opposite of gentleness, softness and tenderness, yet this is not always true.

The concept in our culture that gentleness is weakness is actually backwards. Think about it this way; there is no need to be gentle if there is not already the presumption of strength present.

For example, if you're dealing with dogs or kids playing together, which one do you have to remind to "*be gentle*?" Which one do you say that to? Not the smaller, weaker one - there's no need. The one with the greater strength is the one who needs to exhibit gentleness.

Often, our first inclination when being threatened in some way, is to respond to aggression with an equal amount of aggression; to meet violence with violence and fight our way out. But choosing to meet force with gentleness takes a great deal of strength.

Upon arriving at the scene of his home that had just been bombed with his wife and children inside, Martin Luther King, Jr. chose to respond by telling the mob who had gathered to defend him, "If you have weapons, take them home. If you do not have them, please do not seek them. We cannot solve this problem through violence. We must meet it with non-violence. Love your enemies. Bless those that curse you. Pray for them that despitefully use you." That kind of gentle response comes only from a deep well of inner strength and is much more powerful than any amount of brute force.

Prayer: *"Source of Strength, please allow me to respond to all situations in my life today from a place of true power, which is born of gentleness. Amen."*

PURSUING PEACE

December 7

Gentleness Part II

Affirmation
"Today I understand that strength does not need to be harsh or loud. True strength lies in power that is soft and tender and wielded lightly."

During World War I, British fighter pilots made the amazing discovery that thick layers of silk were very effective at stopping low velocity shrapnel. So they would wrap it around their heads underneath their helmets. Scientists still aren't sure just what gives silk its strength, but it remains true that in certain situations, soft, gentle, tender silk can prove far stronger even than cold, hard steel.

Jesus showed us that the same holds true for human character. Some people try to make themselves impenetrable to the people around them by being hard. Jesus showed us that gentleness, a heart that's soft toward others, and tenderness are, in fact, qualities of great strength.

Gentleness means having great power but choosing to wield it in a compassionate way for the benefit of others. The weak have no need to be gentle. They don't have the ability to hurt anyone.

There is a yoga pose called *humble warrior* that teaches us to find the balance between being empowered, yet full of humility. Strength doesn't always have to be hard and rough. Nor does it have to be loud. Sometimes the most powerful things are said in a whisper.

Gentleness is the perfect combination of strength and softness.

Prayer: *"Gentle God, help me know today that my true power lies in my ability to be gentle rather than forceful or aggressive. May my heart be tender toward others and may I exhibit the strength of humility. Amen."*

Challenge Your Mind. Channel Your Power. Change Your Life.

December 8

PURSUING PEACE

Guilty Peace

> ### Affirmation
> *"The Kingdom of God is righteousness, peace and joy in the Spirit. And, the Kingdom of God is within. Today, from my inner man, I choose peace. I also choose to be at peace without feeling any guilt. Others who are not experiencing peace will attempt to make me feel guilty for my peace. But, if I enter their vibration I will not be able to infect them with my peace. I am at peace with my journey, I am at peace with my God, I am at peace with myself and I am at peace with being at peace."*

The *"peace of God," "the Prince of Peace", a "peace that surpasses understanding," "My peace I give you," "peace be still"*…these are all ways, names or biblical phrases describing peace. So, why is peace so rare in religious circles? Why do we sense a feeling of guilt being subtly placed on us by religious people when we find peace? There are justifications for lacking peace: someone else stole it; I had nothing to do with creating this drama. There are even spiritual ways of describing the lack of peace: I am so important to the Kingdom of God the devil is always fighting me; God is trusting me with a test right now…like Job. Whatever way we find to explain it, we are still making the strong admission that we don't have peace.

The Apostle Paul defines the Kingdom of God as *"righteousness, peace and joy in the Holy Spirit."* These three fruits of the Spirit seem to be missing from the produce sections of most churches. Most churchgoers struggle to accept that they are righteous, peace is hiding somewhere under the pews, and joy is just not appropriate because seriousness is so much more religious. Even worse, when a person truly learns how to create peace and maintain it, those who insist on creating fear, living in jealousy and guarding their turf, project guilt onto the peaceful few. Find peace by creating it. And, don't let anyone make you feel guilty about it!

> **Prayer:** *"Abiding Peace, give me the wisdom to create peace, the courage to keep it and the nerve to resist those trying to guilt me for it! Amen."*

PURSUING PEACE

December 9

Laughing in Difficult Moments

Affirmation
"Today, I will laugh, even in difficult moments, knowing there is a joy set before me. I will surrender to joy and grant laughter permission to soothe my soul, settle my mind, secure my sanity and solidify my serenity. I am persuaded by the truth that all things are working together for my good. And today, my face will reflect my belief."

Growing up I was conditioned to believe that seriousness was equivalent to spirituality, sadness was sacred and a scowl was synonymous with sincerity. My childhood friends and I actually referred to this cultural religiosity as having a "stinky prophet face." Catching a prophet smiling or capturing a pastor laughing was like seeing an endangered species awkwardly roaming around in a busy urban area. Religious leaders laughing, enjoying life and letting their hair down was quite a rare treat and almost made them seem real to us…even human. It took me years to overcome this dysfunctional conditioning. I refused the burden of carrying around a "pain body" in order to prove my commitment to God and others, and to be found "worthy" of my own personal calling.

Before I had broken free of this philosophy, I was a young man, 19 years old, and my world began to crumble around me. I approached this storm with what I had always seen…seriousness, sanctity and sadness. As a result, I almost had an emotional and nervous breakdown…as a teenager. A decade later, I was married, a father of two, and had founded my own church. My world was shaken again. But, this time, I chose to laugh, love and live my life while navigating a ferocious storm that would have overwhelmed me otherwise. I emerged from the storm, happy, healthy and headed toward peace and prosperity. There is an old adage, "A ship can sail through any storm, as long as the storm doesn't get in the ship." Never lose your laughter. It may be the very thing that carries you safely through deadly storms and difficult seasons.

__Prayer:__ "Sacred Laughter, I honor you as a welcomed guest. Thank you for keeping me strong, serene, safe and sane through life's storms. Amen."

Challenge Your Mind. Channel Your Power. Change Your Life.

December 10

PURSUING PEACE

Energy Management

Affirmation
"Managing my energy is my responsibility."

Every time you go into any situation, you bring your energy with you. Sometimes you might think you're feeling fine and that your energy is good, but your body always tells the true story. That's why it's a good idea to do a regular physical check-in, maybe a couple of times each day. Simply stop and see if any part of your body is tense and then consciously release it.

We hold past emotions as tension in our bodies. Maybe something happened hours earlier, or even yesterday, and you think you've moved on and let it go, but when you do the check-in, you notice that your toes are scrunched up inside your shoes, or that your hands are clenched into fists, your shoulders are contracted, or your jaw is tight, and you didn't even realize it. That's your body's way of signaling you that something is off in your subconscious and needs attention.

Even when you're not conscious of it, others are. You may think you're fine when you walk into that meeting, or come home after a long day, but if you have a lot of unresolved tension, everyone around you feels it and their defensive force fields start to go up, which usually leads to arguments and more tension.

So the check-in is helpful because it makes you more aware of your energy status. Even if you can't shake off your tension totally or get yourself into a higher vibration immediately, just being conscious that it's there can be enough to neutralize it, and will benefit not only you, but everyone your energy comes into contact with.

Prayer: *"Peaceful God, help me manage my energy today by listening to the signals my body is sending me. Amen."*

PURSUING PEACE

December 11

I Walk Down A Different Street

Affirmation
"Chapter One of My Life: I walk down the street. There's a deep hole in the sidewalk. I fall in. I am lost. I am helpless. It isn't my fault. It takes forever to find a way out. Chapter Two: I walk down the same street. There's a deep hole in the sidewalk. I pretend I don't see it. I fall in again. I can't believe I'm in the same place! But it isn't my fault. And, it still takes a long time to get out. Chapter Three: I walk down the same street. There's a deep hole in the sidewalk. I see it there. I still fall in. It's a habit! My eyes are open. I know where I am. It is my fault. I get out immediately. Chapter Four: I walk down the same street. There's a deep hole in the sidewalk. I walk around it. Chapter Five: I walk down a different street." (Portia Nelson, There's a Hole In My Sidewalk: The Romance of Self-Discovery)."

I used this short story as our affirmation today because it has powerfully impacted my life and confirmed so much in regards to channeling power and divine creativity. It is a quick journey and quantum leap from being a victim to becoming a victor. See if you can critically follow the evolution and elevation.

Chapter One begins with ignorance, powerlessness, shame and blame. Chapter Two continues with the same ingredients, but by adding dash of denial. Chapter Three takes a powerful turn by awakening from denial, admitting there is a repeating pattern, owning it and then reaping the reward of a quicker recovery. Chapter Four is the fruitful progress and practical application of the knowledge gained in Chapter Three. Chapter Five is total and complete freedom from the past and the full awakening to what is possible when we own what we have created and then choose to re-create something better. Sometimes in life, we innocently and ignorantly create pain. However, the pain is the only teacher needed. The second time we feel the pain it signals our refusal to learn and evolve. The simple truth is that there is no learning from the second kick of a horse. See it, sense it, survey it, shift it and then settle on a new street.

Prayer: *"God of the Second Chance, thank You for showing me the pitfalls on my street and for the courage to choose a new street. Amen."*

Challenge Your Mind. Channel Your Power. Change Your Life.

December 12

PURSUING PEACE

The Power of Choice

> ***Affirmation***
> *"Today, I will exercise my power to choose. I choose to be around people of awakened minds and higher vibrations. I choose to be kind and not invest in relationships fueled by anger or angry people. I choose to be patient and not live my life around impatient people who make everything difficult. I choose to wake up to my divine creativity and to live a life not burdened with pity parties and blaming others for my lack of happiness."*

There is a question that has been asked innumerable times by countless people: "Where did evil come from?" If God is good, and God created all things, did God create evil? This is a question that requires graduation from the lower levels of absolute thought. It is a complex answer. Our Creator created us like Him, Her, It. Which means we have the power to create. Most theologians refer to this as "free will" or the power of choice. With this power of choice, we can create love, peace and joy. Or, we can create hate, war and sorrow. The power of choice is not evil. And, it's actually not good. The power of choice is neutral with the potential to be used for good or evil. So, God did not create evil. God gave us the power to choose that carries with it the potential for good or evil. The real question is not: "did God create evil?" The question that will enlighten our minds, empower our journeys and enhance our lives is this: "why did God trust us with something that carries the potential for evil?" God gave us, trusted us, endowed us, with the power to choose because we are here to learn how to navigate our divine creativity. In other words, we are here to learn how to be like God.

That's a lot of theology for a daily affirmation. So, let's apply this knowledge to our daily lives. We are endowed by God, with the power to choose our friends, spouses, jobs, churches, foods, political candidates. We choose money or the environment, convenience or health, inclusion or exclusion, power or peace. We choose love or hate, fear or faith, joy or pain. Own and hone your power today. God trusted you with it.

Prayer: *"Giver of Freedom, help me choose life today. Amen."*

PURSUING PEACE

December 13

Co-Existing Part I

Affirmation
"Today I choose to co-exist."

Many people are afraid of the term *co-exist* because they are misinformed about what it really means. It doesn't mean a one world government, forced conformity, compromising your principles, or that you're always going to be happy about or completely accepting of everything other people do. It actually means "two or more things existing together in time and space *with* or *without* interaction." That's it.

On the other hand, cooperation is a beautiful concept that has been proven in study after study to be a more effective strategy than competition for accomplishing just about everything. However, we're not always going to get cooperation from everyone in our lives. It would be a much nicer world if we could, but we all have quite a bit more evolving to do before that can be our reality.

So what can we do in the meantime to live, as the Bible says, "as peaceably as we can with all mankind?" First, we must realize that both co-existence and cooperation are choices, and we, as the creators of our own lives, get to choose whatever level we want to live on and with whom.

We can make the choice to cooperate with as many people in our lives as it is possible to. But with others, we're just going to have to settle for co-existing. There will be certain people with whom we're going to have to agree to disagree and keep moving if we don't want to get mired down in a vicious, never-ending cycle of trying to convince each other of our rightness. Instead, we can choose to honor each other's choices, even if we don't agree with them, and live in peace.

Prayer: *"God of Peace, let peace begin with me today. Amen."*

Challenge Your Mind. Channel Your Power. Change Your Life.

December 14

PURSUING PEACE

Co-Existing Part II

Affirmation
"My vibe attracts my tribe."

By the time you become an adult, you are old enough to know which people in your life celebrate you and which do not. You know what environments you're in where you're celebrated and the ones where you're just tolerated. And if you don't know these things, that's step one.

Step two is knowing it's your decision where to put your energy and focus. There are certain people you'll vibe with. Learn to appreciate that and to appreciate them.

There are others who are always going to make the snarky comment. And still others who are basically good-hearted, but the lens they look at life through will always cause them to be on a different vibrational frequency than you. Both groups are the people you need to decide to just co-exist with and let them have their own journey.

Try to limit the drama in your life by remembering that you don't have to show up to every party you're invited to, and you don't have to respond to every on-line post or comment you have an opinion about.

What you do need to do is always show up for yourself by loving yourself unconditionally and honoring your own choices (sidenote: that means you need to make sure you're making choices worthy of your honor). Also, honor the choices others make for themselves on whatever level of life they've chosen to live on - whether you agree with them or not.

The people on your vibrational level will find you. They can't help it. It's a universal law. And that's about as close to a perfect recipe for living happily ever after as you're going to find!

Prayer: *"Source of Vibration, please help me attract my tribe today. Amen."*

PURSUING PEACE

December 15

At Peace with MY Faith Journey

Affirmation
"Today, I will surrender to the truth that Christ authors and finishes my faith. I acknowledge that faith is always new as it comes by what I am hearing and not by what I have heard."

"*The just shall live by faith.*" (Hebrews 10:38 KJV) "*Without faith it is impossible to please God.*" (Hebrews 11:6 KJV) "*Faith without works is dead.*" (James 2:20 KJV) "*Faith is the substance of things hoped for, the evidence of things not seen.*" (Hebrews 11:1 KJV) We have a diversity of biblical references, and a plethora of different definitions, of faith. There is no specific, singular, monolithic definition of faith. Faith is mysterious. And, the faith journey is yours. Own it! It is yours to define! Yours to navigate.

Don't allow anyone else to dictate your faith journey or make you feel like your approach is wrong or somehow inadequate. Be confident that Christ has authored and finished your faith and that we are all working out, and walking out, our own process of salvation. Our faith will and must be shaken so that what remains will be unshakeable. (Romans 12:27 KJV) Faith is not something we figure out. On the contrary, faith is something we surrender to. Today, be at peace with your faith journey.

Prayer: "Faithful God, thank You for the gift of faith. I am grateful that faith is a journey, not a destination. I know You are not limited by my faith. I know I am going to be shaken, and that what remains will be faith. I may waver, wind, wonder and wander, but I will keep walking. Amen."

Challenge Your Mind. Channel Your Power. Change Your Life.

December 16

PURSUING PEACE

My Time and Energy are Valuable

> ***Affirmation***
> *"Today, I will create the life I want to live by guarding my time and by managing my energy. Every person I encounter today has equal worth and value. However, every person does not deserve my time and energy."*

Tapping into our divine creativity does not happen overnight. Often we learn to create our lives by trial and error and at times even by failure. If we are "vibrational creatures in a vibrational universe" then we must be aware that we vibrate, or attract, things to us and also vibrate, or repel, things (and people) away from us.* An important piece of creating our lives is surrendering to necessary adjustments and changes.

As we are shifting, and sifting, we will begin to realize we are not the same person before we started to awaken. Things we once to tolerated become suddenly, certainly unthinkable. Where we once remained quiet, we now speak truth. On the contrary, people we once battled and argued with now only warrant our silence and merit our stillness. We begin to understand the value of our voice and willingly acknowledge there are some situations, organizations, and people that no longer deserve our time, energy and focus. As we resist being drawn into lower vibrations we consciously create joy and intentionally pursue peace!

> ***Prayer:*** *"Original Vibration, give me the wisdom today not to 'cast my pearls before the swine.' (Matthew 7:6) Empower me to reserve my energy for like-minded people and to sow my time into fertile soil. Amen."*

---

* Esther (Abraham) Hicks, "About Vibrational Reality," 2021.

PURSUING PEACE

December 17

Dealing With Stress

Affirmation
*"I understand the vital importance of a daily spiritual practice.
I know in times of stress this is what I can fall back on to
remain in my peace."*

When you find yourself in a stressful moment, what do you do? This is when it's important to have a plan. First, don't be afraid to pause before you react. Rarely do we come across a situation or person who simply must have an immediate response.

If possible, excuse yourself and find somewhere to be alone for a few minutes - even if it's in the bathroom. There's hardly any situation where you can't excuse yourself to go to the restroom.

Once alone, bring yourself back to your center. It's important to note that in order to bring yourself back to center, you have to know where that is. That's why a daily spiritual practice is vital. If you don't know what calm feels like in the first place, it's difficult to get back there.

Regroup, zoom out and see the situation from a wider angle. Is this really an argument worth having? Are you at a family gathering to celebrate something? If so, remember not to give your time and energy to anything that doesn't add to the main purpose of why you're there. Having a mindful plan in place before a stressful moment strikes can help make your life run much more smoothly.

Prayer: *"God of Peace, help me to plan ahead for stressful times so I will not be caught off guard. Help me learn how to protect my peace. Amen."*

Challenge Your Mind. Channel Your Power. Change Your Life.

December 18

PURSUING PEACE

At Peace With My Journey

> ### *Affirmation*
> *"Today, I am at peace with my journey. Spirit has revealed truth to me line upon line; unlocked mysteries through me precept upon precept; transformed me from glory to glory and transitioned me from one dimension to another. I am not where I was. I am not where I will be. However, I am at peace with where I am. And, I am open to whatever is next."*

I have a friend who says, "Christians are a lot like concrete…all mixed up and permanently set." I have witnessed the epidemic of this mental stagnation and spiritual constipation for most of my life. For some reason, we have a strong tendency to find a truth, cherish it, protect it, cling to it and then in an attempt to preserve it, refuse to make room for more truth. Like good soldiers, we stubbornly march with loyalty to what God said while resisting the guilt, and perceived gluttony, of cheating on the last word from God by dating the new or next word. There is a pattern in the Bible, from Genesis to Revelation, of God revealing and unfolding a little more truth each step of the way. While in the wilderness, the Hebrew children ate manna each morning. This mysterious food would only last one day. Each day there was new, fresh, organic food. There is a *"Daily Bread,"* a *"Living Word"* available to us each day as long as we are at peace with the constant transformation. Jesus made it clear, *"Man shall not live by bread alone, but by each word that proceeds from the mouth of God"* (Matthew 4:4). The word "proceeds" is an active verb found in the present tense. In other words, it is always happening…God is always speaking.

The truth that fed you in the last season may sustain you in this one. You can survive on it. But, you are filling your spirit with preservatives, leftovers. Give thanks for yesterday's truth. They are not gravestones to be mourned. They are stepping stones of gratitude and graduation. And, don't throw out the baby with the bathwater. Eat what is eternal. Edit what is temporary. Enjoy the new.

> **Prayer:** "Proceeding Word, I give thanks for where You have brought me from. And, I trust where You are taking me to. Amen."

PURSUING PEACE

December 19

The Name of God

Affirmation

"I will not allow my individual religious beliefs to further separate the corporate human family. The name I call God is not God's name…it is just one of many names humans use in an attempt to name the unnamable; define the undefinable; describe the indescribable, eternal, I Am that I Am! Today, I will neither curse the darkness nor unconsciously add to it. Instead, I will consciously create righteousness, peace and joy by allowing the light and love within me to be manifested all around me! Amen."

According to the Bible, before the erecting of the Tower of Babel, the earth and all of its inhabitants spoke one common language (Genesis 11). We can assume this means there was one universal name for God. Thus, there was no need to argue over the name of God. In early Hebrew law, even saying the name of God was forbidden. Personally, I don't believe God wanted His/Her name to be so revered that no one should dare utter it. I choose to believe that God knew having different names, spoken by diverse languages, would cause division among His children. When Moses finally asks God *"what is Your name?"* (Exodus 3) God continues to remain nameless, or at least refuses to offer Moses a specific name. Instead, God simply answers *"I AM WHO I AM."* In other words, God is attempting to express to Moses that He is more of an essence than a definable name.

How can the global human family be so divided over the name(s) of God? Yahweh, Jesus, Buddha, Zeus, Krishna, Allah… all human names for God and strong points of disagreement and disunity. I believe the segregation that began at Babel was reversed on the Day of Pentecost when the Holy Spirit enabled people of different languages and cultures to understand each other. When we choose to speak in Spirit, not in religion, we will be able to connect with every person we encounter, regardless of their religion, language or name for God.

Prayer: *"Lord, make me an instrument of Your peace. Amen."*

Challenge Your Mind. Channel Your Power. Change Your Life.

December 20

PURSUING PEACE

Good Tension

Affirmation
"Tension can be good."

Normally when we use the word *tension*, it's not in a positive context. Most of the time we're referring to a tension headache or an uncomfortable tightness in your shoulders or back caused by stress.

We use the word *tense* to describe the feeling you get when you walk into a room and people aren't getting along. We talk about there being tension in the air. But tension also serves some good purposes.

A certain amount of pressure from opposite ends is what keeps up what's known as a tension rod that we use to hang our shower curtains and the clothes in our closets on. The element of tension is not only necessary - but vital - in the safety ropes for mountain climbers. The resistance or tension that the earth's gravity provides is what keeps our feet on the ground. If not for the pull of gravity we would all be floating around in outer space!

So if we're going to come here and be born into a physical body in order to have a human experience, we should expect some tension; mainly the tension of knowing we will be in a limited, finite body, playing by the rules of a dualistic world, while at the same time remembering the infinite, eternal soul which is our Christ nature.

I heard someone say once: *Everybody is the Buddha, but everyone is also an idiot.* That's the good tension we have to learn to hold here on earth just as Jesus did - knowing we are fully human as well as fully divine.

> **Prayer:** *"God that is All, help me today understand that I am both fully human and fully divine. I accept this good form of tension as a part of my life. Amen."*

PURSUING PEACE

December 21

The Shortest Day Of The Year

Affirmation
"Today, I proclaim that my happiness, and emotional well-being, is not at the mercy of external conditions like weather or seasons of the year. I will get, stay, and be happy because I am a happy person."

Is your mood subject to change with the weather? Many people experience depression when the sun is not shining. Others long for rainy days. There are parts of the earth that seasonally experience twenty-four hours of darkness and then full days of sunlight. Although we all have a preferred climate, specific temperature and favorite season of the year, should our emotional health be subject to the cycles, patterns or even whims of mother nature?

December 21st, or the winter solstice, is usually the shortest day of the year, or the day when the sun shines the fewest number of hours in a day. For some, this marks a long, dreary, gloomy winter that shifts the moods of people and signals an invitation for short, joyless, dark days. It is a fact that we all need sunlight and even gather essential vitamins from the sun. Which means there may actually be a certain connection between sunlight and our physical health. So, how should we navigate the changing of the seasons?

Awareness is the key to sustaining happiness and mental health as we encounter a climate that is not to our liking. Admit that cold, or hot, or rain, or darkness is not your first choice. Then, after acknowledging this, make conscious choices to be active. Put on warm clothes and still take a long winter's walk. Sit under a covering and listen to the rain. Turn on a fan and sip a cold drink in the heat. Find ways to be proactive rather than unconsciously allowing the weather to steal your joy.

Prayer: *"God of All Seasons, help me sustain joy in every season I encounter. Amen."*

Challenge Your Mind. Channel Your Power. Change Your Life.

December 22

PURSUING PEACE

Addicted to Stress

Affirmation
"Today I declare that my normal state is one of regeneration, creativity, joy, enthusiasm, relaxation and ease."

If you ask people if they'd rather have a life of success and triumph *without* adversity or a life of struggling to overcome obstacles, the majority would probably choose the "no adversity" path over the "struggle" path, yet it rarely plays out like that in real life. So many of us actually *choose* to struggle when we don't necessarily have to. Why is this?

For whatever reason, our culture tends to glorify struggle and to be suspicious of victories won too easily because frankly, struggle just makes for a better story. For instance, it's easy to notice the miracle of someone on their deathbed making a full recovery, or a hopeless drug addict getting clean.

It's harder to be interested in and to give thanks for all those stories of people who never had to experience that kind of struggle because maybe that's just not their journey. But are their lives of good health and relatively smooth sailing any less miraculous?

We're so addicted to stress that the *struggle path* has become the norm, and thus, just like any other drug, we've developed such a level of tolerance that it takes increasingly more of it in order to operate normally. Therefore, we don't consider a story miraculous unless it's overly dramatic.

A life of peace and ease contains little to no stress, and in our current environment we're just not sure what to do with that. Breaking our addiction to stress begins with seeing the miraculous in everything!

Prayer: *"Miraculous God, help me today to appreciate the miracle of the mundane and the wonder of the ordinary. Amen."*

PURSUING PEACE

December 23

The Best Gift: YOU!

Affirmation
"Today, I will not stress myself out, or my bank account, attempting to buy the perfect gift. Each day of my life, I will give the best gift any of my family and friends could ever receive: ME!"

Gift giving can be so stressful and complicated. The questions and protocols seem endless: If someone buys me a gift do I have to buy them one in return? How much should I spend? What did they spend on me? If I buy someone a gift one time does this set a precedent that I have to perpetually follow?

Think about the debt we accrue during the holidays. Also, consider that each person has very specific taste, style and their own body shape and type. Often I have received gifts that I never used because the size was wrong or it just wasn't my style. Buying gifts for others that are not their style is in a subtle way suggesting that your own style is what everyone should follow. The dysfunction of gift giving has gotten so ridiculous that people actually "re-gift" gifts they received, but really did not like. Now, they just pass that gift along to someone else so they don't have to buy anything. Just say "NO!" Stop the madness.

The absolute best gift you can give to someone is you. Your time. Your love. Your understanding. You! One of the best gifts that I offer to others is to really listen when they speak. Listen without agenda. Listen to feel someone else's journey. Listen to connect. Listen with compassion.

Prayer: *"Ever Present Gift, awaken in me the courage to give my very best gift to others: the gift of ME! Amen."*

Challenge Your Mind. Channel Your Power. Change Your Life.

December 24

PURSUING PEACE

The Mad Rush

> ### Affirmation
> *"Today, Christmas Eve, I will not rush to the mall for a last-minute gift. I will resist being anxious over buying the perfect gift. I will avoid stressing myself and others out over creating the perfect meal. Instead, I will intentionally rest in the knowledge that every day of the year I give the best gift, the gift of my love and presence to all of my family and friends."*

It is December 24th, malls are buzzing, supermarket parking lots are jam packed, airports are overflowing, and I am at home, sitting by the fire, watching a holiday movie, drinking a glass of wine and laughing with my loved ones. Sound like bragging? Or perhaps I enjoy the privileged life of someone who doesn't work so many hours that I am forced to do all of my shopping the day before Christmas? However, this image strikes you, there is still one truth that remains. I will not allow precious moments to be hijacked by the expectations of society or ruined by the pressure of others.

How many of us labor under the burden of making sure every person we know has a gift? Or even worse, suffer with having to buy a gift for someone out of obligation because they bought us a gift the previous year? Holidays, religious rituals, special family occasions all retain their sacred nature as we consciously choose to approach them being fully awake to the truth that one gift, one prayer, one song, one meal, one picture cannot make or break any significant relationship.

> **Prayer:** *"Ever-Present Daily Gift of Love, I give thanks that You are the same every day of the year. Today, I desire to live each day consciously and consistently. Amen."*

PURSUING PEACE

December 25

The Word Became Flesh

Affirmation
"This Christmas, I will allow the Word to become flesh and to dwell in, through and as me. I will be open to powerful thoughts and higher vibrations."

When the Word became flesh in John's gospel more was at play than just the birth of Jesus of Nazareth. (John 1:14) In the Greek, the word "word" is *logos*. This Greek word is the root for logic. On Christmas Day, we should celebrate the birth of Jesus (although He was likely born in early April). We should also be aware that the logic of God was made flesh. The thoughts of God incarnated. The Mind of Christ was made manifest in flesh.

Did you know that Krishna, Buddha, Hermes, Zarathustra, Horus, Mithra, Hercules, Dionysus and Adonis were also all born on December 25th, all from virgin mothers, hundreds and even thousands of years before Jesus was born?[*] Obviously, this date is of importance and intentionally assigned to many historical characters with divine attributes. Arguments over birth dates and reasons behind their assignations will detour us from the beauty. What is the beauty? The Logic of God, the Mind of the universe desires to share Itself with us. When we open ourselves to the flow of divine thought the Word becomes flesh in us!

Prayer: "Divine Logic, thank You for sharing Your thoughts with me. Today, I choose to make room for Your Mind to become flesh and dwell in me. Amen."

---

[*] Listverse.com, The World's Sixteen Crucified Saviors: Christianity Before Christ, Kersey Graves.

Challenge Your Mind. Channel Your Power. Change Your Life.

December 26

PURSUING PEACE

Stillness Speaks

> **Affirmation**
> "God has never given me, or His creation, the silent treatment. God is not childish or moody. There is a constant flow, a Living Word, a fresh manna, always coming from the mouth of God. However, there may be times when I am not hearing God or agreeing with God. And, there may be times when I am looking for God's voice everywhere except within. I will not allow circumstances or distractions to convince me that God is not speaking to me. Instead, I will learn to be still and get quiet long enough to connect to the voice of God within me."

The book of Malachi was written somewhere around 400-450 B.C.E. Malachi is the last book of the Old Testament. The first Gospel of the New Testament, Mark, was written somewhere between 70-110 C.E. This gap between Malachi and Mark (over 400 years) is believed by most Christians to be a silent period where God was not speaking or even refused to speak. Years ago, I actually preached sermons promoting this idea and explaining that God wouldn't speak again until people heard the last thing He said. Whatever my justification, I am now awake to the truth that God does not give us the silent treatment.

Sometimes we don't hear the voice of God because It is not screaming at us. The voice of God within us is many times like a *"still small voice"* whispering to us and giving us impressions, intuitions and "knowings" within our hearts. Other times there is simply too much background noise, mindless chatter, family drama, work stress or busy-work drowning out the sound of God's voice. In environments like this, we could benefit tremendously from moments of stillness and uninterrupted quietness.

> "Be still and know that I am God" (Psalm 46:10).
> "In quietness…will be your strength" (Isaiah 30:15).

Prayer: "Still Small Voice, today I will get still, quiet, surrender, connect, breathe, sense and hear Your voice within me. Amen."

PURSUING PEACE

December 27

I Don't Know Anything About That

Affirmation
"There will be times when I am approached with information about something or someone. If the information is negative in any way, and if I have a limited knowledge of it, I will exercise my right to simply say 'I don't know anything about that.'"

There exists an idea that little people talk about people, average people talk about events, and big people talk about ideas. If we are honest, I think we might admit that we are all big, little and in-between at different times in our lives. To talk about people and events is to be human. To ponder ideas is divine. And, we are all hybrids. We are spiritual beings. Yet, we are having a human experience and expression. So, how do we navigate this journey?

Bad news travels fast. Why? Because people love to gossip. Many times, gossip has only a piece of the truth or a small portion of the whole story. When someone approaches you with negative information about a person, a group or an event, unless you have the absolute whole story, reserve the right to say "I don't know anything about that" or at very least "I was not there, and I don't have all the facts." This answer does three things: 1) it keeps you from taking sides, 2) it helps you avoid character assassination of others, and 3) it rescues you from future apologies when you get the whole story.

Sometimes the best answer is no answer. The wisest reply is silence. The peaceful path is an admission of not knowing.

Prayer: *"Panoramic Eye, I admit I don't see it all or know it all. Help me remember to not speak about things that I don't know about. Amen."*

Challenge Your Mind. Channel Your Power. Change Your Life.

December 28

PURSUING PEACE

At Peace With Pain

> *Affirmation*
> *"Today, I am at peace with pain, the pain I create and the pain the world creates. I accept the truth that others will hurt me and that I will hurt others. I know that risking vulnerability and openness is also risking pain. I consciously choose not to allow myself to get stuck in pain or to allow unresolved pain to keep me from life and love."*

"*It rains on the just and the unjust.*" (Matthew 5:45 KJV) We are all going to suffer pain. Some pain comes from what we create for ourselves and some pain comes from being the collateral damage of the lower collective human consciousness. David clearly created his own pain but was also crushed by the betrayal of a dear friend. All of us have suffered lack and also been tormented by the fear of losing something valuable. Pain has many faces and angles. Can we embrace the reality that we will all experience pain?

Why should we accept this difficult truth? When we know that pain is a part of our human experience we are not so offended by it when it shows up. The shock of pain can quickly become a personal offense for us, causing us to take it personally and to become trapped in it. What can we do?

We can view pain as a friend, allowing it to smooth rough edges. Pain is a tremendous teacher. Disappointment can teach us to live in the Now without projecting into the future. Pain can alert us to problems that require our attention. Consciously, actively listening to pain can bring about change that has been awaiting reformation. Don't get stuck in pain. We can allow it to move through us without limiting our capacity to experience life and love to the fullest.

> **Prayer:** *"Very Present Help in my time of need, I give thanks that You are with me in every pain. Today, I pray for the wisdom to see the power hiding in pain. Amen."*

PURSUING PEACE

December 29

End the War

Affirmation
"Today I will view life as a conversation with divinity."

If you begin every day as if you're gearing up for war, guess what you're going to get? War. Let's stop needing someone or something to be the enemy. Let's stop expecting the worst from those we feel are "on the other side" of things from us.

When we approach every situation in our lives as if it is a fight to be won, we will never actually be able to win because we are the one creating the war…not the thing or person we perceive we are fighting.

War is not something that can ever be managed. And that's good, because the process we're all meant to go through here on earth is that of mastery, not management. When you try to manage or manhandle what is, you are constantly trying to either make it better or make it go away.

When you're mastering something, you receive the situation as it is and look at it as a divine gift to help you with this process of mastery. When you say *yes* to the present moment, you realize you are in a conversation with divinity, not a battle with the thing you think of as bad.

When you view your life as a conversation with divinity, you see every experience as being to your benefit. And when you see it that way, everything that comes to strengthen you stays, and that which does not strengthen you moves through you without resistance.

Knowing this, what could there possibly be for you to defend against? What could there possibly be for you to fight?

> **Prayer:** *"God of Peace, help me to learn the art of mastery rather than management. Only I can stop the war within. Amen."*

Challenge Your Mind. Channel Your Power. Change Your Life.

December 30

PURSUING PEACE

Creating God in My Image

> **Affirmation**
> "I will not create God in my own image by projecting my cultural biases, social prejudices and religious experiences onto God. I am willing to surrender to the truth that I am created in God's image, and not the other way around. I have studied to show myself approved. Now, I am ready and able to rightly divide between the word of man and the Logic of God! God is Spirit. And, today I choose to worship in Spirit and in Truth!"

We did not create God. God created us. More specifically, God created us in His image and likeness (Genesis 1:27). Strangely, so many religions, and religious people, get this backwards. They create God in their image. And, they're not alone. Moses, David, the Apostle Paul…many great men and inspired leaders and writers have committed the error of creating God in their image. Does God favor the firstborn son over the other sons? Does God allow us to own slaves as long as they are from a neighboring country and not our own? Does God discriminate against people who wear glasses? Does God sanction a man to speak in church but forbid a woman to speak? I think, or at least I truly hope, that all of us would laugh at these questions and answer "No!" Yet, these are all teachings we can find in the Bible…God's Word. These are all examples of man creating God in his image. The created, projecting its own ideas, cultural opinions and even prejudices, onto the Creator.

When we read the Bible, we must do so with both an open heart and a critical mind. The men who wrote the Bible, and the men who found denominations, have a tendency of projecting their own biases and beliefs onto others, and indirectly onto God, sadly, in the name of God. Ask God to help you rightly divide the Word of Truth. The Holy Spirit will grant you the ability to discern between man's temporary, changing opinions and God's eternal, unchanging truth.

> **Prayer:** "Creative Spirit, help me see when I create You in my image. Today, I surrender to being created in Your image and likeness. Amen."

PURSUING PEACE

December 31

Projecting Happiness Into The Future

Affirmation
"As the year changes, nothing changes. The happiness, peace, love and joy I project into a new year is available to me right here, right now, in this present moment. Today, I choose to end one season with the knowledge that it is connected to the next season."

There is no difference between 11:59 p.m. December 31st and 12:00 a.m. January 1st. Why? Because *you* are the same. Here is the picture: it is New Year's Eve. We are bemoaning all of the misfortune we encountered in the past 364 days. We are also regretting the poor decisions made over the last calendar year. So, we slip into the lower vibration of projecting our happiness, peace, discipline and the realization of a better experience of life into the next year. When the clock strikes midnight, we celebrate a mythical shift of our luck, favor and fortune.

Have you ever considered the idea that time is an illusion? The number of years we hold as true on a calendar are anything but accurate. Who decided that we are in the 2000's while knowing that the earth is millions of years old? Even time on the earth is not an exact science. As we celebrate at midnight January 1st in the U. S., many nations have already begun their new year who are in a different time zone. The magic does not exist with the changing of a calendar year. The magic, miracle and manifestation of all good things is in you!

Prayer: *"Unchanging Presence, awaken within me today the truth that I can change, shift and recreate my life any year, month, day, hour, minute or moment I choose to surrender to my divine creativity. Amen."*

Challenge Your Mind. Channel Your Power. Change Your Life.

Keep reading for a preview of D.E. Paulk's book and manual for rethinking the Bible:

The Holy Bible of Inclusion

SECOND EDITION

If you are like me you have struggled to accept the modern Christian church's portrayal (or betrayal) of God, depiction of the devil and description of hell. Many god-fearing people and good-hearted preachers alike have long harbored unspoken thoughts of a more loving, merciful and masterful Creator. However, just about as many who subscribe to this grander vision and version of God also admittedly and even ashamedly lack the ability to reference the Bible and specific passages of scripture in order to publicly validate these privately held higher concepts of God.

If you are looking for *chapter and verse* that will both quickly and completely rescue a big God from the smallness of fundamentalism, *THE HOLY BIBLE OF INCLUSION* is precisely the tool you need! *THE HOLY BIBLE OF INCLUSION* will scripturally, extensively and even exhaustively confront theological myths, misrepresentations and mistranslations of *the Bible and its Origins – Universal Salvation – the devil – the Purpose of hell and the Fire of God – Sexual Orientation* and many others. Join me on this worthwhile and rewarding spiritual journey as we research, rethink, recover and then re-present the awesome and awe-inspiring God of the universe.

> *Who is going to harm you if you are eager to do good? But even if you should suffer for what is right, you are blessed. "Do not fear their threats; do not be frightened." But in your hearts revere Christ as Lord.* **ALWAYS BE PREPARED TO GIVE AN ANSWER TO EVERYONE WHO ASKS YOU TO GIVE A REASON FOR THE HOPE THAT YOU HAVE.** *But do this with gentleness and respect, keeping a clear conscience, so that those who speak maliciously against your good behavior in Christ may be ashamed of their slander. For it is better, if it is God's will, to suffer for doing good than for doing evil. For Christ also suffered once for sins, the righteous for the unrighteous, to bring you to God.*
> **I Peter 3:13-18 NIV**

Second Edition Update from the Author...

What is the survivability of inclusive religion? This was the question haunting me when I first published The Holy Bible of Inclusion in 2010. Specifically, how do you transition a traditional, Evangelical Christian church into expressions of LGBTQ+ affirmation, universal salvation and interfaith oneness / openness without losing the church? Pragmatically, can a church shift in thought and still pay the bills?

Current scholarship and pew research reveal that American Christians are opening to a greater sense of inclusivity while more than 20% of Americans who formerly identified as Christian no longer wish to be identified with any single religion. However, problematically this shift in theological opinion is mostly held in a scared space of secret devotion. This awakening to inclusion seems to be trapped in personal journey, encountering a number of roadblocks when attempting to manifest itself openly in American church settings. Can individual, personal leanings toward inclusion, pluralism, and LGBTQ+ affirmation survive the transition from private spiritual ascension to public articulation and systematic actualization? Can these personal, individual "aha" moments emerge into corporate church modality? I believe they can. And, as a pastor who has successfully transitioned a traditional Pentecostal Christian church into a more inclusive, even pluralistic expression, I speak from experience...this shift is possible! However, knowing how to "rightly divide the Word of truth" is the key to survival.

Christians do not speak English. They speak Christianese, or better, the King James Version of Christianese. What does this mean? In order to survive the shift from tradition to inclusion, you have to know the Word of God and then be able to explain it in a nuanced way that satisfies those who have been conditioned to worship it. I wrote this book to save my church over a decade ago. Many were ready to walk out the door at the time of this book's arrival. As we investigated hundreds of scriptures justifying inclusive expression, many turned around, sat back down, and are still with me today.

This is my exhortation to you: If you know God is bigger than any religion or human construct, and want to survive the transition from private thought to public expression - study this book, salvage your church, save your marriage, secure your family and friendships, and "show it to them in the Word" - all from your deep knowledge of the Bible!

Fully Awake,

D. E.

> *Then He opened their minds so they could understand the Scriptures.*
> **Luke 24:45 – NIV**

In his book, *THE HOLY BIBLE OF INCLUSION*, Pastor D. E. Paulk does a much more thorough and comprehensive job of probing the critical concepts of *Inclusion* than I do in my book, *THE GOSPEL OF INCLUSION*. The delicate theological, scriptural and spiritual balance my friend D. E. Paulk walks and writes in this book, is an artistic, tactful and tasteful treatment of some of the most sensitive aspects of both modern and ancient religious doctrine, dogma and discipline.

The subject of *Inclusion* deals more with being and feeling spiritually and mentally *safe* than being and feeling religiously *saved*. I am proud of the expanded consciousness this book embraces and embarks upon in further discussion. During this journey you will inevitably enjoy renewing and re-knowing God (and yourself) all over again - or perhaps for the first time.

Peace is possible.

~ Bishop Carlton D. Pearson

THE HOLY BIBLE OF INCLUSION
CONTENTS

Part I - INTRODUCTION

Part II - UNIVERSAL SALVATION
   (Ultimate Reconciliation, The Restoration of All Things, "Inclusion")

Part III - THE DEVIL

Part IV - THE PURPOSE OF HELL ... AND THE FIRE OF GOD

Part V - SEXUAL ORIENTATION

Part VI - END TIMES (from a Scriptural Perspective)

Part VII - JESUS and THE CHRIST
   NO MAN COMES TO THE FATHER EXCEPT THROUGH ME

Part VIII - GROWING AN INCLUSIVE CHURCH
   (Wisdom for Inclusive-minded pastors)

INVITATION OF TRUTH

As we journey through the Word of God together, searching for hidden truths that have remained concealed for many years, we must invite the Spirit of God to guide us into TRUTH. If you are in agreement, read aloud this simple Invitation of Truth:

My mind is alert and my Spirit is open to receive Truth. I acknowledge that Truth is not reserved only to what I already know and is not merely restricted to concepts with which I am already familiar. As beauty is in the eye of the beholder – Truth is in the ear, heart and mind of the perceiver.

INTRODUCTION

I could say "the glass is half full" and then say of the same glass that it is also "half empty" – and each of these opposing statements would be strangely true, correct, accurate. It is true. The same glass that is half full is also half empty. Both of these statements are "right." Whether we see the glass half full or half empty does not reveal accuracy or correctness or rightness about the water or the glass. How we view the glass only brings to light our personal perspective and level of consciousness.

In many Christian circles, there has been much theological debate around the doctrine of *Universal Salvation*. Other "less threatening" offshoot names associated with Universal Salvation are: *Ultimate Reconciliation*, the *Finished Work of Grace* and the *Restoration of All Things*. However, *INCLUSION* is the name (at least for the past decade) that has received the greater majority of attention. From an exhaustive, thorough study of the scriptures (including both Old and New Testaments) – we can, and will, accurately prove that Universal Salvation is an original, sound and recurring doctrine throughout the whole Bible. Yet, we also find a consistent biblical pattern that would line up with a more fundamentalist or evangelical expression and interpretation.

So, how do we choose?

Which Bible do we read?

The Universal, Progressive, *Inclusive* Bible?

The Fundamentalist, Evangelical, *Exclusive* Bible?

The Bible is a holy book (or a collection of 66 holy books) containing contrasting (even contradicting) truths. And, it is designed that way. The contradictions are there intentionally to encourage growth and a greater depth of understanding. They are meant to catapult us into higher revelations. The Bible is a progression of man's process of wrestling with the unending truth of an eternal God. The Bible is a beautiful story of humanity's struggle and surrender to becoming divine. And, along this journey we utilize the Bible, not to declare or prove specific doctrines as absolute truth – but, we corporately use the Bible as a mirror to show us where we are individually on the path to enlightenment. If the Bible contains purposeful contradicting truths…then the Bible we choose to read (whether inclusive or exclusive) only reveals our personal level of spiritual growth and our degree of awakened consciousness.

In the final analysis, this "argument" has proven to be counterproductive to achieving a cohesive collaboration and a closer common union in the greater Body of Christ. As long as the ultimate goal, from either viewpoint, is to prove someone or something to be right or wrong (the glass to be half full or half empty) we will never see the beauty and necessity of celebrating a diversity of expression and function in the same Body.

Inevitably, when theological arguments ensue, people become polarized to one position or the other, allowing very little room for open-minded discussion, thus effectively preventing any possibility of learning anything from someone who may have a perspective other than their own. As a fourth generation preacher, I have seen my share of doctrinal schism, and have heard of even more. Biblical argument is just about as old as the Bible itself. And, Christianity is an extremely scripture-driven religion. Someone who has been raised with the Bible as if it were a long-standing trusted family member will usually not even give consideration to an unfamiliar spiritual concept without first being shown some sort of foundational scriptural reference or evidence. If I had a dime for every time I have heard someone say – "Show it to me in the Word" – I would… well, have a lot of dimes.

Visit www.mytruthsanctary.com for ways to purchase the entire book and more.

Keep reading for a preview of D.E. Paulk's book and journey toward surrender, self-awareness and the evolution of consciousness:

I DON'T KNOW...

the way of
KNOWING

SECOND EDITION

I Don't Know is the required confession needed to be granted admission to the path of enlightenment and to The Way of Knowing. I Know is conclusive, ending, finite and therefore devastating. I Know is an enemy of immortality and nemesis to The Way of Knowing. We are all infinite spirits and the offspring of the Infinite Creator. When we discover the I Don't Know within we unleash our Infinite nature and unearth the Endless Us! Are you ready to put on immortality?

All Truth flows to us from One Divine River. From that One River many wells form and are fed. We might call these wells religions, cultures or philosophies. All wells sustained by the One River contain beauty and truth. However, we make a grave mistake when we declare any particular well as being the One River. I Don't Know dissolves religious division, bridges cultural chasms and dodges philosophical divorce originating from the I Know. I Don't Know is the Repairer of the Breach. In a day when the I Know is to be charged with so much human suffering - I Don't Know shines brightly as an ancient idea whose time has come of age.

Foreword
Dr. Carlton Pearson

Knowledge is both the most intriguing and most ambiguous of realities. It is and isn't; simultaneously. I am actually, for the first time in my life, more curious about what I don't know than what I believe. I think we all believe too much and know too little.

What you know, what you think, what you feel and what you believe are all interrelated, but not equal. The combination of all of them facilitates *Being*. The segregation of them facilitates the dysfunctionalism and desperation we see all around us.

I believe that authentic truth is not so much learned or taught, but remembered. It is more recovery than discovery. In the deepest recesses of our individual souls, we know everything, because we *are* everything. God made us this way. We were created in the image and likeness of Divinity. This would be Divinity with us, in us, for us and ultimately as us!

In some ways, knowledge and knowing might be different. Knowledge is usually based on information while *knowing* is based on transformation. One is based on fact the other on faith, which is inner persuasion. It is less external and lives both internally and eternally with and as us.

As I am now over half a century old, for the first time in my life I feel as if *being* has more essence and more importance than knowing, after all we are called human *beings,* not human doings or even knowings. Both are part of our *Being*, but in many ways we've neglected being, choosing knowing and doing over being. Being is our first and foremost Self. Knowing and doing come out of Being, but if Being is ignored, negated or neglected, knowing and doing become counter-productive and imprecise. It is this inaccuracy of emphasis that causes most of the pain and pathos of human disease and/or dis-ease.

I studied five and a half years in university seeking knowledge, but while doing so, my *Being* was shrinking and shriveling because that's the only way it could fit in the smaller garments and wardrobe of knowledge.

I majored in Biblical Literature/English Bible and minored in

Theology and Historical Studies. I know the history, but I am, in my being, *the mystery*. Being is both who you are and who you are not, the part of you that is and is not. It is both sides of YOU-ness or YOU-niverse!

Being doesn't need clothes. It is the truest, purest and original form of nakedness. It is the nakedness Adam and Eve (the male and female in us all and that we all indeed are) had before they felt shame. The only darkness there is the Light you are and aren't... Selah!

The shame and sham religious pre-supposition can be is what robs us of our sense of being and prevents us from knowing, beyond knowledge acquisition. Institutionalized religion fills us with knowledge of the doctrines, disciplines and dogmas that pervade human culture worldwide and often cause and then activate the war of the worlds. This knowledge often hinders and hampers "Knowing" which is the essence of being, who we are and are becoming.

The sense of self and soul is what I call *Self Actualization*. Learning, or should I say, remembering to be actually, factually, functionally and punctually YOU is what *being* really is.

Pastor D. E. Paulk, my friend and colleague in ministry, has tackled an issue few even acknowledge exists. The over certitude of many and most of the world religions have kept us from accessing, experiencing, expanding and expressing the greatest of the ethereal disciplines, the discipline of *Not Knowing* and being at peace with, and actually becoming, one with the *Unknown*. Anything else is probably an illusion!

I pride my self in not knowing anything except that I know little... but remain open and eager to know more, which means essentially, to know ME. Knowing you is being you. Being you is experiencing God! And for most of us, Knowing begins with the simple admission – *I Don't Know*.

Second Edition Update From The Author
D.E. Paulk

When I first published I DON'T KNOW…The Way Of Knowing in 2008, I had not been introduced to the wisdom traditions of Zen bardo space, Buddhist emptiness, Beginner's Mind, or to the Judaic, Kabbalistic Chabad ideal of celebrating nothingness. I knew Jesus. I had studied the Gospels my entire life. But, I had not yet seen the mystical Christ. In my desire for mastery of doctrine, I had not allowed myself to become "like a child" to enter the Kingdom. My entire life I had "heard of old" but was not hearing what Spirit was saying. I had not yet begun to celebrate the not-knowingness resident within Jesus, who explains that the children of the Kingdom are "like the wind…blowing here and there…no one knowing where it comes from or to where it is going."

I just said these three simple words, "I DON'T KNOW!" All of a sudden the knowING began to flow to me, through me, and most importantly, from within me. Whatever was necessary for the evolution of my consciousness began to show up. Somehow I had opened a portal to the wisdom of the Universe, not by way of reading or research, but by removing the obstacles of presupposition, conditioning and the know-it-all-ness that had kept the knowING from awakening within me.

Eventually, I stumbled upon Taoist ideas like "When the student is ready, the Teacher will appear." Lao Tzu showed up and reminded me that "knowing, without knowing, was true enlightenment." But, at the time of my awakening, I only knew I had surrendered what I thought I knew in my hunger to know more. Since that time, I have found that truth is a journey, not a destination. I have realized that I am not my beliefs, but the spirit capable of having, changing and considering beliefs. I have detached from any false identity of being my mind and have surrendered to the idea that I am not my thoughts, or even the thinker of thoughts, but the observer of the thinker having thoughts. It is from this approach that the Holy Spirit is granted complete permission to guide into all truth. It is in this methodology, not in a specific doctrine or truth, where safeguards against spiritual stagnation and mental constipation can be realized.

If you are reading this book in quest for specific truths or concrete answers, you will end up dissatisfied. Religion tells us what to think. But, spirituality teaches us how to think. This book is not designed to teach you anything. It is designed to remove the obstacles that keep you from seeing what you already know. Or rather, to teach you how to think and provide an approach that will open an eternal channel where truth(s) are always available. You are neither destined to get stuck on a specific truth nor fated to be tied to a specific teacher - "When the student is truly ready, the Teacher will disappear."

The fifth word in the Bible is "created" (Genesis 1:1- "in the beginning God created"). Created in Hebrew is bara – which means to "carve away" or "clear out space." In essence, when God was creating the earth, God was actually re-creating the earth. God was carving away and clearing out space in order for something else to emerge. As we begin this creative journey, find some available space for God to create. I offer this affirmation as a temporary guide, leading us to the emptiness that fills us, to the nothingness that is the all-ness and to the knowledge of not knowing:

"I am not my thoughts. I am not the thinker of my thoughts. I am the observer, witnessing the thinker, thinking the thoughts. I am not the voice in my head or any limitation of an inherited collective cultural conditioning, religious indoctrination or even my past experiences. Wisdom of the ages and sages, grant me the surrender to mind my mind, free my mind, be free of my mind and surrender to practice no-mind."

*There is nothing better than to know that you don't know.
Not knowing, yet thinking you know, this is sickness.*
  - Lao Tzu

Visit www.mytruthsanctary.com for ways to purchase the entire book and more.